You were good at your job, right?

*If you're having a difficult time finding
a new one, we can tell you why...*

We bet your job search focuses on Resumes, Job Boards, Online Applications, Recruiters, and Traditional Networking -- Okay, you have a LinkedIn profile, too.

*In the Social Media Era, Job Search has evolved dramatically.
What once worked so well is no longer as effective.
So many new tactics can be confusing. But*

Employment
Recommendations
Personal
NetworkingResumes   Business
Brochures
Voicemail Time   Resume Endorsements
Assessments Brand Tactics·Closing   Traditional
Matter   Pitch Media Signature
Transition Job   Online B2B   Work
Video   Interviewing BrandingBranding   Workforce
Omaha Blogs Words Codes Systems   Events QR   Interview
Executives Applicant Planning   Profile Preparation Google
MarketJob Search   Career   STAR   Thank
Interviews Launch Paths HIRED Social   Existing
Twitter   Tracking   Boolean Networking
Dirt Grammar RedOut Groups Bag Questions
Companies   Myths
Contacts Phone Era SEO Future Boards
Targeting   Boomer Stand   Functional
Hidden DISC Profiles Negotiation Email LinkedIn
Coaches Assessment Stories Keywords Facebook
Aboutme Searches Differentiation   Gorilla
FacetoFace   Market ATS Marketing
Connections   Hybrid
Cards·StructureBaby
Branding WordstoWork
Professional

HIRED!

Will clear your Paths to Employment in the Social Media Era

i

HIRED!

Paths to Employment in the Social Media Era

Jeff Sheehan   Alfred M. Smith

Published by Trinity Press
Norcross, GA
www.HIREDthebook.com

HIRED! *Paths to Employment in the Social Media Era*

www.HIREDthebook.com

Published by Trinity Press
Norcross, Georgia

www.HIREDthebook.com
ISBN: 978-0-9914389-0-7

Printed in the United States of America
Trinity Press, Norcross, Georgia
Editing, direction, and insight by Al Cole
Front Cover photo and design by Tarik Fojnica
Portrait photos by Bruce Kromer
Illustrations by Tanya Leon Tyeva

Table of Contents

Chapter 1: One Size Fits All ?!?   **1**
"*Omaha! Omaha!*"
Great, but will this work for me?
What is it with you guys?

Chapter 2: State of the Job Market   **7**
The State of *Confusion*
What You Don't Know <u>Can</u> Kill You
Fact vs. Fiction
Natural Selection and the Evolution of Job Search
       Look Beyond Your Resume, By Tyrone Griffin

Chapter 3: Get Ready, Get Set...   **17**
Lookin' Under the Hood
Harvesting a Bounty of Riches
Recommendations
Contacts
Red Flags
Ground Rules
Get to Work, You Lazy Bum!

Chapter 4: Mental, Physical, and Fiscal Fitness   **34**
Planning
The *Real* Cost of Job Transition
Financial Preparation
       How to Survive Financially After a Job Loss,
       By Lee Pence, CFP AAMS
       Budgeting During Transition, By Karen Vining
Time Ain't on Your Side
Time Management
       Time Tactics for a Successful Job Search,
       By Gene Griessman
Assessments: Personal & Professional
       Personal Assessment

Creating Passion and Purpose in Your Work,
By Asha Lightbearer
Professional Assessments
The DISC Assessment System,
By Jon Newman
Go to Health!
*Reducing Stress During Job Transition; A Holistic
Approach,* By Marilyn Pierce, RN BSN
Psychology of Job Search
How Job Loss Affects the Family,
By Katherine Seifert, PhD

Chapter 5: Keywords and Boolean Searches   52
Words Matter
The Hidden Job Market
Boolean Searches
Applicant Tracking Systems
How to Stand Out When Dealing With ATS,
By Rick Sullivan
S.E.O. Ho! Ho!! Ho!!!
Words to Work
Bits 'n' Bites

Chapter 6: Personal Branding   64
Howdy, Pardner!!!
Branding = Differentiation
7 Myths of Personal Branding,
By Joellyn 'Joey' Sargent
The Fulcrum
Marketing Brand Managers
Symbolism
Tell Me a Story
S.T.A.R. Stories
Something to Consider
The Parent Trap
*How Stay-at-Home Parents Can Enter or Re-Enter the
Paid Workforce,* By Dr. Michelle Hutchinson
Elevator ~~Speech~~ Pitch

Chapter 7: Targeting   80

  A Quiver Full of Arrows
  Target Industries
      Companies
      Dirt Bag Companies
      Executives
  Networking

Chapter 8: Assembling the Puzzle   88

  Putting it all together
  Resumes: 'A Career Obituary'
      Functional Resume
      Chronological Resume
          Career Highlights
      Hybrid Resume
      Infographic Resume
      Video Resume
      Miscellaneous Thoughts on Resumes...From Someone
      Who Writes Resumes as a Profession,
      By Tim Morrison
  Social Media Profiles and You
  Gimme Whatcha Got
  LinkedIn: Everything You Need to Know to *Get Started*
  Google+ Profile, About.me, Facebook & Twitter
  Marketing Brochures
  Marketing Brochure Formats
  Marketing Plans
      Conducting the Business of Job Search Like a Business,
      By Nadine Walley
  Business Cards
  QR Codes

Chapter 9: Pre-Launch Checklist   131

  Spelling & Grammar
  Editing & Proofreading

Want To Look Good In Social Media? Then Spell Words Correctly and Use Correct Grammar,
By Betsy Rhame-Minor
Voicemail
Email Signature
Online Reputation
Contacts
'Now Playing in Poughkeepsie'

Chapter 10: Light This Candle!   141

'Let's Do Launch'
Voicemail, Email Address, & Email Signature
Resume
LinkedIn
    LinkedIn Views
    LinkedIn Connections
Google+, About.me, Twitter Profiles
Job Boards
Marketing Brochures
Contacts
Other Necessities

Chapter 11: Maximizing Your Effectiveness   147

How to Maximize Your Efforts
Organize Your Files
Word Document Folder
Google Email Account
LinkedIn
    LinkedIn Endorsements
    LinkedIn Groups
    LinkedIn Connections
Daily/Weekly Activities
Job Boards
Purple Squirrels
Human Resources
Marketing Brochures
Contacts
Google Alerts

Networking
>>>> Traditional Networking
>>>>>> Current Contacts
>>>>>> Career Events
>>>> Non-Traditional Networking
>>>>>> B-2-B Events
>>>>>> Associations
>>>>>> Conventions
>>>>>> 'Executive Cultivation'
>>>> *Networking to Best Effect,* By Emile Paradis
>> Blogs & Personal Websites
>>>> *There's More to a Candidate Search than LinkedIn,* By Jim Stroud
>> Job Fairs
>> Targeting
>> Recruiters
>> Career Coaches & Job Coaches
>>>> *Why Hire a Career Coach?* By Chris Gilliam
>> Volunteerism
>> WwwwwwwwwwwwwwwwwwlA!
>> Calendar
>>>> *10 Job Search Ideas,* By Caron Atteberry

Chapter 12: Advanced Social Media   181

>> Social Media Footprint
>> Online Audit
>> Age of Aquarius?
>> LinkedIn
>>>> Recommendations
>>>> Endorsements
>>>>>> 6 Tips for Using LinkedIn's Endorsements
>>>>>> Getting Rid of Unwanted Endorsements
>>>> Groups
>>>> Connections
>>>> Planning Your Work and Working Your Plan
>>>> Updates
>>>> Path (Formerly LinkedIn Today)
>>>> Network-Contacts
>>>> Your Activity Feed

Google+
It's All About.me
Twitter
    Profile
    Adding Followers
    Posting Information
Facebook
Other Directions
    Digital Marketers: Learning How to Use Their Online World to Job Search, By Raegan Hill
Websites & Blogs
    Blogging: The Inside Scoop on How to Mesmerize Your Potential Employer with Your Expertise; By Melissa Galt
You've Got Klout
The Future
    The Now & Future of Social Media's Role in the Hiring Process, By Vala Afshar

Chapter 13: Interviewing   216

Interview Overview
Questions, Questions, Questions
Phone Script
Phone Screen Interviews
'Planned Spontaneity'
Salary Prep
Face-to-Face Interviews (Initial)
Panel Interviews
Interviewing 101
800 Lb. Gorillas
    How Do You Answer the Standard Question, 'What's Your Greatest Weakness?', By Abby Kohut
Face-to-Face Interviews (final)
Overcoming Internal Candidates
Skype & Video Interviews
Cocktail Umbrella Questions
Negotiation
Thank you, Thank you, Thank you
Dressing for the Occasion

Job Interview Tips, By Joanne Blake
10 Interview Tips, By Caron Atteberry

Chapter 14: Alternatives to Traditional Jobs   251

Your Next Job: Your Own?
   Franchise Ownership
      Should Your Next Job Be Your Own?,
      By Bill Williams
   Existing Business Purchase
      Purchasing an Existing Business,
      By Art Lennig
   Starting From Scratch
      Two Things I Know About Being an Entrepreneur,
      By Dee Doanes
      Take Your Career to Another Level – with Multi-Level!,
      By Peter Gibson
'Stringers'
'The Trades'
Government
Catching the Next Wave
   Green Dimension, By Holly Henderson

Chapter 15: Future Mountains to Climb   268

Where Have We Been?
What We Can Expect
What can you do to NOT go through this Again?
Mighty Morphin' Power?
   MORPH or DIE, By Bob Zartarian
Future Climbs

Referenced Experts   276

Resources the Authors Recommend   286

Acknowledgements   294

"Omaha! Omaha!"
-Peyton Manning

Chapter 1:   One Size Fits All ?!?

Bull $#!+

You've heard the expression in the clothing business where some products claim to be "One Size Fits All." Well, we're here to tell you that one size may fit some; one size may even fit many; but one size does NOT fit all. And despite what you'll hear from the "Job Search Experts," there is no *One Size Fits All* method of finding a job either.

That's one of the biggest problems we have with most how-to-get-a-job books, systems, and coaches. Too many authors will try to make you believe that they have uncovered the *"One-and-Only"* way to get a job in this rapidly changing job-search environment. They want you to believe that their method is the Holy Grail, the one size that will fit all.

We say BULL Shhhhh...well, you get it.

No matter how good an individual idea may be, that idea may not be right for your personality, profession, or principles. People get jobs in many different ways. All of them are right (other than lies or deceit), but none of them has a corner on the market. For that reason, we plan to introduce you to every method of finding your next position that we're aware of—even methods we're not crazy about. Because even though we might not like a method, it could work for you. We also won't claim that our more novel methods will work for everyone.

In the same way that no single method is perfect, no one person knows everything. That's why we've asked a variety of experts to share their thoughts with you. Not only will we offer our own methodology, we think you should have the perspectives of others, as well. We often tell our clients, "We don't give a darn *how* you get a job; we just want you to *get* a darned job!" That holds true here too.

[1]*Omaha! Omaha!*

You may find yourself in a situation where you need to call an audible (a deviation from your original plan). Just ask Peyton Manning (Al's mother's most famous student.) Fired, downsized, consolidated, unhappy, or just seeking a better opportunity...No matter how you arrived here, here is where you are. Peyton Manning was unceremoniously fired (technically released), but he came back. Boy did he! And you will too.

In the 2013 season, Manning led the league (U. S. football) and set two all-time records. True, he didn't win the championship (how many greats in any profession ever get the chance?). But like a Phoenix, Mr. Manning rose from the ashes. We (Jeff and Al) did, as well. And now, you will too.

Over the past several years, we have personally spoken with and helped thousands of people through their job transition, and we want to share what we've learned with you. We want you to know *everything*. We want you to know every method of securing a job because what fits one person perfectly may not fit you. This is not professorial theory. This is real-world stuff.

Great, but will this work for me?

Here are some examples of the varied nature of what you will learn in this book:

- A former news editor and producer had been out of work for over two years and was severely depressed. We were able to take a single accomplishment she had totally discounted to brand her as an Emmy Award Winner.
- Another client applied some of our social media instruction to obtain considerably more interviews (and a job) than he had previously gotten. He's often said, "This ---- works!"
- A third client used one of our suggested questions that made the president of a company speak nonstop for 35 minutes. That company president later commented that he was really impressed with the client's intelligence. (Our client had barely uttered a word).
- Still another client who had been jobless for over two years, partially because of brain cancer, was able to present herself in a way that her former health issues were never even questioned.
- One person who had lost her job after 20-plus years of service wasn't getting a nibble, even though she was in an industry where skilled people like her were in high demand. When we uncovered the correct keywords that industry recruiters were seeking, she got two offers within a week.
- When a well-qualified client agreed to include bits of past recommendations with her qualifications as evidence of her abilities, she quickly got exactly the type of position that allowed her to pursue her other ambitions.
- We have twice helped a man without a degree who was in his late 50s and now early sixties secure jobs.
- We've been able to help people at every level: Staff, Managerial, Executive, and C-Level. Our methods work for doctors, lawyers, laborers, teachers—you name it. Of course, there are no guarantees in life, but there's no reason you can't enjoy the success our former clients have experienced.

What is it with you guys?
Although our stories are a bit different, we've both lived what you're going through now and have a great deal of empathy for each and every job-seeker.

This stuff is highly personal.

Jeff's Story:

This is personal to me because it's what I've experienced over the past four years. It's the reason I got involved with helping people in job transition.

For many years, I had traveled all over the world so much that I had little time for volunteering. I had a real passion for marketing and social media, so when the opportunity came to help others by utilizing my skills in this area, I jumped at it. Even though I thought it might also help me gain the exposure to locate a new job myself, that was not my main intent.

I continue to provide coaching on the job-search process, with a focus on using LinkedIn, Twitter, Facebook, Google, and other tools in job search. Over the past four years, I've made presentations to thousands of people through church ministries, Webinars, and Face-to-Face (F-T-F) meetings. I've also been involved in a variety of entrepreneurial ventures.

I, like you, have my down days. And there have been times when I wanted to take the advice of a former hockey coach of mine: "If you're not serious about hockey, hang up the skates, go home, and watch cartoons." Instead, I continue to move forward, engaging and helping as many people as I can.

Al's Story:

I've been at the executive level for many companies in five different industries and have won more awards than I have fingers and toes, yet a number of years ago I found myself without a job for more than two years. I couldn't get a nibble for any of the Vice President of Sales positions I was well qualified for, so I decided to take a step back and apply for directors' positions. Nothing. I love field management, so I went after that. Zip. I couldn't even get an interview for a sales job.

To say the least, I was not a pleasant person to be around and could find the bottom of a bottle of booze in a heartbeat!

A neighbor dragged me (kicking and screaming) to a career event. The next morning I went to their Website and stumbled onto its prayer request page. Now, I am NOT the sort of person who reads other people's prayer requests, but that day I read four. The last one changed my life.

The guy wrote, "I've lost my job, I'm virtually penniless, my wife has left me, my house is about to be foreclosed on, and I'm in total despair." It scared me to think what he might be capable of doing to himself because that guy could have been me—and I knew what I had contemplated. I swore at that moment that as soon as I got a job, I would help other people get jobs. When I landed a position, volunteering was a part of my employment agreement.

Yes, this is personal to Jeff and me because we've lived it. Which is why I got into the business of helping people in job transition in the first place.

This book is not a theoretical exercise from some self-proclaimed expert with no practical experience. This is real to both of us because we've lived it and come out the other side. We don't want you to have to endure what we've had to when there are better options. As we've said, it's personal to us—and to you.

Finding a job may feel like you're climbing Mt. Everest; job-hunting in this era can seem like that daunting a task. But if you did find yourself in the Himalayas, you'd hire a Sherpa guide who knows every way to reach the summit because his experience is that every climb is different. That's our intention: to teach you every way to the top, to be your Sherpa guides. We encourage you to use as many of our methods as possible so you can get there more quickly. More logs make a bigger fire.

Most books of this genre are as dry as dirt. We hope this isn't the case here. Besides offering a lot of useful information, we hope you can have a laugh or two at our expense (mostly Al's), accept our solace and understanding—and a kick in the keister when necessary.

Enjoy the intended humor, but remember the words of Winston Churchill, who said, "A joke is a very serious thing." When you read one of our jokes, there will almost always be a VERY serious message behind it.

> *"...I dream of things that never were,*
> *and ask why not?"*
> -Robert F. Kennedy

P.S. There's one common mistake we want you to avoid. In your reading, don't focus so much attention on the areas where you're strongest. Instead, closely examine the **weakest** elements of your job search—the things you hate doing most. If you work hard on the methods you're the least comfortable with, you will become the strongest of all candidates—and people. Let us help you strengthen your candidacy.

Chapter 2: State of the Job Market

The State of Confusion

You're going about this whole job-search thing wrong.

Don't misunderstand. We're not saying that you're dumb or that we're particularly smart. It's just that you're almost certainly looking for a job the same way you and practically everyone has *always* looked for a job. That's what's wrong. Times have changed and your search methods likely have not. It all seems so confusing, doesn't it?

It's not your fault. Until now, no one has brought all these changes to your attention. And there's an entire industry built on selling you products based on those old methods. Besides, virtually everyone else is doing the same thing. And there's some comfort in numbers. But is what *They* say working for you?

We're going to introduce you to some uncomfortable truths. And while the pundits may rant and rave, we're in good company. Consider what Plato said more than 2,000 years ago: "Strange times are these in which we live when old and young are taught falsehoods in school. And the one man that dares to tell the truth is called at once a lunatic and fool."[1] Sometimes we question our own sanity, but the matter of our lunacy should be settled in your mind if you agree that you have the qualifications to be an asset to a company. What *They* say hasn't worked for you so far, so maybe it's time to try something different—especially if *They* call it lunacy.

Do you want a job?

No, really. Do you want a job or do you want to continue doing the same things you've been doing because that's all you know? If the answer is, "Yes, I want a job," then let's get started.

Like mountain climbing, every successful journey starts with proper preparation and planning. A job search is no different. Your successful job-search journey begins now. Hang on to your hat!

What You Don't Know <u>Can</u> Kill You

Because of our traditional role as bread-winners, we men too often associate our self-worth with employment. But don't worry, guys, our female counterparts are catching up. Maybe we can all have a "One foot in the grave and the other on a banana peel" party. And we're only joking a little.

In a *National Journal* article, staff correspondent Brian Resnick presents some frightening statistics about the relationship between job loss and physical health: "Losing a job because of an establishment closure increased the odds of fair to poor health 54%...[and] it increased the odds of a new likely health condition by 83%."[2] If that's not scary enough, get a load of the title of Resnick's article: *Unemployed Less Likely to Receive Kidney Transplants.* This ain't hyperbole! He quotes a 10-year study that shows a 75% increase in end-stage renal disease and increased dialysis. And a case could be made that the unemployed have a higher incidence of being denied transplants because the jobless are a greater overall health risk.

Have we gotten your attention yet?

Let us share a bit more that might prompt you to seek a "combination of medications" to get well (and employed) again.

Fact vs. Fiction

We're willing to bet that you were good at your job. We're also willing to wager that you're not nearly as good at getting a new one. A job search is foreign to most of us—and for good reason. Who wants to lose a job and then be forced to look for a new one? Most of us would rather endure a root canal without an anesthetic than go through a job loss and job search. One thing is for certain: the concept of a job for life is something for a display case in a museum. As *New York Times* columnist and author Thomas Freidman said: The world is flat.

According to former Georgia Commissioner of Labor Michael Thurmond, the average job tenure in the United States is a mere 2.4 years.[3] Think about that for a minute, fill in the blanks below, and let's do some simple math. How old are you? At what age do you want to retire? (If the geniuses in Washington get their way, you can hope to retire no earlier than 72). Subtract the former from the latter then divide that number by 2.4 years.

____(retirement age) minus____(your age) equals____(# of work years to go)

____(# of years to go) divided by____2.4____(avg. years at a job) equals

_____ # jobs to come

That's the number of times you may be looking for work until you can retire. We forgot to include a little tidbit: the amount of time it takes to actually get a job (presently 9-plus months on average). Okay, let's say you'll buck that trend and stay at every job twice as long as the average Joe. You'll still be looking for a lot more jobs in your professional career.

Do you want to go through this job search crud again?

Let's get most of the frightening statistics out front, examine them, and then formulate a plan of action so they will only affect the other people, those who aren't as serious about getting a job as you are. (For the most current data, go to your country's Labor Department/Ministry. For the United States, the Web address is: http://www.bls.gov/ces/.)

But no matter how positive or negative the current job market might be, we believe that both your search prospects and income potential will be enhanced by what you learn in this book.

Note: If you find yourself becoming discouraged by the statistics, skip over them and go on to the next section.

State of the job market:
- Unemployment in the United States 6.7%[4] (~1.5m stopped looking)
- 10.3 million Americans remain unemployed[5] (officially)
- 36.1% have been unemployed for over six months (Long-term Unemployed)[6]
- Actual U.S. unemployment is estimated as high as 26 million[7]
- 26.9 million are jobless in the European Union (EU) countries[8]
- Overall EU unemployment stands at 12.2%[8]
- Greece (27.6%) and Spain (26.6%) remain extraordinarily high[8]

Let's pick our own personal poison to break down the official unemployment numbers (US) further:

- Adult Men 6.8%[5]
- Adult Women 6.5%[5]
- African Americans 11.9%[5]
  - Black Men 11.5%[6]
  - Black Women 10.4%[6]
- Asians 5.2%[5]
- Caucasians 5.9%[6]
  - White Men 5.6%[6]
  - White Women 5.3%[6]
- Hispanics 8.3%[5]
  - Hispanic Men 7.8%[6]
  - Hispanic Women 8.1%[6]
- Teens 20.2%[5]
- Recent college graduates 12.6%[9]
  - *underemployment* Rate +40%[9]

- Veterans 8.0%[6]
- Baby Boomers 5.9%[6]
- Generation-X 5.8%[6]
- Generation-Y (Millennials) 7.3%[6]
- Multiple Job Holders 3.7m[5] ("Stringers" +2.2% Dec. 2013 vs. Dec. 2012)
- Long-term Unemployed (27 weeks or more)
  - 4.1Million[5]
  - 36.1% of the total of the unemployed in the USA[5]

In 2011, CNN Money reported that the average time in job transition was 40.4 weeks.[10] That's over nine months! Those numbers have improved recently, but with 4.1 million still among the *officially* long-term unemployed, we have a long way to go.

And the longer you remain unemployed, the harder it may become to get a job.

Cynthia Shapiro, an often-interviewed former HR executive and author of *Corporate Confidential,* offers this chilling statement: "Once you are unemployed over six months, you are considered pretty much unemployable. We assume you were already passed over and no one else wanted you either."[11] Isn't *that* lovely? And according to Joshua Bjerke's article at Recruiter.com, [12] those with a criminal record are more easily employed than the long-term unemployed. Some companies simply will not hire someone who is currently unemployed, even though many of them deny that they do this.

Time magazine's Christopher Mathews writes that "[T]he depth of long-term unemployment in this recession far surpasses that of the recession in the early 1980s."[13] In that recession, long-term unemployment was only 25%, as opposed to today where those who remain jobless more than six months remains close to 40%, even four years into the current recovery.[13] Economics writer Michael E. Kanell notes in an amazing feature article in the *Atlanta Journal-Constitution* that Georgia has the fifth worst long-term unemployment in America, as 56% of Georgians have been unemployed for over 13 months. [14]

Affluent communities haven't been immune. In Roswell, a northern suburb of Atlanta, more than half the residents (children included) have a four-year college degree. Yet the January 18, 2012 edition of the *Wall Street Journal* reported that the need for subsidized housing in Roswell increased from 40 families to more than 500 over the previous year; the number of children eligible for free lunch increased 50%; and a Methodist church there has begun offering marriage counseling for couples experiencing stress due to job loss.[15]

Nobel Prize-winning economist Paul Krugman stated in late 2013 in the *New York Times* that there were "three times as many people looking for work as there are job openings."[16] And on top of an official unemployment rate in excess of 7%, the Gallup Organization estimates the rate of those who have taken lesser jobs just because they had to have something—what they call the "underemployment rate"—to be 17.4%.[17]

Would you like fries with that?

There might be worse news for those in job transition, but we can't imagine what that might be. There's this perfect storm of persistent long-term unemployment combined with an anti-unemployed bias that must be shattered. But it won't be broken if candidates limit themselves to familiar job-search methods.

But there's good news for **YOU**...

Neither the currently employed nor the majority in job transition have a stinkin' clue about how drastically the job-search playing field has changed. And THIS is to your advantage.

Natural Selection and the Evolution of Job Search

When did everything change? And what has it changed into? It doesn't matter whether you're currently employed and looking for something better, just lost your job, or have been in transition for quite a while. Here's what you probably did to start your search process:

1. Updated your resume
2. Looked through the job boards
3. Applied
4. Waited, and waited, and waited some more

Have you ever wondered why this is what everyone always does? The answer is simple: It's what we've always done; it's what everyone says to do; and it's always worked in the past.

This is what we call the "Spray 'n' Pray" method of job search. You spray your resume everywhere and pray that you get a call.

When Al gives speeches, this is about the time he normally does his Dr. Phil imitation: "So, how's that workin' for ya?"

It's hard to believe just how much and how quickly the job-search process has evolved. Here's a short history:

A scant 15 years ago, going to the classified section of the newspaper was the way most of us found jobs. This made sense because back then companies and recruiters posted the majority of jobs in the paper. When we found an interesting job posted, we put a resume and cover letter in an envelope, added a couple of stamps, and marched off to the post office.

Do you even get a daily newspaper anymore?

Job search began to move toward the home computer in 1994 when Monster® was founded. CareerBuilder® and Hot Jobs® soon followed. Companies began creating career pages there, so instead of one place to find posted jobs, candidates could look in several places. Job aggregators such as Indeed and SimplyHired took advantage of the available technology to bring virtually all jobs posted anywhere to a single site. (We think that using an aggregator is your smartest move to search for posted jobs.)

Today's job-search darling is LinkedIn, which celebrated its 11th birthday in May 2014. But in its early years, it wasn't the 300 million plus member juggernaut it is now. It was mostly reserved for Silicon Valley tech geeks.

At the height of the major job boards' popularity, recruiters and talent acquisition (HR) departments were required to pony-up five-figure annual fees. So recruiters began to look elsewhere. Since LinkedIn was free, it quickly morphed into the single most important tool for people on both sides of the job-search equation.

Two caveats:
1. Merely having a LinkedIn Profile means about as much as just having a posted resume (not a lot).
2. LinkedIn is now a publicly-held corporation, and as shareholders demand greater profits, some new entity is bound to supplant it as the job-search leader (their clock is ticking; Facebook is rumored to be considering an aggressive entry into this market).

Let's look at a couple of examples to illustrate why traditional methods are no longer as effective as they once were.

Open up a deck of cards. What do you see? If you're like most people, you just see 52 cards in your hand. We, however, see a stack of resumes. From one side, every card looks exactly the same. It's only when you turn them over and fan them out (read the resumes) that you see that every card (every resume) is unique.

Let's take this metaphor a bit further. Pick a card, any card (no, seriously). Jot your card's value and suit here _____. Now, submit your resume (return the card to the deck), shuffle the deck (like the resume-scanning software), and choose another card. If you picked the exact same card you had before, you "get an interview!" If your chosen card is what we've written a few paragraphs down, you just got to the second interview.

Back in the *Good Old Days*, 50:1 was about your odds of applying for a job and getting an interview. Although terrible odds when betting horses at the track, they are far better than your odds from an online submission in today's market. According to HR and talent acquisition executive Abby Kohut's book, *Absolutely Abby's 101 Job Search Secrets,* you have only a 5% chance of getting someone to even notice your online submissions, much less get an interview.[18] That's a 95% chance of NOT getting noticed!

In today's job market, you could easily be going up against more than a thousand other applicants. We're not exaggerating. (We'll share a real-life example later.)

Bet you thought we forgot to tell you what our card was…

Was your card the 9 of clubs? No? Darn, you didn't get that second interview after all. On the plus side, there are lots of jobs out there, and a lot of people are being hired. Odds are you've just been looking in the wrong place.

According to a 2009 CNN Money report by Jessica Dickler, of all available jobs, 82% are never posted.[19] Voilà, the Hidden Job Market everyone talks about. You (and just about everyone else) apply for the 18% of jobs that are posted, never getting a hint about the remaining 82% (other sources such as *Forbes* report similar Hidden Job Market numbers). To make matters worse, many of the posted jobs are predestined to go to internal candidates. They're posted merely to satisfy government regulations.

Now you see why they call online submissions the "Black Hole." You keep sending applications in, but nothing ever comes out!

Another example of how traditional job-search methods fall short: Tyrone Griffin has gone through job transition and has the scars to prove it. After a successful career came to an unexpected and abrupt halt, he went through the same kind of roller-coaster ride you may be enduring. In the end, he returned to the land of the employed, but he (like us) became determined to help people like you avoid many of the pitfalls that he encountered.

Tyrone is a talented speaker and an avid volunteer. His *Bunny Slippers are Evil* presentation is both funny and informative. He is the first of many experts who will share their insights with you throughout this book. In his article, "Look Beyond Your Resume," he offers his thoughts:

> One thing I've noticed with many job-seekers is an over-reliance on the resume. They think it is the last step in job search, instead of a first. They tend to focus all their efforts on getting the resume perfect, and less on the other aspects of job search.

It doesn't matter if your resume is written on gold leaf paper and imprinted with the king's signet ring in a wax seal. If it's buried in a stack of 500 similar resumes, you will have a major uphill battle.

My experience shows that networking and helping others is far more important. After being out of work for over a year, it was not a stellar resume that got my foot in the door; it was the fact that someone I'd helped get through transition walked my resume to a Hiring Manager and made a recommendation.

Yes, the resume was important, but if it was not for the fact that I had networked with and helped someone in their transition, they would never have helped me. Networking is important because that's how you get your name and experience known. Helping others is important because you will quickly realize the more people you help, the more will want to help you. And transition is a lot less lonely place when you have a group of people trying to help you.

Don't get us wrong. Like Tyrone, we're not telling you to throw out the baby with the bath water. Don't abandon the traditional methods of job search (resumes, cover letters, traditional networking, and recruiters). People still get jobs that way. But we're going to show you how to maximize your results and minimize the time you invest in those methods.

And in the chapters to come, you'll learn how to look beyond the traditional by also using the following:

Branding	Contacts	QR Codes	Interview Training
Positioning	Contacting Executives	Social Media Positioning	• Phone
Differentiation	Networking & "New Network"	• LinkedIn	• Panel
Targeting	Keyword Loading	• Google+	• Face-to-Face
Red Flags	Resumes & Cover Letters	• Twitter	• Skype
Assessments	• Choices	• Facebook	• Hidden Objections
Marketing Brochures	• Content	• About.me	• 800 lb. Gorilla Questions
Business Cards	• Structure	Baby Boomer Tactics	• Closing & Negotiation
Hidden Job Market	Job Boards & Aggregators	Job & Career Coaches	"Next Job" Preparation

From the above, you can see there are many tools for getting a job. As we said earlier, "We don't give a damn *how* you get a job; we just want you to *get* a damn job!"

Now let's get down to the business of getting you a job.

Chapter 3:   Get Ready, Get Set...

*"Your visions will become clear only when
you can look into your own heart.
Who looks outside, dreams;
who looks inside, awakes."*
-C.G. Jung

Lookin' Under the Hood

Unlike what you've been taught and what virtually everyone else will tell you, your first move should NOT be to update your resume. You're not ready for a meaningful resume yet. So let's not go off half-cocked. Besides, in today's job-search world, a resume is considerably less important than your LinkedIn Profile because the vast majority of jobs are never posted. But let's set that aside for a moment and take a look under the hood.

One of the first things that happens when you find yourself jobless is that you tend to lose your sense of value. We can speak from personal experience, unfortunately. We tend to minimize or forget all the great things we've done over the years. We tell ourselves, *"That's nothing; anybody can do that."*

But the truth is that *everything* you've done has value. For one thing, you earned a paycheck. They probably even gave you paid vacation time and other benefits. This wasn't done out of the goodness of the boss's heart. You EARNED it. You did valuable work. Those accomplishments, credentials, licenses, responsibilities and skills are worth something—namely, another job. But we all tend to minimize the value of what we've done, especially if our position has been taken from us. Even if you're presently employed, you will tend to think less of what you have done than others think of you.

It's time you reclaim your value here and now!

Sales people of any mettle keep a brag-book; those in other fields may maintain a portfolio or keep some sort of history of their accomplishments. You may not realize it, but you have a treasure trove of valuables. Grab a shovel, because the map below will lead you straight to that buried treasure. It's time to begin gathering the tools you need for a speedier, more effective Job-Marketing Campaign.

Harvesting a Bounty of Riches

Start by gathering the following:

1. **Old Resumes**
   At minimum, old resumes provide a timeline of your professional history. More likely, though, they will remind you of things you did in previous positions that you had forgotten about, such as projects or assignments you liked and would want to do again. Or they may make you aware of things you would want to avoid in the future.

2. **Performance Reviews**
   Many an annual review contains long-forgotten tidbits that can help you paint a picture for your future employer. These documents can include strengths, awards or consideration for awards, work you did as part of a team, areas for improvement, and much more. They are candid assessments of some of your key qualities.

3. **Group Accomplishments**
   If you were a member of a group that was given a task and the goals of that assignment were accomplished, those accomplishments are yours to claim! This is one of the most difficult concepts to convince some clients that they should include. Many insist, *"I was just part of a group."* This is true, but when you're in an interview situation and are asked about it, you will be prepared to give the Situation, Tasks, Accomplishments, and Results (S.T.A.R.) of the event.

An example: A former client of ours had been a television news editor and producer for over twenty years but found herself out of work for more than two years. She had worked for most of the local television news stations, in addition to the major three-letter all-news network based in Atlanta (CNN). She was convinced, however, that she had done nothing of value in her entire career. We gave her an assignment to write a short biography of her professional history. In it she happened to mention that she had been a member of a group that had won a regional Emmy Award. We said to her, "You buried the lead!" In the Marketing Brochures she created after she completed the process you're now going through, we branded her "Emmy Award Winner." Not only did she get a job quickly, she went to work for the company of HER choice.

What groups have you been a part of? This includes districts, branches, regions, and companies that had achieved positive results. Did your group's efforts save time, money, or manpower? Increase productivity or the bottom line? These are the types of accomplishments employers see as predictors of what you will do for them if they hire you. We'll discuss accomplishments in greater depth later.

4. **Examples of Your Work**
   Examples of your work might include marketing pieces, samples, awards earned, words-per-minute, pictures, speeches, presentations, brochures—what you assemble is limited only by your imagination and experience. FYI: LinkedIn allows members to post any number of presentations.

5. **Reports**
   Sales reports are near and dear to our hearts because we spent most of our professional careers as salesmen, trainers, managers, and sales executives. As such, we can still put our hands on reports that document our early successes. Other reports could include overall company results and Federal Trade Commission filings.

   Note: None of these reports should be shared directly with your new or prospective employer; they should be used only to document your work. (Not only is it in poor professional taste, it might be illegal.) They may also be used to calculate the return on your former company's investment (ROI) in you.

6. **"Atta-Boys"**

For those of you not from the south, an "Atta-Boy" is slang for any written praise of your work. It could be in the form of a note, email, or letter. These can be used as a third-party proof-source for any statement or claim you make.

7. **Articles About You**

Were you mentioned in a work-related article? Luckily for us, we've been written about often throughout our professional careers (some even good!). Many companies have newsletters, which are great morale boosters. Any time you're written about in a company newsletter you should hold on to it for dear life!

This may also include any mention of or reference to you in any publication. It will differentiate you from other candidates and help establish your position as an authority.

8. **Publications**

Many of us have written articles. Some have written technical manuals, books, blogs or published reports. Whether you're the principal author or a minor contributor, you should claim your expertise and creativity.

9. **Assessments**

Many of us have taken professional or personality assessments over the years. Some of us have taken so many that we can predict the graph we know we'll chart. If you have retained copies of yours, they can be a useful tool to help you foresee your future or change direction. We have a separate section about the desirability of investing in a professional assessment.

In addition to a formal assessment, we suggest that you make a list of your likes and dislikes. On a sheet of paper, draw a horizontal line across the top and a vertical line down the middle. Put a (+) at the top of the left column and a (-) at the top of the right. Now, list every task you have ever undertaken throughout your career. When you're done, closely examine the entire list to determine whether there are things you really want to have included in your next job or tasks you absolutely do not want to do. The results may surprise you.

10. **Recommendations**

More than likely, you've received formal recommendations during your career. Once you get a recommendation, you will want to retain that written praise of your work for life. You also will want to seek additional recommendations. (We'll discuss ways you can add to your collection of recommendations later in this chapter.)

11. **Associations**

There is an association for almost every profession. And many of these associations have national, state, and local chapters. Associations are an excellent way to uncover corporate insiders and possibly meet with employed members of that industry. The last time we went to their site, Weddles.com listed 97 broad associations. You should check to see if there is an association in your geographic area and area of expertise:

http://www.weddles.com/associations/[1]

12. **Accomplishments**

Many clients are unclear about what is meant by accomplishments. Simply stated, an accomplishment is anything quantifiable. For our purposes, accomplishments are anything that can be noted in the form of any of the following:

a) Dollars   (Increased bottom line by $2MM)
b) Percentages   (Customer satisfaction increased 22%)
c) Numbers   (Followers increased by 25,000)
d) Time   (Saved 642 man-hours)
e) Before & After (Compare before & after implementation)

13. **Skills and Certifications**   Examples:

a) Licenses   (Commercial Driver's License)
b) Software   (Microsoft Office, Excel, PowerPoint, Word)
c) Machinery   (Forklift; Crane)
d) Advanced Degrees (MBA Fuqua School of Business)
e) Specialized Training (Black Belt Six Sigma)
f) Certificates   (Systema Train the Trainer)
g) Formal Training   (American Management Association)

14. **Languages**

There's an old joke that goes like this:

What do you call someone who speaks 3 languages?   *Trilingual.*
What do you call someone who speaks 2 languages?   *Bilingual.*
What do you call someone who speaks only 1 language? *American.*

If you speak a second or third language, put it down! Let an interviewer ask about your level of fluency.

15. **Attributes**

How would others describe you personally and professionally? If you could, wouldn't you want to get a feel for a person in just a few words? Create a list of your attributes. They should be single words or short phrases (3 words maximum). Some of these attributes could be used on the back of your business card and/or in your Marketing Brochures. Below is a link to one of many lists of potential attributes. A good example is from the Missouri State University system:

http://www.missouristate.edu/assets/bms/AttributeComp.pdf [2]

16. **College Activities**
    a)   Degree Attained
    b)   Sports
    c)   Clubs
    d)   Employment
    e)   Internships
    f)   GPA
    g)   Greek Societies

17. **Volunteerism**

Volunteering shows an employer a number of things, including, but not limited to:
    a)   Strength of Character
    b)   Civic-Mindedness
    c)   Activity During Unemployment

Volunteering can lead directly to employment through people you meet. Many employers volunteer and prefer those who share similar values. It can also fill in gaps in your resume and get you away from the computer.

18. **Childhood Activities**
Especially if your background is thin, a list of these activities can go a long way toward landing that first or next position. You never know what it will take to make a connection with a hiring authority. Some childhood activities might include:
   a)   Scouting
   b)   Farm Employment
   c)   Talent Show
   d)   Sports
   e)   Clubs
   f)   Academics

We'll bet you didn't realize all the things you've accomplished in your lifetime. Pretty impressive when you put them all together, isn't it? The best part of this exercise is realizing that you deserve a pat on the back. Besides, you never know what will turn the head of a potential employer. And if you like what you've read so far (and are still in the process of putting your list together), hang on. What's coming up a little later will blow you (and Hiring Managers) away!

Recommendations

It's virtually impossible to get a job without recommendations. The more recommendations you have, the more confident the Hiring Manager will be that you're the right choice among all the candidates to be hired. Recommendations help minimize their fear of making a bad hiring decision.

Once you have a recommendation from someone, you have that gold star for life.

We encourage you to seek out and reconnect with many of your contacts. Reach out to former and current colleagues, former bosses, vendors, and clients; ask them for a recommendation. These are people with whom you have had a relationship. Many, if not all, will probably be glad you're reconnecting and be happy to help you out. They might even have a job lead for you. You never know.

LinkedIn has made it relatively easy to accumulate recommendations, but instead of just sending a cold, impersonal email, we suggest you pick up the phone. After making nice, let your contact know how much you appreciate something they did or something you especially liked about them. Whatever you say will most likely be both unexpected and deeply appreciated. This sets the stage for you to seek a comment in kind and/or ask for a recommendation.

One way to get more recommendations faster is to offer to write the recommendation *for* them—e.g., *"I know how busy you must be...."* Then tell them to review the recommendation and if they approve, all they need to do is send it back to you. (Be sure to load the recommendation with the keywords necessary for your desired position. Much more about keywords throughout this book.) This can all be done through LinkedIn, but we suggest that you make and keep a hard copy for your files.

Here's how to request a recommendation from a LinkedIn connection:

1. Go to your LinkedIn Home Page.
2. Move your cursor over **PROFILE** then click on **EDIT.**
3. Scroll down to the **Recommendations** box then click on the **EDIT** icon (the pencil thing).
4. Click on **Ask for a recommendation.**
5. Select a position from the **"What do you want to be recommended for?"** dropdown list.
6. In the **"Who would you like to ask?"** section, enter the name of the connection, then click **Finished.**
7. Enter your request in the **Create a Message** section. (Always personalize the message.)
8. Click **Send.**

We suggest you write the recommendation in a Word or similar document, proofread it carefully, and send it in an email or as an attachment. Remind your connection that all he or she needs to do is cut and paste what you've already written for them then click Send. This not only makes it painless for your connection but it also ensures that the recommendation says exactly what you want it to say using the terminology and keywords you've chosen.

Bits and pieces of these recommendations can be sprinkled throughout your Marketing Campaign to showcase your talents, expertise, and experience. You could, of course, simply tell people that you're the greatest thing since sliced bread, but someone else saying it carries a lot more weight.

Contacts

We never know where our next great job will come from. We each have thousands of contacts. These are people with whom we have *any* degree of association. Any one of your contacts might hold the golden ticket or be able to give you some insight into how to get in touch with a potential hiring authority. We want you to start assembling a list of contacts, with a goal of 300 individuals with whom you have some degree of relationship, not just social media.

No, we're not kidding. Leave no stone unturned!

Why?

> *Al: There was a couple who lived across the street from me; we were the closest of neighbors. David and I could often be found in the middle of the street sharing bad jokes or ribbing one another. The last job he had before they moved to a condo closer to town was lead engineer/architect for the world's largest aquarium.*
>
> *My wife and I hadn't seen them for a few years when we received an invitation to their 36th wedding anniversary celebration at the aquarium. He had become the President of the Georgia Aquarium, and we were one of only 14 couples invited—most of whom were corporate big shots.*
>
> *In the interim, I had been in job transition and never thought about contacting him. What a dope I was! Can you imagine how many big*

honchos he rubs elbows with every day? I never thought about it because my background and his were so different.

Everyone is a potential breakthrough contact. *EVERY* contact.

While LinkedIn is the main tool you should be using for your job search and managing contacts, you want to be sure that you have its latest update, which includes a feature that functions as a rudimentary "Customer Relationship Manager" (CRM). If you don't have it, you can send a request to http://contacts.linkedin.com[3]. It should only be a matter of days before you're added. This will benefit you tremendously by helping you stay organized.

In addition, we highly recommended that you download your current LinkedIn contacts into an Excel file, which will give you more control over your contacts and ensure that you have them in your possession in case LinkedIn ever decides to suspend your account for some reason. It doesn't happen often, but it does happen from time to time. We can't think of anything in the world worse than losing a contact list that has taken months, if not years, to compile. We also suggest that you download this monthly—more frequently if you're adding a large number of contacts—so you can properly save them.

Simply merge the new file with the old in Excel to maximize its usefulness.

Regardless of whether or not LinkedIn Contacts is live, you'll want to make sure you start "Tagging" each and every contact as soon as you connect with them. It's fairly simple to do whenever you review someone's profile. You'll see a section with Relationship and other criteria. To the far right is the Tag icon, which you simply click on to initiate the Tag function.

The reason we stress using Tags is that you want to be able to manage your contacts and be able to access the ones that fit certain criteria in your job search. For instance, you could set up the following Tags on LinkedIn:

1. Recruiter
2. Talent Acquisition Manager
3. Hiring Manager
4. Former Colleague
5. Friend
6. Relative

7. Career Event Contact

The list can get quite extensive, so please be strategic in creating Tags. You want to be able to manage them and not have so many that it becomes difficult to assign Tags and/or find ones you've already created.

In addition to the categories listed above, we suggest that you also set up separate Tags for the following:
A. People Who Have Recommended You
B. People Who Have Endorsed You

An added benefit of Tags is that you can search by Tags and find all the people you've listed for a specific category. This allows you to use these lists for creating email or other targeted campaigns.

We should note that LinkedIn limits mailing to no more than 50 people at one time. So if you find that you have more than 50 people in any one category, consider creating new categories such as Recruiters A, B, C, D, etc. that contain a listing for 50 people or fewer. It's unfortunate that LinkedIn is currently structured like this, but their goal is to prevent it from becoming nothing but an email marketing tool for spammers, which is to everyone's benefit. These limitations help tremendously.

We also believe you should create a contact spreadsheet on your computer. Outlook, Excel, or similar contact management system (CRM) would work equally well. A loose-leaf notebook is an alternative, but at a page apiece for every single contact, you could end up killing a lot of trees! All joking aside, what you want to record is:
- Name
- Address
- Phone Number
- Email
- Company
- Make room for
  - Current Date
  - Follow-up Date
  - Notes

Your list could include:
- Friends
- Relatives
- Address Book Members
- Rolodex Listings
- Former Bosses
- Colleagues (current or former)
- Classmates
- LinkedIn Contacts (the ones you actually know)
- Business Cards
- Clients
- Vendors

Like David, even people who seem off the wall should be included.

Think about it. Isn't it in the best interest of your cleaner, insurance agent, and financial analyst for you to be employed? Your kids' ball coach might be a contact who has a contact who can help you. How about your Christmas card and email lists? Write everyone down. You can always remove them from your list.

Red Flags

While we're in the introspection mode, we may as well face the fact that Hiring Managers are likely to discover real or imagined Red Flags about your candidacy. If not anticipated and addressed, Red Flags will sink your chances of being hired. It could be something you say during an interview, but more likely they will perceive that you're lacking some desired ability or trait.

Not to fret. Everyone has Red Flags. But if you prepared for them in advance, there is virtually nothing that can't be overcome with a story. We assume, of course, that you're not an axe murderer.

The only way to overcome Red Flags is:
   A. Assess what your potential negatives might be
   B. Create a plausible story that minimizes or eliminates that Red Flag
   C. Uncover a "Hidden Objection" during any interview
   D. Address the real or perceived Red Flag with a pre-planned story or explain that their concern is misplaced

In the chapter on interviewing, we'll discuss in depth how to judiciously uncover hidden objections without creating new ones. Right now, however, you should make a list of potential Red Flags a Hiring Manager might raise about your candidacy. You may also want to enlist the help of a trusted former employer or coworker to give you a candid appraisal. If so, be sure not to take offense or become defensive. Accept their comments as *positive criticism.*

What Red Flags might you have?
   • Gaps in your Resume
   • Odd Jobs (ones you took to pay the bills during your transition period)
   • Job History (too many or too few)
   • Education
   • Technical Skill
   • Licenses
   • Experience (too much or too little)
   • Qualifications (over or under)
   • Geography
   • Age
   • Physical
   • Drastic Change of Professional Direction
   • Non-Transferrable Skills

How might you address and overcome these potential shortcomings?

Examples: Did you leave the marketplace to raise children, aid a sick family member, move with a spouse who was transferred? Did you take a seemingly odd job because you had bills to pay and refused to go on government assistance? Were companies merged or moved? Did your employer downsize? Even though you don't have a degree, do you have extensive experience? Are you willing to acquire the necessary education? Do you have similar experience where the skills transfer?

Often a perceived negative can be turned into a positive in the eyes of an astute Hiring Manager. It all depends on how you package and convey your message. Red Flag stories should be succinct, meaning no more than sixty seconds long and delivered in a matter-of-fact manner. More about this in the interview chapter.

Ground Rules

Rule 1: **Job Search is Your Job**

Just because you're in job transition doesn't mean you don't have a job. You do. Your job is to find new employment, which means you should conduct your daytime activities as if you were employed. You do NOT have enough time on your hands to finally complete those chores on your "Honey-Do" list. Would you be painting the house or sitting with the neighbor at the doctor's office if you still had your last job? You should not feel any obligation to change your WORK behavior merely because your employment ended.

- Get up and get dressed! (In a later chapter we'll share a job-search secret that is best done before breakfast.)
- Work the time zones (there are four 8 a.m.'s and four 5 p.m.'s in the continental USA).
- Consider joining Toastmasters International. (If uncomfortable speaking, it will help you perform better during interviews.)
- Schedule time around EMPLOYED people (they have jobs!).
- Get buy-in from your loved ones that these are MUSTs to get a job faster. (Don't play computer games when you're supposed to be working.)
- Plan the work and work the plan. (Create a game plan and stick to that plan!)

Rule 2: **Designate a Search Space**

An orderly work place is essential. You become less efficient if you have to continually move, sift through, or put away your search tools. The sofa or dinner table is not conducive to a good search space, nor are those spaces private. You will certainly be conducting phone or Skype interviews, so a designated, professional search space is important.

- Claim all or part of a home office to conduct your search.
- Assemble all your tools in one spot (computer, files, printer, office supplies, planner, etc.).
- Keep it clean (Your space will be visible during Skype interviews, so know what will be in the camera's view.)
- Keep it quiet! (You can't conduct a phone interview with noise in the background.)

Rule 3: **Go to Health!**

It's easy to become ill during a job search. We can enter into depression without noticing it. Even casual questions from loved ones that are meant to be positive can get under our skin.

- Schedule exercise time (it helps reduce stress, maintain your weight, and take your mind off searching).
- Take all your medications and vitamins (you can't get a job if you're sick).
- Drink lots of water (staying properly hydrated helps you remain lucid and control your weight).
- Eat properly (fresh fruits and vegetables are better than carbs and fast, fatty foods).
- Get sleep. (Not too little or too much; besides, there's nothing good on TV at 3 a.m. We know this.)
- Go easy on caffeine and booze (the former can overstimulate and the latter is a depressant—need we say more?).

Rule 4: **Celebrate Every Win**

It's easy to get down, but most days you can find someone who has it worse than you. Your attitude matters. The clients that are hardest to help are the ones who always see the glass as half-empty, who see only the negative. We call these folks "Eeyores," after the donkey in the Winnie-the-Pooh books that was always losing his tail. Who wants to be around, much less hire, someone who's a downer?

- Write down EVERY positive happening for review on a weekly basis.

- Write every negative occurrence, read it once, then immediately tear out the page, rip the sheet to shreds, and throw the pieces away.
- This too shall pass! (Know that you're not the only person to ever lose a job.)
- Remember that you have people on your side.

We've given you a "Do List" of Ground Rules, so we believe we should include a list of counterproductive things you should NOT do, as well.

Do Not Do List

- **Don't rush this process**
  - Your search is a Marketing Campaign; a bad launch is costly.
  - You have only one chance to make a first impression.
- **Don't do chores** you would not normally do if you were at your regular job
  - Do weekend work on the weekend!
    - Housework
    - Repairs
    - Taking the neighbor to the doctor
    - Honey-Do's
- **Don't take advice** Everyone thinks they're experts at job search, so always consider the source
  - Search has changed. (A resume alone just doesn't get it any longer.)
  - How long has it been for them? (Remember the changes in the past few years.)
- **Don't go to too many Career Events**
  - Accountability groups are great, but if they turn negative, RUN!
  - Avoid *Pity Parties.*
  - Network with **employed people** (business-to-business events).

- o Calculate the cost/value relationship for a career event (otherwise you can spend hundreds per month).
- o Too many well-meaning amateurs give **BAD** advice!
- o Avoid "Career Event Overload" (1-2 per week maximum).
- **Don't go to resume reviews**
  - o Once you're satisfied with your resume, stick with it.
    - ▪ Everyone will have an opinion and will make suggestions.
    - ▪ You may become a professional resume-changer. The pay stinks and the benefits are lousy!
  - o A resume won't get you a job, but it can keep you from getting one.

Get to Work, You Lazy Bum!

While we're at it, let's debunk the notion that you're lounging around in the lap of luxury and are therefore a lazy piece of garbage if you're collecting unemployment insurance benefits. *You* know it's not the truth, but it really ticks us off when we hear it from holier-than-thou people who claim that the jobless aren't working hard enough at finding a job or only want to live off their unemployment checks.

In an article entitled, "Do Jobless Checks Subsidize Laziness? Research Shows…," *Atlanta Journal Constitution*-Constitution editorial writer Jay Bookman quotes a study conducted by economists from the San Francisco Federal Reserve examining the longevity of unemployment for individuals collecting unemployment benefit payments versus those who, for whatever reason, do not. "As of the fourth quarter of 2009," he writes, "the expected duration of unemployment had risen about 18.7 weeks for job losers and about 17.1 weeks for leavers and entrants, using the years 2006-2007 as a baseline. The differential increase of 1.6 weeks for job losers is the presumed impact of extended UI benefits on unemployment duration."[5]

In our state, Georgia, unemployment benefits max out at about $300 per week—BEFORE TAXES! What a windfall! Time to retire on that unemployment check. Meet you on the beaches near Rio...

"Tall and tan and young and lovely..."
(Apologies to Stan Getz and Astrud Gilberto)

Chapter 4:   Mental, Physical, & Fiscal Fitness

"A dream doesn't become reality through magic;
It takes sweat, determination, and hard work"
-Colin Powell

Planning

Virtually every job requires you to meet specific goals, expectations, mandates, and other targets. Job transition is no different. But since job search is foreign to most of us, thank God, planning is essential. Every hour of your daily/weekly search period should be planned and accounted for, even though you may only be accountable to yourself. Be a tough boss!

There is a set of ground rules you should adopt and stick to.

Full-Time Search

Part-Time Search

Let's assume you're in job transition, since that's the situation most of you reading this book are in. (Note that we didn't say "jobless" because TRANSITION is now your job.) You must determine if this is to be a full-time or a part-time job.

The current length of time the average candidate in the United States can expect to remain in job transition is 40.5 weeks, or nine and one half months.[4] That's the *mean* number (pun intended). Let's also assume that the above duration is based on people working their keisters off to land a new position.

Although it may seem simplistic, you must realize that you have a choice to make: Will your search be a full-time or part-time endeavor? If you choose to make your job search part time, it will probably take you twice as long to land your next position, right? So, what's is going to be? Before you answer that question, let us share a touch of reality with you.

The *Real* Cost of Job Transition
You owe it to yourself to determine what your actual cost of transition is. Many people believe that their cost of being unemployed equals the income they are losing based on their former salary. Nothing could be further from the truth. True, your cost does include your lost income, which may be mitigated slightly by a severance or unemployment benefits. But this isn't the complete picture— and it ain't a pretty picture.

As stated in the previous chapter, some companies won't consider someone not currently employed. Others tend to think you are of no value (our term) if you're unemployed for more than six months, even in an era where the average duration of unemployment lasts more than nine months and where scores of highly skilled individuals are jobless well over a year. (Have you noticed that this really ticks us off?)

To calculate your **actual** cost of Transition, here's what we suggest:

_____ Former Monthly Salary (take-home)

+_____ Actual Monthly Expenses (leave nothing out)

=_____ Monthly Loss of Wealth

This can add up quickly.

In economics there is a theory called "The Paradox of Thrift,"[1] which states that if consumers stop buying during a recession, the downturn gets worse and lasts longer. Even if you're totally against Keynesian Economic Theory, the "Paradox of Thrift" is certainly true in job search.

Like a turtle, most of us tend to hide in an economic shell during a period of job transition. But contrary to our natural instincts, it may be wiser to invest in ourselves when we're searching for a job. Things you should consider as wise investments include: additional training, advanced education, personal assessments, and/or a job coach. It may seem counterintuitive that spending money can actually save you money, but in this case it's true.

Consider this illustration:

> If your previous salary was $60,000, your monthly take-home pay was about $3,500, give or take a few bucks. If you're like most of us, you spend practically everything you bring home. So let's say your monthly expenses are $3,000. In this example, each month you're unemployed you're losing $6,500 of your personal wealth (based on lost income added to continuing monthly expenses).

> Remaining unemployed for the U.S. average of nine months would actually cost you $58,500 of your personal wealth. That's what we call the destruction of your future. Compare that to an investment in yourself of a thousand or so dollars to potentially get a job six months sooner. Your "net gain" would be close to $40,000 bucks!

And it's not the lost income that's the most harmful. It's the lost time.

Here's what one of our former clients had to say:

> *"After a few months, I wondered why I wasn't getting the results I expected. I stepped back and realized that at 59 it was costing me over $25,000 a month to cover living expenses and loss of wages for retirement."*

He determined that his actual cost of eighteen months in transition was nearly $320,000. Paul sought our help after nearly a year and a half of searching on his own. After a small investment in coaching, he got a new job within four months by following our suggestions.

Financial Preparation

The example above is not extreme. You must prepare to weather the storm. If you don't believe us, consider what a couple of financial professionals have to say. First is Certified Financial Planner Lee Pence, AAMS. We know you'll find his article, "How to Survive Financially After a Job Loss," helpful:

1. Talk to your family first. Don't panic and make hasty decisions. Job loss is a fact in America and you will get through it.
2. Develop a Financial Plan and put it into place. Start looking for work immediately, but remember that you need to set up a budget before you do this. You do not have as much income now, but your expenses continue. Which expenses can you reduce or eliminate?
3. Reassess your Career. Are there job opportunities available in your chosen field? If not, you may want to consider a new career with more potential and job satisfaction.
4. Severance packages are often negotiable. Ask! The worst they can say is no. Check out your benefits: Often outplacement assistance is available and paid by your employer.
5. Maintain health insurance at all costs. You will probably have to terminate your participation in a retirement plan, so use the extra funds to keep insurance in place. Consult an Insurance Professional if you qualify for COBRA.
    NOTE: Most of the time, this is very expensive, and an individual policy may be cheaper, especially with the implementation of the Affordable Care Act.
6. Continue life and disability insurance, if possible.
7. Avoid dipping into your retirement funds. Distributions before age 59½ may contain a penalty, plus you have to pay income taxes. Roll over your retirement funds tax-free into an Individual IRA if you're eligible.
8. Avoid short-term investment decisions. You may want to shift some funds into shorter-term investments with less risk.
9. Do not let debt become a burden. It's very easy to live off credit cards. If you find that the cards and debt become a burden, seek help from a reputable organization like www.Credabilty.org. Do not pay someone to get you out of Debt!
10. Seek Professional help. A Certified Financial Planner ™ Practitioner can help.

We believe that financial planning during a period of job transition is so important that we felt the need to let another pro further emphasize this point. In her article, "Budgeting During Transition," Karen Vining, a registered financial advisor, offers more practical wisdom:

> **A** budget is basically an estimate of income and expenses for a given period of time. As a job-seeker, it's more important than ever. A budget can be done on paper, a spreadsheet, or with software or an app such as Quicken or Mint. It's a tool and needs to be done based on what is easiest and works for the individual. Use whichever method is most comfortable for you. Keep it simple and it will be easier to adhere to.
>
> To begin, make a list of your expenses. It's that simple.
>
> Start with those bills that must be paid. These are the "have to" or most critical expenses such as the mortgage, food, and utilities. Next add the "want to's," those expenses which are not a necessity. For example, groceries are a "have to," but dining out is a "want to." Do this on a month-to-month basis. Also, be sure to allow some for miscellaneous items.
>
> Once you get this list done, you will have a much better idea what it costs you to live.
>
> Next, list all of your sources of income. Then subtract your expenses from your income to see what is left over.
>
> If you're currently in the process of a job search, that number may be negative. You may need to live very frugally until you find employment. If this is the case, it would be a good time to review your expenses and really scrutinize your "want to" list to see what expenses can be eliminated or reduced. Start by reviewing insurance and getting new quotes to see if it can be done at a lower cost. Review cable and telephone bills to see if there are ways to lower those expenses. There are many ways to save money, and Google is always a good place to start to get ideas.

Each individual and family is different, so once you have your budget on paper, you can prioritize what is most critical for your situation. And of course, once employed it's so important to start your "rainy day" fund for unforeseen expenses or in the event unemployment should happen again.

Time Ain't on Your Side

You must determine whether your job search schedule will be a full- or part-time process. Will you set aside 40 hours per week to this job search? If so, there are some things you must commit to and get the buy-in from your family members if you plan to succeed quickly.

While we're on the subject of time, managing the time you spend productively searching during transition is a problem for us. It's easy to begin the research process, find something that diverts our attention (that seemed important at the time), and at the end of the day wonder where all the time went.

Gene Griessman was once a cube-mate of media mogul Ted Turner. As the years passed and the Turner Empire evolved, Gene's position with the company expanded. He was an institution during the early years of CNN, interviewing many of the most important figures of the day. He has written a number of best-selling books and, as you can imagine, had to learn how to manage every hour in his deadline-filled days. In his article, "Time Tactics for a Successful Job Search," he has adapted some of those methods to help you not only during a job transition but for life in general:

> During the job search, like anything else in life, you need to properly manage your time. You need to come to a realization that if something is not worth doing, you shouldn't do it just for the sake of doing it. Although you might enjoy a momentary sense of satisfaction that *something* was done, it's a fleeting and false sense. Going through the motions is counter-productive.

You need to realize that much of life is a zero-sum game. One activity that you're involved in is always at the expense of something else you could be doing. That time spent in the other could be invested in activities that are much more valuable, so you really need to make a determination before you undertake an activity.

As part of this, you should make sure that the job that you're looking for plays to your strengths and not your weaknesses. Part of your success in life is living with, and maximizing, your strong points while working within the parameters of your weaker points. For example, if you don't have any skills in or like selling, if you choose that as a profession, you will always be uncomfortable at it. It's highly unlikely that you'll be successful either.

You also have to realize that sometimes you'll have to think outside the box to get a job and shouldn't just be relying on posted job listings, job boards, or social media sites. I know first-hand how you can be successful in so doing, as my daughter once employed such tactics in getting a sales job.

She came up with a very aggressive game plan for a company that she wanted to work for. Knowing that sending a resume to a company often resulted in placement of the resume in a revolving file and that calling resulted in unreturned calls, she took it upon herself to learn about the comings and goings of the VP of Sales she so desperately wanted to meet. After finding out from the receptionist what time he generally arrived, she decided to camp out at the business to see if she could somehow get the opportunity to introduce herself to him. One morning, she lucked out and she was able to greet the VP as he entered the building. Yes, it did startle him, but he was impressed with her approach and invited her for a formal interview. The rest was history.

Activities such as this may lead to that next position. So it's important that you manage your time and focus on those activities that are going to produce results and not just provide you with a false sense of accomplishment.

Assessments: Personal & Professional

Personal Assessments

One of us made Asha Lightbearer's acquaintance through her singing, the other at a networking event. She is more than talented—she's impressive. Soon after we met, she discovered that we are directors of career ministries and asked to speak at one. At first we were skeptical, but we saw that recent leaps of faith in Asha's personal and professional life parallel the challenges job-seekers face.

Still, it was the conviction of her vocational message with a *yet to be discovered* audience half a continent away that was the overall decision-maker. Asha's passion for that message prompted us to want to share both her passion and her message with you. We believe we should take stock of ourselves, determine on a gut-check level where we want to go, then follow up with a professional confirmation. We hope you can use what she suggests in her article, "Creating Passion and Purpose in Your Work." If so, we believe you will add a powerful tool to a soul-deep fulfilling future that also pays the bills. Here's Asha:

In order to be satisfied in your work, it's not a requirement that your vocation is your passion. However, if you wish to have a happy, healthy, balanced work life, there are a few simple rules to consider when making career decisions.

First, it's a good idea to commit to either:
- Doing what you love, or
- Learning to love what you do.

Many people live a life of trading days for dollars so they can keep up with the Joneses, have the luxury items and lifestyle they desire, or sometimes just pay the bills. However, true prosperity comes from being in alignment with your core values and the needs of your essential self.

Having material abundance is terrific! But it's also important to keep in mind the personal factors involved in creating a complete experience of prosperity and well-being. When you do, you will find yourself making more money and having a more enjoyable and peaceful life, including a better work experience.

So how do you know which employment or income opportunities will create this higher level of peace and prosperity? You can start by identifying the needs of your essential self. What inspires you? Motivates you? Brings you joy and passion?

Ask yourself these 6 questions:
1. What did I love to do when I was six years old?
2. What do I love to do now?
3. What makes me smile?
4. If I had plenty of money, energy, and time, how would I spend my days?
5. What do I most value in my life?
6. What would I like to experience more of every day?

Write down your answers. Make a list of all the different responses that come to mind for each question. Be sure to include a minimum of ten items for each—the more the better. This will stretch you beyond your limited everyday thought processes, so that you can begin to see what's truly important to you.

Now review your answers. Are there any common themes?

Also consider...
· What do I need to incorporate into my life to feel complete?
· What service would I be willing to do for free if I had the time and energy?
· What am I naturally gifted at?
· What was I born to do or feel I ought to be doing?

For each question, circle the top five or six answers that you resonate with most strongly. These are the answers that, if they had a voice, might call out to you.

Most likely, you will begin to notice a trend in your responses and priorities. This trend will often identify one or two specific skill sets and ideas for using those skills in a way that will bring you ease, prosperity, and satisfaction in your work.

If you cannot see how your responses could apply to any specific, viable work situation right now, I would encourage you to set your intention on being open to see broader solutions that allow you to use your innate gifts and passions vocationally. Over time, you will inevitably begin to notice how these skills can be used in a variety of applications.

When looking for a new job, carefully assess each opportunity against your circled responses above. Review the company's values and culture, job duties, commitment requirements, and any other relevant factors. Use a simple checklist to compare opportunities side by side against your identified skills and interests.

If an opportunity does not meet a requirement on your list, is there a way you can satisfactorily fulfill that requirement in your personal life?

You will find that some opportunities you were strongly considering do not line up with your personal requirements for a happy, balanced, complete life. Yet others, which you might have otherwise overlooked, seem to line up perfectly.

Do not try to make your values and requirements fit the job opportunities you're exploring. Doing so will have undesirable results. In the end, you will not be able to best serve yourself, your family, or your employer due to a fundamental breakdown in meeting the needs of your essential self—which has powerful control over your success. You cannot out-reason or bargain away your core values to make space for a more logical view. Instead, embrace and honor your essential self, its needs, and its desires. Commit to finding right-fitting jobs that work *for you*—not just you for them. You will find yourself happily making more money, having better relationships, and enjoying your work and your life more than ever before.

Professional Assessments

So, what do you want to do when you grow up?

Has anyone ever asked you that? Or have you asked yourself that question since entering this job transition? If so, don't feel bad. Not everyone wants to continue doing what they have been doing.

Right now is actually the perfect opportunity to take an in-depth assessment of where you are, what you want to do, what your personality says about you, what your strengths and weaknesses are, and whether you can make a living at it. If this sounds familiar, you may want to take a professional assessment.

We can't stress highly enough how important the small investment in a professionally conducted assessment can be for your future. We both have taken many assessments over the years, and of all the formal, professionally conducted assessments available, we recommend the DISC assessment systems. There are many other assessments available, but in our experience DISC is among the best.

Jon Newman has spent a lifetime at all levels of sales. As such, he, like all outstanding sales professionals, is a student of human behavior. He has transitioned from sales into training and now conducts formal, professional assessments. His article, "The DISC Assessment System," describes this useful tool:

> As you continue to prepare yourself in your career search, there are a few tools that will enable you to differentiate yourself from your competition. Specifically, the use of a widely established behavior-indicating tool called DISC is a method employers use to find out how a person can adapt his or her communication skills within the workplace. It accurately measures a person's communication styles in both their "natural style" (how they act naturally without stress), as well as their "adapted style" (the style they adapt at work and other stress-related environments).
>
> To more clearly break down the **DISC** model of human behavior, I've explained it in its most basic form.
>
> **D** stands for the **Dominant** Type, who is outgoing and task-oriented.
>
> **I** stands for the **Inspiring** Type, who is outgoing and people-oriented.

S *stands for the **Supportive** Type, who is reserved and people-oriented.*

C *stands for the **Cautious** Type, who is reserved and task-oriented.*

As you become *more* aware of these behavioral differences in people either at work or in life, the more you will adjust your behavior style to become an effective communicator. If you expect a naturally reserved person to act in an outgoing manner, you may wonder why they seem so hesitant. If you expect an extremely task-oriented person to be very people-oriented, they will disappoint you. However, people can adjust and grow in terms of their behavior skills, and everyone is a mixture of all four behavioral styles. Recognizing a person's normal behavior style allows you to adjust your own expectations when relating to them. You will find that recognizing other people's normal behavior styles allows you to better meet their needs and increase effective communication.

As a professional who is aware, you can adapt the way you relate to better meet the needs of others. How can you use DISC to better prepare yourself within the interviewing process? There are a several companies offering individual DISC assessments. Most often the assessment is administered online and feedback is returned within a few hours. In many cases, for an extra fee, a DISC behavior specialist will summarize the findings in a simple and easy-to-understand format. The assessment should provide an action plan and recommendations for personal growth. By understanding the assessment and ultimately utilizing its content, you will be able to pinpoint your communication strengths and create actions for improved communication skills.

As mentioned in the first paragraph, you need to assess how you can differentiate yourself from other prospects within the job market. Taking the DISC assessment and creating a personal action plan for improving communication is one method. Sharing your DISC summary with your prospective employer can further differentiate you from other candidates since many employers want their new hires to be on a constant track of self-improvement. And excellent communication skills are most often the key variable to becoming a valued employee.

We believe that having a formal, professional assessment enables you to position yourself for a brighter, more fulfilling future, as opposed to the dread of *just another job*. Job transition is a "Sales Situation." And although you may not like salespeople, you are now a salesperson. Knowing sales techniques will help you get through transition more quickly and prepare you for a more fruitful career.

For a fun and informative way to incorporate sales techniques into your professional life, seek out Dan "the Deej" Jourdan. Dan has made a video just for this book and YOU! Go to www.HIREDthebook.com and click on the link.

Note: Throughout this book we attempt to present as many perspectives on job search as space allows. Although we believe fully in the DISC assessment system, we invited other companies to present an argument as to why theirs should be the assessment of choice, but none responded.

Go to Health!

Not long ago, we met Marilyn Pierce, a registered nurse who works for an outstanding healthcare system. She knows the stresses of job search and its effects on the well-being of those in transition. We look forward to her upcoming book and thought it important to include her article, "Reducing Stress During Job Search: A Holistic Approach," in which she shares some thoughts on a subject most of us tend to overlook when we're seeking a job:

> **S**tress is a normal psychological and physical reaction. Job transition is stressful, yet one must be looking and feeling his or her very best to impress and project the value they bring. Imagine interviewing someone who wants a position with your company and looking into the eyes of a tired, pale, anxious person who is out of breath from a brisk walk down the hall? Stress can cause THIS person to show up to the interview, but this is not who needs to be there. Knowing that stress is a factor during job transition and implementing a plan to override the stress responses that includes health and wellness is a pro-active way to bring the best person to any interview.
>
> There are three basic areas of wellness that can easily be improved to manage stress responses during job transition:

1. Healthy eating
2. Regular exercise or movement
3. Plenty of rest

These three areas are essential to supporting wellness, but are the first to be abused and mismanaged during times of stress. Planning for ways to improve this will lead to pleasantly unexpected, positive results in all aspects of life.

Healthy eating does not mean going on a diet and losing weight; now is not the time. Instead, eating food that is high in nutrition and balanced in categories is a way to support healthy skin, good metabolism, and general health. Healthy meals and snacks should include a variety of deeply colored vegetables, citrus fruits and berries, beans, whole grains, and whole-grain breads. Incorporate low-fat proteins such as fish, poultry prepared without the skin, as well as lean meats. Also choose dairy products that are low in fat. Planning and shopping for these types of meals will be habits that can continue to maintain health and wellness into the future.

Move each day and get plenty of rest. If exercise was once a part of life, this is the time to remind those muscles how good it felt. Make it a daily habit to spend time getting the heart rate up with movement such as bike rides, taking the stairs instead of the elevator, or dusting off the exercise machine in the basement. A gym membership is not needed for a walk. Listening to music is a good way to get things moving, and dancing is a super-fun way to get the heart rate up and a smile on one's face. Regular brisk movement is one of the best ways to improve one's outlook on life. It releases the right chemicals that can uplift the spirit and supports the immune system during this stressful time.

Sleep is essential to supporting good health. Getting 6-7 hours of sleep nightly can help prevent illnesses such as heart disease and cancer. The hormones released during the stress response make it harder to sleep, so if it's difficult to get to sleep, use deep-breathing and relaxation techniques to calm and center your mind and body. Techniques such as meditation, yoga, and biofeedback can be used before bedtime. Try to go to bed and wake up at approximately the same times, even on weekends, to allow your body predictable times to sleep. The right amount of regular sleep will improve memory and allow better processing of thoughts and information. Napping during the day can lower stress, improve memory, and can provide a mood-lifting experience. The correct amount of sleep provides for more availability of serotonin, which decreases depression. While sleeping, the body has time to make repairs to systems affected by stress. Making regular sleep habits a part of life is an essential element of managing stress.

Job transition is undoubtedly a stressful time, but eating wholesome foods, exercising, and proper sleep habits will lessen its negative effects and can actually improve your overall physical and mental health.

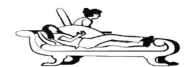

Psychology of a Job Search

Equating a job search to an emotional roller-coaster does a disservice to roller-coasters. Unfortunately, you *will* encounter some of the highest highs and lowest lows of your life. You will find jerks who will yell at or hang up on you, won't take your calls, or respond to your emails. The priorities of other people will not match yours, or the business of their business will get in the way of your search. You may feel like you're behind the eight ball or a square peg in a world of round holes. Or that *everybody hates you, nobody likes you, so you want to sit in the garden and eat worms!!!* (Did we hit every cliché?) Frustration can become a way of life in job search.

Neither your family nor your friends can know what you're going through, even if they've gone through a job search themselves. You may have heard the old saying, *"The definition of a recession is when a neighbor loses his job; the definition of a depression is when I lose MY job."*

Be aware that when a loved one asks, "What did you do today?" you might hear it as, "What the hell have you been doing all day? What's wrong with you? and Why haven't you gotten a job yet?" (Hmmmm...Wonder where we came up with that?)

All joking aside, job loss can make even the strongest of relationships suffer. And it's more than just the financial pressure. The loss of a job throws off a family's equilibrium that produces an emotional strain that can bring out the worst in some folks. So acute is the problem that a large church-based job-networking ministry we know of has added couples' counseling.[5]

One way to minimize this negativity is to celebrate any and all the victories (See Rule 4 above). Go back and read the good-stuff weekly or whenever you feel the need. Violently rip or even burn the bad stuff. It may sound hokey, but, believe us, it helps. Keep in mind that wins and losses are a natural part of life—including during a job search.

We take the mental health of you and your family as seriously as we do helping you get a job faster. Katherine Seifert, PhD, a psychologist and an expert on mental health, has graciously agreed to add a clinician's perspective to the effects of job loss on the family dynamic. We hope that her article, "How Job Loss Affects the Family," helps you and your loved ones avoid the pitfalls:

> **A** parent losing a job can affect the entire family. In addition to financial insecurity, it can cause a change in lifestyle. The stress caused by job loss may also lead to conflict among family members. Some family members may become depressed or anxious. Children may worry that something horrific is about to happen from which family members cannot recover. Some family members will have headaches and stomach aches that are probably stress-related.
>
> Stress can be a good thing or a bad thing. The right amount of stress can motivate us to work on solving a problem. It's like the amount of effort one needs to pick up a large load. The larger the load, the greater the effort that is needed. However, if the load is too heavy to lift, you can hurt yourself trying to pick it up alone. Too much stress that overwhelms us for a long period of time can hurt us, too. That is why family members helping each other makes the load lighter and is really essential in this situation.
>
> There are great ways to reduce the stress of job loss on family members. Relax and play together as a family often. Talk about the joys of the family as often as you talk about the hardships. Problem-solve new issues by holding regular family meetings. Say encouraging things to each other. Children need to know that everything, while different, is all right. They need to know that the family will love and help each

other in every way possible. However, if a family member has moderate to severe problems with sleeping, eating, mood, concentration, activity level, school, or relationships that lasts more than 2-3 weeks, he or she may need an assessment to see if individual or family therapy is needed.

The number one thing that helps people cope with hard times is support from the people who care about them. It's called social support, and it helps a person put a hardship into perspective, reduce worry, maintain self-esteem, and solve problems. Look for loving things you can do for each other that do not cost money. Families supporting each other through a job loss with encouragement and love can actually bring a family closer together.

God forbid you should find this necessary, but just in case:
Suicide Hotline 1-800-273-8255

Remember that a job search, like sales and baseball, is a numbers game.

Ted Williams was the greatest hitter baseball ever had, and in his best year he missed getting a hit about sixty percent of the time. And there are many others in the Baseball Hall of Fame who were successful at the plate only about 25 percent of the time.

You will swing and miss, too. You'll feel like a little leaguer. But if you follow our suggestions and keep practicing what we teach, you will succeed. And you're much more likely to get your next position months faster than the average candidate.

Keep in mind is that our worst day during transition is probably better than the best days for most people in the world. For example, Jeff's son got married a while back, and he traveled halfway around the world to his new daughter-in-law's native country, Cambodia.

It's a miracle in itself that she was born, given the atrocities of the Khmer Rouge and its leader Pol Pot, whose minions imposed "Social Agrarianism" on his people. Through virtual slavery, executions, rampant malnutrition, and a total lack of medical attention, somewhere between one fourth and one third of its population died in what became known as "The Killing Fields." As many as three million Cambodians perished.

Though the country is quite beautiful, the depth of poverty is overwhelming. During Jeff's time there, he took a picture of a beautiful little girl who, with her sister, was begging through a fence for pennies as their mother worked in the adjacent rice fields.

We understand your plight. We've been where you are. But a job search is a passing phase. You WILL get a job-and sooner rather than later. In the meantime, try to keep your current situation in perspective.

Chapter 5:   Keywords & Boolean Searches

> *"Words are, of course, the most powerful drug used by mankind."*
> -Rudyard Kipling

Words Matter

"A rose by any other name would smell as sweet,"[1] uttered the naïve Lady Juliet Capulet regarding her love, Romeo Montague. A single word, "Montague," turned out to be the death of them both. Similarly, using the wrong words in the job-search world of today can poison your candidacy.

Come on, guys, you gotta be kidding me!

Think so? Consider this: A new president was named at the company where a former client of ours had worked for over twenty years. The two didn't get along, and she was soon fired.

Her experience was exceptional, the industry was booming, and her location was perfect (safety training in the petrochemical area of Louisiana known as "Cancer Alley"). Still, she couldn't find a job. The problem? The terms she was using in her LinkedIn Profile and on her resume were not up to date.

Doris came to us on a Thursday and we scheduled a "Words to Work" session on Friday. We discovered the currently used terms for what she did every day as opposed to the terms her former employer used. She uploaded her revised LinkedIn Profile on Saturday and began getting calls from companies on Sunday to schedule face-to-face interviews. She had an interview on Monday and another one on Tuesday. She received two job offers on Tuesday.

No, that's not typical (we wish it were), but it's just one of many examples of how using the right words can help your job search.

Another example:

A former client, a naval communications officer, wanted to exit the military and enter the corporate world. But it wasn't until we uncovered the civilian terms for what he did in the military and added them to his LinkedIn Profile and to his resume that he began getting calls and interviews. He soon had his choice among a handful of job offers.

What's so important about the words you choose?

By now you should have assembled the elements of what you've done for other companies. It's time to understand how today's job search works—and why.

The Hidden Job Market

Hidden Jobs
Posted Jobs

Source:
CNN Money 2009

According to numerous Internet sources, more than 80% of all available jobs are never posted. In 2009, CNNMoney reported that the Hidden Job Market accounted for 82% of all jobs.[2]

How can that be?

In Chapter One we promised to share a story about why there are so many hidden jobs. And how, when you apply for a posted job, you may be in competition with hundreds or even more than a thousand candidates. Here it is:

A talent acquisition executive at a Georgia-based Fortune 150 power generation company (not hard to figure out which one) was speaking at one of the larger career ministry meetings at a local church. She told the audience that the company recently had a requisition number for one administrative assistant (that's HR jargon for one secretarial job). Her department received more than 1,200 applications for that one position. That's right, one thousand two hundred people applied for that single job.

We're certain that the person they hired (#1) was outstanding, and we're equally certain that candidate #1,200 was probably pretty lousy. But think about it: How much worse could #100 have been compared to #1?

How many times have you applied for a posted job that you were perfect for and didn't get any response? How much worse could you have possibly been than the people they interviewed, much less the person they hired? Blame this guy, why don't you...?

Boolean Searches

George Boole (1815-1864)

You've probably hated this guy for years and didn't even realize it. As a matter of fact, we can tell you when and where your hatred of George Boole began. You were a high school freshman sitting in algebra class. George Boole was an English mathematician, the guy who created Algebra's Order of Operations— you know, that wretched braces, brackets, and parentheses thing.

$$\{\ \}, [\ ], (\ )$$

That's probably not where you *learned* to curse, but it may have been when you elevated cursing to the level of an art form. It may make you feel better to know that Boole only lived into his forty-ninth year. We can't confirm this, but our theory is that Boole was murdered by freshman math students hurling their algebra books at his head.

Years ago, some IT wizard created a program that allowed computers to scan for specific words by adapting Boole's Order of Operations theory. You employ this technology every time you do a search. You type words, the computer searches for those terms, and within a fraction of a second you get a gazillion search results. Remember the line we used from *Romeo and Juliet* to start this chapter? The link we clicked on after we entered our search words was one of

111,000,000 (that's million) results. (By the way, we didn't go past the first page—but we'll get to the importance of THAT in a little bit.)

A typical Boolean search begins with open quotation marks, then the desired keywords are added with plus signs between them, and unwanted keywords are entered with a minus sign in front of them. The search is concluded with closed quotes. A search might look something like this: "keyword+keyword+keyword-keyword." Putting a series of keywords in quotes tells the computer to search for that exact phrase. On the other hand, entering keywords without quotes produces keyword matches found anywhere, in any document, in no particular order—thus, the gazillion results.

Whether you like them or not, people in Human Resources are no dummies. That scanning technology was adapted for their benefit, better known as Applicant Tracking System software (ATS). An HR person can conduct a search based on a handful of keywords and/or phrases to find as many qualified applicants as he or she wants within seconds.

Don't believe us? Read on:

> I (Al) was presenting on this subject to a skeptical audience (like you), so I did a Boolean search live. I told the attendees that I was looking for a Vice President of Sales for a fictitious pharmaceutical company that was launching a blockbuster new product. The candidate had to reside within 25 miles of postal code 30317, which is Sandy Springs, a northern suburb of Atlanta where I was speaking.

> I began my LinkedIn advanced search by opening quotes and typing in "Vice President." I got 56,455 results! (Can you believe that there are more than 56,000 people with the title of vice president within a 25-mile radius of that postal code?) I added "+Sales" to my search and the number was reduced to about 22,000 people. Adding "+New Product Launch" drove the results to a bit less than 1,200. The inclusion of "+pharmaceutical" and "+medical" dropped it to 91. This is where most recruiters would stop, about 10 pages of LinkedIn. But I wanted to eliminate more, so I typed "–Insurance."

> I ended up with nine individuals: eight brilliant people and me.

If this had been an actual search, it's virtually certainty that a great hire could have been found using that search criteria. And it took only a few minutes.

So maybe now you see how important using the right words can be. Just in case you're still not sold, let me make it simple. Many years ago I (Al) worked for a small medical manufacturer's rep company (Neat job, I got to see my first chest cracked open) that sold disposable products and capital equipment to hospitals. Guess what? Hospital Capital Equipment is no longer called "Hospital Capital Equipment." It's known as "Durable Medical Equipment" (DME). No medical device company or medical recruiter seeking a *Jim Dandy* sales person would do a search today using the term "capital equipment." today. It's "DME" or death!

You might be the world's number one medical capital equipment salesperson, but you would never be found in a Boolean search like the one above and the ones being conducted every day because you used the wrong words to describe your accomplishments. The same applies to what you've done in the past and what you want to do next. As cited earlier in this chapter, the words you choose may be the difference between getting found and floundering.

Is it becoming clearer that specific words added to your profile and your resume just might be important?

Every day recruiters are using Boolean searches to find people *like* you. Wouldn't you prefer that the above sentence read, "Every day recruiters use Boolean searches to find YOU"? Discovering the terms they're using is essential to getting found.

Words matter!

Applicant Tracking Systems (ATS)
Companies can receive more than a thousand applications for a single position. And as we've demonstrated, a method to sort through the onslaught had to be created: Applicant Tracking System Software. Rick Sullivan is an HR Professional and ATS expert. In his article, "How to Stand Out When Dealing with ATS," he offers an insider's perspective on how you might best deal with scanning software when applying for posted jobs:

In today's world of hiring, the larger companies and recruiting firms use Applicant Tracking System (ATS) software. The reasons are obvious:

1. These organizations receive hundreds to thousands of resumes, both solicited and unsolicited. So the use of ATS saves them a lot of time and hassle to sort through those resumes.
2. The results of an ATS search give the Hiring Manager or recruiter a reasonable number of resumes to sort through to select candidates to be interviewed.
3. The Equal Employment Opportunity Commission (EEOC) likes these systems because they are a non-discriminatory way to select candidates.

So what does this mean for you?

For starters, you have to have a resume that can "pass muster" in an ATS search and be selected. First, do your due diligence on the company before you hit the "send" button on your computer or fill out an online application. Your objective is to tailor your resume to show that you're familiar with the company and its industry. Second, make use of keywords in your resume and cover letter.

Where do you find keywords?

There are no dictionaries of keywords. You're going to have to take the time to read and study the job ad, job description, or the input of an insider networking contact.

One way to help you find these words is to make use of a "T" analysis. On the left side of the T, lay out what the company wants, using their words and phrasing. On the right side of the T, list your skills and experience that match each item you listed on the left side, as well as point out gaps (items you do not match up to). Then sprinkle these words into your cover letter and resume. Bud Bilanich, author of "Climbing the Corporate Ladder," noted that if the job ad says the company is looking for a "self-starter," make sure you insert "self-starter" somewhere near the top of your resume.

Next, review your online presence to ensure it's consistent with your Personal Brand. Also Google and Bing yourself on a monthly basis to see what comes up.

Finally, use a font like Ariel or Times New Roman (size 10 to 12). Do not use special, unique, or obscure fonts because many ATS software systems may not be able to read it. In the same vein, do not use graphics or include pictures on your resume. Your resume needs to be in a professional format. Do not submit a functional resume, as it may not be able to be correctly read by the ATS.

Keep in mind that the purpose of a resume is to get the coveted interview. So the point of this job is to do your homework up front and tailor your resume with keywords to show the ATS (and then a human) that you're worth their consideration for an interview.

Let the other candidates get sucked into the Black Hole while you cruise through space in your Starship at warp speed.

S.E.O. Ho! Ho!! Ho!!!

S.E.O., for those who don't know, stands for Search Engine Optimization. That is at least part of what companies and products (individuals too) use to reach their goal of position one, page one when any search is done. To make an exceptionally complex concept simpler, there are algorithms in place that use key search terms in descriptions to move that entity higher or lower in a search return based on the number of terms used. (More of that darn math we swore we'd never use again.) These could be single words or what's known as *long tail strings* of multiple words in a specific order. (There's more to it than that, but that's close enough for our purposes.)

Generally speaking, when you do an Internet search, how many pages do you research before moving on?

According to Jessica Lee's June 20, 2013 article in *Search Engine Watch*, Google #1 position gets 33% of total search traffic.[3] It's largely the same with a job search. Wouldn't you like to be found every time a recruiter does a search for someone with your background? What's good for Google is great for you!

Guess what? Recruiters do pretty much the same thing on LinkedIn and any other sites they choose. They search for the requisite number of qualified candidates then end the search and try to fill the position. No one else from that point on is even considered.

The Black Hole returneth!

Where do you want to be?

In a job search, as in business, your goal should be page one, position one. The higher you are on LinkedIn for your specific area of expertise, the more likely you will get viewed and have your profile read. After that, it's a question of, "Are they seeing what they're seeking?"

As we've been trying to hammer home, one of the key elements is using the right words—the words companies with posted jobs are using. Even more important would be the companies that don't post their jobs. Remember that 82% Hidden Job number we showed you earlier? Many of the companies that do not post jobs search for the best candidates without the hassle or expense of sifting through hundreds of resumes. They use Boolean searches.

S.E.O. for Y-O-U

But how do I find the right words?

'Words to Work'

Vichyssoise may be nothing more than cold potato soup, but look at how much more a French restaurant charges versus your neighborhood diner—and the diner serves it hot!

In our opinion, the best first step to find the right keywords words for the job you want is to start with your specific job title. In the Boolean search demonstration above, the more refined the search got, the closer the matches came to the "ideal candidate." The same is true for you.

Some time ago we began a program with new clients that we dubbed "Words-to-Work" since one of the many methods we espouse is to use the specific keywords that companies are using in their searches to find qualified candidates. Every new client goes through a Words-to-Work session within their first week to discover his or her particular keywords and phrases. These are personal coaching sessions. You bought this book, so you're getting the generic version. But don't worry. You'll be able to follow along just fine.

In our maiden Words-to-Work class, one of the clients was seeking a new Director of Supply Chain position. So that was the initial search. Here's part of what we found doing a LinkedIn advanced search for both jobs and people (example first, then we'll get to your specifics).

We found three jobs that were interesting to the client after he reviewed the job descriptions. From the job requirements, skills and expertise, and preferred skills we created a word cloud. Our client came up with a handful of words, terms, and acronyms from that word cloud that **he knew were important** to the type of position he was seeking. (A little analysis on your part is required). He also had a vast list of words that he knew were being used in his industry—then we did a bit of comparison.

In the title box of a LinkedIn people search, we entered "Director of Supply Chain" and got 1,644 people from our moderately large network. (We saved that screen's results to review later). Using only first names, the page 1 results we received included "Stephen, Robert, Rick, Diana, and Bill." Then we added a few of the client's known keywords into the keyword box. Of the original 10 people, only Stephen "survived" the addition of the keywords!

Let's back up for a moment. There are a few things you need to do before we start YOUR keyword search. This will be some live practice. You can go back and do it again later.

1. Crank up your computer and go to your LinkedIn home page (go now, we'll wait).
2. Note the number of views you're presently getting per week (bottom right-hand side of your screen); take that number down to compare in a couple weeks.
3. Then move the cursor to your tiny picture on the top right-hand side.
4. A dropdown box will appear with six lines including your name. (If you're reading an older copy of this book, LinkedIn may have changed the operation slightly.)
5. Click on **Privacy & Settings.**
6. Enter your password when prompted.
7. Look at the column below the yellow Upgrade button.
8. Find Privacy Controls then click on "Turn on/off your activity broadcast."
9. A box will appear that includes a small box that reads, "Let people know...."
10. If there is a check mark in the little box, click to remove. You'll be making a lot of changes to your LinkedIn Profile, and you don't want the whole world to know what you're doing (especially if you're currently employed). You also don't want people to think you're a spammer. You can change back later.
11. Click on Save Changes.

That little tidbit aside, we can get down to work.

You already have LinkedIn open. You'll also need to open a Word document (or the Apple version). We'll have a couple of other things going on simultaneously.

1. On your LinkedIn home page, click on **Advanced.**
2. On the new screen, click on **Jobs.**
3. Where the box reads **Title**, enter your desired job title in quotation marks. If you don't put them in quotes, every permutation of each word will appear in the search, and you will curse us like we cursed our algebra homework back in high school.
4. A number of jobs should appear from all over your country. That's what we want!

   Note: We DID NOT enter a Zip code (postal code) because we're not looking for jobs at this point; we're looking for the words associated with the jobs you're interested in.

5. Read everything about each job to determine whether that job is something you would hire yourself for if you were the Hiring Manager. If it is, copy the skills, qualifications, and requirements, then paste it into your Word document.
6. Repeat step 5 until you have 3-5 such jobs. Post all that info into the same document.
7. Go to a Word Cloud generator. (There are a lot of them: Wordle.net is a big one, but we prefer ABCYA.com. It's a word cloud generator for kids, but we like it better for a number of reasons.)
8. Copy ALL the stuff from your Word document and paste it into the box that reads something like *Type or paste text here.* (There are character limitations.)
9. Then click to generate your word cloud.

   Note: With ABCYA.com you can make numerous adjustments to the word cloud. You can change the font type to something that's easier for you to read; change the color (we suggest black on white so you can print the word cloud without having to buy a new printer cartridge); and adjust the direction of the words (we don't know about you, but *we* don't read in circles). There's one more major adjustment available: you can increase or decrease the number of words in the word cloud as desired. Please see:

   http://www.abcya.com/word_clouds.htm

10. Print your word cloud.

    Note: Generally speaking, the larger the print in your word cloud, the more important it is to use that exact word numerous times in your profile and resume. Use these words to describe similar things you have done elsewhere in your professional history. Use these exact words over and over.

11. Review carefully, seeking specific keywords, phrases, and acronyms that you know or believe are important for securing your job.

    One last thing...

12. Do a people search throughout all of LinkedIn for people with your title and note that number. (Just repeat steps 1-3 above, EXCEPT click People

instead of Jobs.) Try to avoid 1st-level connections as they can bias your results.

Because you have multiple sets of keywords from a number of companies, you now possess a close approximation of what companies seek when they are searching for someone like you. In short, you're no longer shooting in the dark. You'll use these keywords to populate your resume and online profiles. This will also help you create your own Personal Brand.

Just before you launch your campaign, you'll be able to compare yourself to other professionals with backgrounds similar to yours—your competition. And without scamming the system, you should be able to out-keyword virtually all of them, thus increasing your LinkedIn views and maximizing the chance of making it through the Black Hole.

Bits 'n' Bites
A couple of final words to this chapter. We recommend that you sign up now for and use the following two free services:
1. "Bitly" account at: https://**bitly**.com/.
2. HootSuite account at: hppt://**hootsuite**.com

Bitly will allow you to shorten links to Internet sites while HootSuite lets you copy and post the links, add comments regarding the posts, and schedule them for times where they are most likely to be viewed.

Hootsuite will allow you to set up and schedule your postings to a number of social media sites. You will not only be more productive, but it will minimize the possibility of your being viewed as a "spammer" by posting one update right after another. Furthermore, it will allow you to monitor "conversations" on Twitter streams so that you can really understand what is going on with target companies, industries, and other areas of interest.

Chapter 6: Personal Branding

Howdy, Pardner!!!!!!

You've gathered the herd, that vast amount of professional and personal information about what you've done throughout your career to date. You've decided on a desired job title and have a good handle on the traits companies are seeking in people of your caliber and that title. Now it's time to establish your Personal Brand based on all the above.

We know what you're thinking: *"Whoa, Cowboy! I'm not some steer. What does Branding have to do with me?"*

Let's face it. To most companies, you're just like any other product, just another member of the herd. It's actually worse than that, because you're looked at as being as replaceable as any other commodity. To them, we're disposable components.

My first *real job* (AI) was with Kimberly-Clark Corporation, a very good company with outstanding training. I was hired while I was still in high school, and after eight years, four transfers with as many promotions, and numerous awards, we parted ways. Not long before I left, the company created an airline that was to become Midwest Express. My facts may be off somewhat, but the content is basically accurate here. Anyway, two Venezuelan-owned DC-9's became the initial fleet. Early on, one of the planes lost an engine just after takeoff and went down, killing everyone aboard. A couple of days later, I called a former coworker and asked if we knew anyone on the plane. The reply was, "No, but every one of those men was replaced by 8 a.m. the next morning."

Granted, it's an extreme example, but consider that the Personnel Department at many companies has been replaced with Human Resources and that at some companies, that department has devolved into something called "Human Capital." Heartwarming, isn't it?

"Tote that barge and lift that bale..."[1]

And what's the first thing companies do when a downturn occurs or they want to show short-term increased profitability? They "reduce headcount." Every time we use that term, the guillotine scene at the beginning of the movie *Papillon* comes to mind. Gulp.

You must, of course, remember that we're capitalists, and that there is this thing called a profit motive. After all, these companies have shareholders (and their own jobs) to consider. Besides, if we were in their position, would we do anything differently? Well, maybe the head-chopping part.

Okay, so you want a job. We can probably agree that you don't care if you "find" the job (active pursuit: through HR, job boards, recruiters, networking, or via direct contact with a corporate executive) or "get found" by a company that's looking for someone with your skill set (passive pursuit).

To get a job, you must first get interviews. And if you want to get interviews, you must do something to differentiate yourself from all the other candidates. But if you merely go about your job search in traditional ways, you're no different than every other candidate—just another resume in the queue. You're like every other card in the deck. Remember that "Card ~~Trick~~ Truth" we did earlier? We want them to flip you over and see what's on the other side. We want you to get categorized as a real person as opposed to all those paper people (resumes).

So how do you differentiate yourself? Personal Branding

Personal Branding is similar to branding a product or service, where marketing executives ask: "Does the name have meaning or possess intrinsic value? Is the brand unique, thus separating itself from the wannabe competitors? How will someone remember the product or service?"

Do you remember a product called Dow Bathroom Cleaner (Yawn)?

In 1997, Dow Chemical Company sold many of its consumer products to S.C. Johnson Wax, including Dow Bathroom Cleaner. Obvious, S. C. Johnson had to change the product's name. Why promote another company, right? Besides, the name stunk. What name could they come up with to differentiate this cleaner from all the others? What would be a memorable name?

Hmmmmmm...

Dow's product name notwithstanding, their marketing department and/or advertising agency had some smarts, and the people at S.C. Johnson were bright enough to use the product's ad to great advantage. Have you ever used "Scrubbing Bubbles"? A product that *tells* you exactly what it does—it's *"Scrubbing bubbles so you don't have to."* Not only can you "see" the product's symbol in your mind's eye, but you probably can recite the commercial's tagline.

A brand is born.

Branding = Differentiation

What is branding?

Adapting the American Marketing Association's (AMA) definition of a brand to the job-search arena would go something like this: a *name, term, sign, symbol or design, or a combination of them intended to identify the goods and services of one candidate and differentiate them from those of other candidates.*[2] So it makes sense to understand that branding is not about getting your target market to choose you over the other candidates, but it's about getting your prospects to **see you as the _only_ candidate who provides a solution to _their problem._"**

Objectives a good brand will achieve:

1. Confirms your credibility
2. Understands the needs and wants of your prospects
3. Delivers the message clearly
4. Connects your target prospects emotionally
5. Motivates the Hiring Authority

You will accomplish each of the above when you establish your own personal brand and other elements of this process. Here's how the Transition Sherpa methodology will work for you:

Branding Efforts Must	Action Items
1. Confirm Credibility	Professional History (Accomplishments, Credentials, Assessments, etc.)
2. Wants & Needs Understood	Requirements-based Word Cloud creation & Keyword loading
3. Clear Message	Personal Brand throughout Marketing Campaign (Profile, Resume, Brochures)
4. Emotional Connection	Personal Brand, STAR Stories, Marketing Campaign, Interview Training
5. Motivation to Hire	Marketing Brochures & Interview Training

In "7 Myths of Personal Branding," Joellyn "Joey" Sargent, principal and founder of Claravon Consulting Group, clears up the most common misconceptions about branding and you:

There is a lot of confusion about personal branding, what it is and what it means. This can trip up job-seekers who are unsure if they have a brand or how to create one, so let's clear things up.

First, you already have a personal brand, so you don't need to worry about creating one. You might want to freshen it up a bit and in order to do so, you'll need to understand what a personal brand is and is not.

Some people equate personal brand to reputation, but the concept is much broader. Others mistakenly assume it's an artificial

7 Myths of Personal Branding
1. It's all about selling yourself.
2. It's all about you.
3. It's all about your image.
4. It's all about self-promotion.
5. It's about being something you're not.
6. It's about treating yourself like a product.
7. It's about giving people what they want.

construct, designed to present someone in a more positive light, whitewashing character flaws or blemishes on a career. It's not that either.

The idea of personal branding has become quite popular in recent years, bringing out many self-appointed experts. Unfortunately, some of what these so-called experts are preaching is marginal advice that's not about branding at all. Instead, they're promoting sales techniques or self-promotion strategies that do not help you build your personal brand.

Branding is not selling. Branding is creating value.

There is a big difference between simply selling yourself and fostering an enduring personal brand. Branding is all about creating value through your interactions with others. When you deliver value, your personal brand becomes a tool for career growth, helping you achieve your personal goals.

To help you better understand how to cultivate a strong personal brand, let's debunk seven myths you may have heard about. These myths are dangerous misperceptions that undermine your efforts to grow. They disregard the value created by a strong brand. If you overlook that critical element, you'll end up with a glossy veneer—all shimmer and no substance—instead of a brand that draws others to you.

Let's dispel these myths right now...

1. **Personal branding is all about selling yourself.** A strong brand will sell itself, so you don't need to sell at all. Instead, make it easier for people to "buy." Be authentic and the results will follow.

2. **It's all about you.** The strength of your brand lies in the value you create for others. It's not about what someone can do for you or how to get what you want. Your brand is about showing people who you are and how you make a difference *to them*.

3. **It's all about image.** Sure, how you look, speak, and carry yourself plays a part in your brand, but image without substance is worthless. Image alone is not a brand. Branding is a way to express how you want to be seen, an outward reflection of what you are inside.

4. **It's all about self-promotion.** When you have a great personal brand, others will promote you. Instead of focusing on promoting yourself, focus on sharing your value and the buzz will take care of itself.

5. **It's about being something you're not.** Your brand is not a costume you wear when you feel like it, something to be donned or shed as circumstances change. Your personal brand is a representation of who you are every day, and authenticity matters.

6. **It's about treating yourself like a product.** You're a person, not an assembly-line product. When packaging your brand, don't mistake yourself for off-the-shelf goods. It's better to be uniquely you than to try to fit into a mold of someone else's making.

7. **It's about giving people what they want.** Of course you want others to be happy, but first be true to yourself. Bowing to pressure to meet someone else's agenda is a sure way to eradicate your own brand.

What exactly IS a Personal Brand?

Simply put, a personal brand consists of three components, each of which you can influence over time. The key components that add up your personal brand are:

Reputation + First Impressions + Delivery = Your Brand

Your brand is the combination of your reputation, how you're perceived in that crucial first interaction, and how you conduct yourself on an ongoing basis.

Thankfully, your personal brand doesn't have to be over the top to be effective. One of the most important elements of an effective brand strategy is believability. A brand needs to be credible or people won't accept it, no matter how hard you try to sell them on it.

When we talk about Personal Branding, we're not creating a theatrical character. You won't be playing a part or turning yourself into someone you're not. It's critical that people be able to see through the brand persona to the person underneath.

As you work on developing your personal brand, highlight what is best about you. Let your best traits shine while showing your human side. We all make mistakes and live through times we'd prefer to forget. That's part of what makes you unique. You don't need to expose your innermost secrets, but you must be open and accessible in order to be authentic.

Be yourself, weave in your hopes and aspirations, tell the world who you are, and constantly add value. That's the best recipe for a strong personal brand.

Two additional resources for Personal Branding ideas include Karen Kang, author of "Branding Pays" and Dan Schwable's "Me2.0".

The Fulcrum

Archimedes said, "Give me a lever long enough and a fulcrum on which to place it, and I shall move the world." Given your talent and the newfound knowledge of what your future employer is looking for (keywords), creativity is the **long lever** and your personal brand is the **fulcrum** on which to place it. After that, all that's required from you to move heaven and earth is some concerted effort.

In the August 1997 issue of *Fast Company*, Tom Peters, best-selling author of *In Search of Excellence,* wrote about the importance of branding: "We are CEOs of our own companies: Me, Inc. To be in business today, our most important job is to be head marketer for the brand called **You**."[3]

Let's rename you. For the purposes of this exercise, your new name will be "You, Inc." (Jeff claims that with the naming skills Al has, his daughter is glad her mom named her before he met and eventually adopted her.).

Remember Step 12 at the end of the last chapter? What was the number of people you wrote down who have the same title as you? Holy Schmoly, there's lots of competition for You, Inc.! (If there's neither a lot of competition nor a fair amount of jobs nationally, you might want to make some adjustments).

Why would someone hire You, Inc. over any of those other "Them" companies? What separates You, Inc. from "Them"—your resume? Hahahahaha!!!!! Until you differentiate yourself, you're just another one of "Them." Seriously, they don't know you from Adam's house cat. In fact, to a Hiring Manager you might as well be hog belly futures on the Chicago Mercantile Exchange. Your bacon is fried!

What are some of the more pressing needs common among the companies looking for someone like you? Which among them are you strongest at meeting? Can they be expressed in symbolic form? Maybe it takes a Marketing Brand Manager to figure that out.

Marketing Brand Managers

According to the Association of National Advertisers, "Brand management is more than a marketing job. Brand managers are responsible for the overall performance of their brands, which includes managing and developing their brand's Profit and Loss (P&L), image, and positioning in relation to their competitors[2]." So welcome to the first of your three jobs as a candidate: Marketing Brand Manager. (The other 2 are Recruiter and Commission-only Salesperson—you will become expert at all three).

Let's start with your brand's—that is, You, Inc.'s—image. Go back to the last paragraph of the previous section. What is it about you that satisfies a compelling need of your future employer and can be expressed symbolically? Remember that there are many "something specials" about you.

Symbolism

Let's uncover a symbol (like the Scrubbing Bubbles) that can visually represent you as "something special." Go to Clip Art in PowerPoint or Word (click on **Insert**; then click **Clip Art** or **Online Pictures,** depending on the version you have). Based on what you've learned so far, type in one of those "something specials" about your job, or what you do, or a need you satisfy.

When we tried "accountant," for example, we got 33 results that included juggling numbers, ledgers, and adding machines. If you were a Hiring Manager, would an image like that make You, Inc. more memorable? If you're a plumber, wouldn't a pipe wrench or a drippy faucet make it clear what you do?

Some examples from our files: We had a client who was a legal secretary. The symbols she chose were the scales of justice and a woman at a desk. Those symbols shouted: Legal Secretary. An executive used clip art of a guy in a suit with a factory in the background and gears attached to his head, which proclaimed: Business Operations Executive—the image conveyed the idea that the gears of business were always moving in the back of his mind. A new product launch specialist used the Space Shuttle.

Other clients have spelled out three to four keywords using Scrabble® tiles. Remember the lady who had been a member of a group that won a regional Emmy? Want to guess what symbol she used to make an instant and long-lasting impression?

The symbol(s) you choose will become part of your brand's identity. You'll use it (them) on your business cards, Marketing Brochures, and possibly even in your email signature. The symbol will support your brand on your online profiles and some types of resumes. You will use it throughout your Marketing Campaign.

The symbol you use will help satisfy Personal Branding effort requirement #3 above: (A Clear Message). It's based on the science of keyword discovery and is only limited by your level of creativity. Your goal should be to find something that grabs attention, holds it, and makes people want to know more. What's You, Inc.'s symbol going to be? Perhaps you could be the missing piece of a puzzle. Charts with arrows are also good possibilities.

Play with it a bit...and have some fun while you're at it!

Tell Me a Story

Believe it or not, you're about to begin interview preparation!

If you haven't yet been asked something like, "So who is <u>Your Name</u> and what are you interested in doing?" or "So, tell me about yourself," you will be soon. Having a *"So tell me about yourself"* story is essential to your campaign. Surely you've endured a laundry list of the standard questions in previous interviews, right?

There are lots of others you need to prepare for:
- Red Flags.
- Where do you see yourself in 5 years?
- What are your weaknesses?
- Give me an example of a time when you had a disagreement with a subordinate/supervisor and how you resolved it.
- Tell me more about a_____ situation (an accomplishment you've cited or a claim you've made).

A great list of typical interview questions you should prepare for was written by recruiter extraordinaire Abby Kohut in her pamphlet, *Absolute Abby's Top 12 Interview Questions Exposed.*[4] We recommend it highly. (More from Abby later.)

We believe that the single best way to answer questions, overcome Red Flags or objections, and make an emotional connection with the interviewer is to do it in the form of a story (see #4 above). When we say story, we're not talking Faulkner, Tolstoy, or Melville. Our Point—*and we do have one* — is that you need to get to the point. We're talking SHORT stories here.

K.I.S.S.! "Keep It Simple Stupid" and you can become a S.T.A.R.

S.T.A.R. Stories

Most of us don't know how to answer questions. We either respond flatly, *"Just the facts, Ma'am"* or *"First I slithered out of the primordial ooze, and eventually grew legs...."* If either of these describes your story-telling ability, let us introduce you to STAR stories.

STAR stories have been around for as long as we can remember. STAR stories, in most interview (and personal) situations are the best way to answer questions. The acronym S.T.A.R. stands for Situation, Tasks, Action, and Results. The STAR method is a great template for organizing and creating a compelling yet concise answer. It also helps you make the emotional connection with your Hiring Manager/Interviewer that we're seeking.

Here's where you should take each of the typical questions you can anticipate being asked by an interviewer, the key highlights or accomplishments of your career, and ALL of your Red Flags and turn them into STAR stories. All of your stories will contain each of the following four elements:

S. Set the situation you found yourself in or what was happening at the time.

T. Name the tasks of the situation (what needed to happen).

A. Share all the actions you've taken toward those ends.

R. Speak to the results of the actions taken.

A good rule of thumb to follow with STAR stories is to write everything down first. Then time yourself as you practice telling the story. Better yet, tell the story into a recording device (we suggest a hand-held digital recorder or Smartphone) and then critique the content and time yourself afterward. Your goal should be to tell each story in a friendly, conversational tone in one minute or less. You should get used to the format fairly quickly.

Companies like to ask situational questions because they see them as a good predictor of your future behavior as an employee working for them.

There are lots of Internet posts on STAR stories. Lehigh University's career services Web page[6] is one of the best.

Something to Consider

It should be fairly easy for you to create STAR stories for the typical, anticipated questions and for your success stories. But since you might not feel comfortable addressing your Red Flags, let us offer some thoughts:

As in any sales situation (which every interview is), you'll want to accentuate your "product's" strengths and minimize your "product's" weaknesses. (Your "product," of course, is you.) If you're lacking something the Hiring Manager desires, you can address that weakness by saying something like, "Although I don't have that specific _____, I have worked in similar situations. In fact…." Then go on to lay out your STAR story that features something positive.

If you did something "wrong" and they're aware of it or ask about it, it's best to admit to the offense then explain the situation from your perspective and what you learned from the experience. "Why did you leave your last job?" might be one of those hard-to-answer questions.

A perfect example of addressing a negative situation was the way Johnson & Johnson handled the 1982 Tylenol® tampering case.[7] Although the company was not at fault, it chose to "do the right thing" in the eyes of its customers, knowing that a multimillion-dollar hit to the company's single most profitable product line would result. But J&J was eventually able to regain both consumer confidence and its market strength largely because of the proactive approach it took. The company told a compelling story of "what they learned" and what changes they made so that the same situation would never happen again. You will do the same.

As with anything you want to be good at, practice is essential. And while it may seem dumb, practicing your STAR stories will make them appear to be well-thought-out and believable. You'll also be more at ease during your interviews, instill a level of camaraderie with your interviewer, and make the emotional connection you need to properly present your brand, You, Inc.

The Parent Trap

What if your brand is Stay-At-Home Parent? You may question what your value proposition is or what you bring to the table—besides dinner. You're not alone. An increasing number of parents want to enter or re-enter the workforce but aren't sure how to begin.

We met Michelle Hutchinson separately, but when we raved to each other about some gal we had recently spoken with, we quickly realized we were talking about the same person. As such, we immediately agreed that she was the perfect person to add her expert opinion on how parents should rebrand themselves when they're considering entering or returning to the workforce. Michelle is the founder of Wordhelper (wordhelper.com) and has a great deal of experience preparing resumes and cover letters that open doors to interviews. In "How Stay-at-Home Parents Can Enter or Re-enter the Paid Workforce," she gives an interesting take on an often-overlooked segment of job-seekers:

> Fortunately, it's been many years since either one of my kids has needed a diaper change, but no matter how old my children get, I will always be a mom. It's one job title that never gets retired.
>
> Unlike most jobs in our economy, parenting is one position that has no financial remuneration. That's why many stay-at-home parents think they don't have the skills or experience to enter or re-enter the paid workforce. They're wrong.
>
> *A parent is the ultimate small business.* Okay, maybe changing diapers doesn't exactly qualify as having maintenance expertise, but parents definitely have marketable skills. Let's identify some and see how you could highlight them on a resume.
>
> Parents certainly have experience utilizing training and instructional strategies. Heck, they've taught their kids how to use a toilet, ride a bike, and make their beds.

They know how to use motivational skills too. After all, once parents teach their kids how to make their beds (and stack the dishwasher and vacuum the carpet), they have to motivate the children to do those chores on a regular basis. And if kids are doing those chores on a regular basis, then parents are increasing the productivity of the teams they manage. They could back that up with a bullet point on their resumes that reads:

- Increased productivity of 3 maintenance team members via training and motivational sessions in
  - vacuuming,
  - dusting,
  - bed-making, and
  - dishwashing.

I'll bet many parents also have financial management experience. After all, don't they have to oversee the household budget? They could present that with bullet points on their resumes that read:

- Reduced travel expenses by X% in spite of Y% increase in trips, by
- Pre-planning routes,
- Maintaining speed limit, and
- Decreasing weight carried.
- Decreased household expenses by X% by
- Instituting 4 energy-conservation measures and
- Engaging in comparison shopping for goods and services.

Do you get the idea? You have the qualities that employers are seeking, so don't sell yourself short.

Elevator ~~Speech~~ Pitch

Under every rock, there's another snake that claims that a candidate must have an elevator speech. Unfortunately, the vast majority of the ones we've been forced to endure are long enough to last the time it takes to get to the top of the Empire State Building. (We can't tell you how many times at career events, when asked to give an elevator speech, we hear people first stumble "hamina-hamina-hamina" then they start reciting their resume.) The length of most elevator speeches causes people's eyes to roll back in their heads. Since we believe in sharing every method for finding a job—even the ones we're not crazy about—how about we discuss the elements of an effective elevator PITCH as opposed to a speech?

Think about a baseball diamond (field). The distance between the pitching rubber on the pitcher's mound to home plate is sixty feet, six inches. An effective elevator pitch should be shorter than that in seconds. As a matter of fact, your goal should be somewhere between thirty and sixty seconds.

An elevator pitch should contain the following:
1. Your name (see, this isn't so hard)
2. What you do (SPECIFIC)
3. What you bring to the table FOR A COMPANY (this ain't about you!)
4. Why you would be an asset to a company (your value proposition)

Some people insist that you need to include a list of companies you're interested in, but it has been our experience that candidates only mention large corporations. We believe this is a mistake. More important in our view is to clearly state what it is you do for people. Add an example of how what you do is used in companies. The more specific you can get without being overly technical the better. Strangely enough, the more specific you are about what you do, the more likely someone will be able to "see" you doing that something or be able to make an association.

Most of us have worn a lot of hats in our professional careers. Unfortunately, few companies (especially big ones) are seeking generalists. They're looking for specialists. The best way we can explain this is to picture yourself holding a funnel and looking through the small opening then through the large opening. You can see more when you look into the small end than you can when you look through the large end. Similarly, if you give people a laundry list of things you "can do" they probably cannot actually see you doing any ONE thing.

For example, there are a lot of different accountants, IT professionals, sales people, etc. What kind are you and what do you do that makes a difference for companies?

Most of all, as with your STAR stories, you should:

✓	**Write it**	(so it can be distilled to the essentials)
✓	**Rehearse it**	(so it comes naturally)
✓	**Recite it**	(to everyone you're near)

Even though the title may overestimate the importance of Elevator Pitches, the *Forbes* article, "The Perfect Elevator Pitch to Land a Job,"[8] written by Nancy Collamer is a very good piece on elevator pitches. Titles aside, she is an excellent source for job-search material.

Chapter 7: Targeting

> *"The odds of hitting your target go up dramatically when you aim at it.*
> -Mal Pancoast

A Quiver Full of Arrows

Most of us go into search mode believing that as soon as we update our resume, the next logical step is to "target" the job boards, apply, and submit. While it might make you feel as if you're accomplishing something by applying for jobs willy-nilly, in short order you will come to realize that your effort was mostly busy work and a waste of time. Avoid this mistake. Today's job search requires more than the same old soup. Targeting requires work, research, and discipline.

You already know how to target posted jobs (and probably have been unsuccessful landing one that way), so let's move on to methods you may not have tried.

Targeting

Industries

What industry or industries would you want to work in?

Many of us have been in the same industry for much of our professional careers, are satisfied to remain there, and know companies in that sphere to pursue. Okay, have at it! Just be certain your industry hasn't gone the way of the buggy whip. Unfortunately, that was the fate of Jeff's industry a few years ago. He literally travelled the world selling the microprocessor guts of computers to most of the largest computer hardware manufacturers in the world. Virtually all of those jobs are now located in the Far East. Jeff is in Atlanta.

Others, like Al, have a more varied background. He's been at the executive level with seven companies in five different industries—all in the sales and marketing arena but in very different industries. The principals of sales management, sales training, and marketing in those disparate industries differ not one iota—a widget is a widget is a widget. That's common sense. Unfortunately, common sense seems to be in short supply these days.

You may face a similar challenge in that you have to overcome narrow-minded recruiters or talent-acquisition executives and Hiring Managers that want, or prefer, only industry-specific experience. (In later chapters we'll discuss in great detail how to overcome those lummoxes with marketing material, social media positioning, and interview techniques.)

But since most professions readily cross industries flawlessly, let's assume yours does too. So we ask the question again: What industries would you like to work in? Choose one or more industries that appeal to you then we'll move on to the next step in the targeting process: Companies.

Companies
Now that you have the most general targeting accomplished, let's focus on companies you would actually like to work for, as opposed to wandering aimlessly through job boards looking for jobs to apply for. There's nothing worse than going to work for a company where you dread every hour of your employment. Regrettably, we have experience here:

Al's company just "went away." (Actually, we were so good at what we were doing that we ran ourselves out of business.) Here's Al:

> I was approached by the Vice President of Human Resources of another pharmaceutical company, and although I knew the company's reputation was lousy, I figured, "What the hell. I need a job." So I accepted the interview. They flew me up to New Jersey where I met

with the HR person, the company's Founder and President, the Vice President of Marketing, the Vice President of Product Development, the Director of Sales, and the President again.

The charm offensive was on!

The president said, "The Company needs to change our management style, and I think you're the one who can best do it." Then he asked how much I was looking for. I gave him my highest number (I didn't want to work for them so if they wanted me, they'd have to pay!). When he added $40,000 to my number, the hook had been swallowed and it was set deep!

Two and a half weeks later I was fired. I was told, "Your management style is different than ours." Duh! I never felt so relieved in my life to get away from those crazies. (Even though the company no longer exists, I still don't put it on my resume.)

Now that you have the opportunity to get a new job, let's look for one that isn't filled with nutjobs like the one Al went to work for. You'll want to research companies where your personality, ethics, and experience blend with their corporate culture, reputation, and needs. You, and they, will be much happier.

One place to learn about a company is their website's home page. At speaking engagements, we like to use two companies for this comparison. Look at Facebook's and Intel's home pages. (We're not trying to denigrate or promote one over the other, just to compare their different corporate cultures). The people on Facebook's home page are all below the age of 30 while the people on Intel's home page represent all ages, races, sexes, and nationalities. If you were looking for a job in that industry, which would fit you best? (Note: website images are subject to change.)

Research the companies' products and services. Do they go against any of your cherished sensibilities? Not too long ago a university fired a professor who otherwise was in good standing when they saw a Facebook page of his that showed him holding what appeared to be an alcoholic beverage in his hand. The man was on vacation at the beach, not at school, but what he was doing in that picture violated the signed morality clause in the professor's employment contract. (My father, a former professor, would have been unceremoniously shown the door there!)

Let's not get crazy about this stuff, but while you're going through the process of creating a target list of companies, you might as well start out aiming high then work your way down the line.

Lisa Rangel is a Certified Executive Resume Writer. In a LinkedIn article, she offers six ideas on how to build a list of target companies:[1]
1. Look at industry peers
2. Consider vendors and clients of previous employers
3. Check out "Best-Of" lists
4. Perform a geographical search (of companies)
5. Pursue companies that fuel your passions and match your hobbies
6. Seek out like-minded co-workers who share your Interests

Dirtbag Companies
Although this sounds crazy, we want you to target 3-7 companies that you DO NOT want to work for. We want you to go after them with all your energy, as if they were the perfect companies created just for you. And we want you to do this first!

You'll have to trust us with this for now. There's method to our madness.

Executives
Ever get an email from a friend who asked a bunch of silly questions? I (Al) used to get them all the time. One time I made the mistake of answering one of them. The question was: "If you were stranded on a desert island with only one other person, who would you want that person to be?" The answer made me the laughingstock of the quiz's writer and a number of my mutual friends.

Instead of answering that I'd want to be stranded with the hottest celebrity of the day, I gave the guy the name of the most interesting politician I had ever heard speak. The guy was in tears from laughing so hard. I tried to explain that after the "rumpus room time" was over with the hottie, there was probably going to be a lot more time on that island and that he might prefer a little intellectual stimulation over the long haul. Although he was ribbed unmercifully, the guy had to admit it made perfect sense.

All joking aside, wouldn't it be preferable to work for someone you *respect* rather than someone you disdain? So research and target those sorts of people. It gives you one heck of a story to tell during interviews when they ask why you want to work for the company. They'll immediately know that you've done your homework and that you bring passion to the job.

Through this targeting exercise, you'll be asked to directly contact these executives. Not all will accept your overtures, but many will appreciate your chutzpah, creativity, and passion. This will greatly expand your list of contacts and form your "Executive Network." This new network will be essential to your professional future because jobs simply do not last as long as they did in the past, and executives maintain a file of people who have impressed them in the past—one of them should be YOU.

Networking
According to statistics from CareerXroads, somewhere in the neighborhood of 75% of all jobs are filled through employee referrals, social media recruiting, and Hiring Managers' personal networks.[2] (That about covers everything, doesn't it?) Let's review them:

1. **Social Media Recruiting**: We've established that 93% of all recruiters use LinkedIn as their primary search tool. This is where the largest percentage of the Hidden Job Market is hiding. Recruiters can literally, and within minutes, find 10 LinkedIn pages of qualified candidates (100) by doing a Boolean search of requirements, desired skills, and preferred qualities. But like you, they can't find you if you're not properly positioned through keyword discovery and loading.

   Keywords are so important in today's job search universe that we devoted an entire chapter to it!

2. **Hiring Managers' Personal Networks**: Every manager worth his or her salt keeps a file of people who the manager would be interested in hiring should the opportunity arise. Often, being in a Hiring Manager's personal network enables the preferred candidate to learn about an upcoming job before anyone else. Also, Hiring Managers and executives have been known to add specific qualifications into a job description

that only the candidate from their network possesses—a so-called Purple Squirrel requirement. They can also have a job posted for only a couple minutes—just long enough for their candidate of choice to begin the application and then the job is taken down. (No kidding!)

Put me in the game coach!

In upcoming chapters, you will learn ways to expand your network, gain entrance into the personal network of executives, and maintain contact without being seen as a nuisance.

Note: There is no "Job Fairy." Few, if any, of the executives you contact will have a job for you at the moment you initially make contact, but don't give up. They may not have a job for you today, but if you become a member of their inner circle, you may find yourself hired for a dream job or an "opportunity position" where you're seen as an improvement over an underperforming current employee (the two lower-percentage—but best—possibilities in the hidden job market).

And there's always normal turnover to consider.

According to a Society for Human Resource Management (SHRM) 2012-2013 report, overall corporate turnover for all industries averages 13% annually.[3] But keep in mind that executives change jobs too. And when they land, they tend to surround themselves with people from within their personal network. John Zappe of Execunet, an outfit that helps senior-level executives find rewarding new opportunities, reported in a 2009 survey that the average executive's tenure in any position declined steadily between 2005 and 2008 to just 2.3 years, a 15% dropoff.[4]

Still, these are the people who typically have the wherewithal to create jobs because they're the ones who have the "juice" within a company and the budget to do so. When you gain access to the personal network of an executive, you are in reality cutting out all the middlemen.

3. **Employee Referrals:** We all know that one of the best ways to get a job is to be referred to the Hiring Manager by a connected, well-thought-of employee of that company. That recommendation, along with your resume, go directly from your connection to the Hiring Manager. You

get an interview, wow him or her with your confident manner, and get the job. (We love it when a plan comes together!)

We always suggest that you seek an insider who can champion your cause. You want to find that person (or persons) for either a posted job, a Hidden Job, or an introduction to an executive (See #3 below). More often than not, this is a net positive.

Most companies promote employee referrals. They want to feel that the referral is legitimate and that the employee has the best interest of the company at heart. And that's usually the case. Because it's so helpful, the employee often will receive a referral fee. Unfortunately, this can create the potential for abuse.

Although the benefits for the company far exceed the potential negatives, we suggest that you thoroughly vet your insider, even if he or she is a close friend. If the insider is not well-thought-of, your chances are damned from the start. Still, the chances of getting hurt by a company insider are slim, whereas your chances of making it through the Black Hole without help are even slimmer.

Practically all your contacts could be insiders or at least people who can put you in contact with potential insiders. You should mine your contacts thoroughly. In fact, during the launch process we're going to be asking you to contact and follow up with all these folks on a regular basis.

The referrals you want to seek are from employees of your competitors, vendors, and clients. Even former colleagues may have inside information and connections at *their* former employers. Of course, you need to be especially careful about these relationships. (We prefer using those connections to gain insight about the people they know inside your target companies, not for direct referrals.)

According to Nelson D. Schwartz's *New York Times* article, "In Hiring, A Friend in Need Is a Prospect, Indeed," employers increasingly rely on current employees to refer new hires to bypass reams of applications from job-search sites such as Monster.com.[5] As we've said before, companies who post job ads can receive in excess of 1,200 applications for a single position. Talk about cutting out the middlemen.

Even using elaborate ATS software can be cumbersome and time-consuming. So it should come as no surprise that companies seek to increase employee referrals in their overall acquisition process. In his article, Schwartz cites the accounting firm of Ernst & Young, which he reports actually has internal referral hiring goals. "As a result," he writes, "employee recommendations now account for 45 percent of non-entry-level placements at the firm, up from 28 percent in 2010."[4] At a time when Hiring Managers are under great pressure NOT to make a bad hire, a direct referral by a fellow employee is seen as an excellent way to minimize the risk of making a bad choice.

Developing, increasing, and maintaining your network has never been more important. Indeed, it may be the single most important task you undertake in your professional career. For many of us, it will mean having to acquire a new skill that may seem uncomfortable and unnatural, something that has almost become a lost art: Human Interaction.

Step away from the computer. Put down the phone. Have a meaningful face-to-face conversation. Ask questions (then listen more than you talk). Attend business conferences with a secondary goal of making contacts. Go out of your way to speak to people. Follow up meeting someone by sending a brief note or email and a request to connect. We're amazed at how seldom otherwise smart people do these simple, common-sense things.

We speak and make presentations on a weekly basis. At every talk we implore the attendees to connect with each of the other attendees and with us. Only a small percentage follow up on this. They have no idea what a professional grave they're digging. If you don't believe us, re-read the stats in the Schwartz article. (BTW: *We'll* connect with you if you send us a request.)

What about you? Are you willing to take the simple steps we suggest to expand your network?

A spider needs a large web to catch many flies.

Chapter 8:   Assembling the Puzzle

> *"Even if you're on the right track,*
> *you'll get run over if you just sit there."*
> -Will Rogers

Putting it All Together

In this chapter, all the work you've done previously will come together. Like assembling a jigsaw puzzle, every piece has a specific place and each one is necessary to create the finished product. One missing piece and your next employer will know that something is not altogether right. And as with a jigsaw puzzle, we suggest that to avoid frustration you take on this chapter a few pieces at a time.

Piece by piece, we'll guide you through the process of choosing a winning resume, building remarkable LinkedIn & Google+ profiles, assembling creative Marketing Brochures, and adopting effective business cards. Each of these documents will support the others and showcase your talents, as opposed to merely regurgitating companies, titles, duties, and dates. We'll also suggest a couple of things that may be new to you but will help differentiate "You, Inc." from the other candidates.

Even though we know your LinkedIn Profile is more important than a resume in today's world in terms of getting you in front of a Hiring Manager, we realize that you've been chomping at the bit to re-write your resume, so we'll start with resumes—or as we sometimes call them...

Resumes: 'A Career Obituary'

Most resumes read like a career obituary, a term we ~~stole~~ borrowed from our friend and excellent photographer, Bruce Kromer. They all seem to start with a flowery and meaningless Career Summary or an equally nonsensical Career

Objective, both of which resemble some of the vapid statements made at beauty contests: *"My life's goal is world peace where we all drive a solar-powered Lexus, never again eat red meat, and everyone is as blonde and beautiful as I am (eyelashes all aflutter)."*

Next comes the obituary itself, starting with the most recent job (typically cataloging job titles and responsibilities rather than accomplishments and meaningful credentials), sometimes dating as far back as cutting the neighbor's lawn as a child or when the Dead Sea only had the sniffles. Education and other training usually come next, with *References Available Upon Request* bringing up the rear.

C/V = Cut Veins!

Of course, what we've just described is a typical Chronological Resume—your *grandfather's* resume. It's the standard-bearer, but it can be your death! In our opinion, a Chronological Resume is best used by someone presently employed, out of a job for no longer than six months, or a C-Level executive who is directly contacting a company president or CEO.

Don't panic! It gets better.

We get a kick out of some of these people on the Internet who claim that their resume ideas will double your number of interviews. Double? Oh, really?!?

Some say you must customize every resume to the job you're applying for. This nonsense assumes two things:
1. You should go after only posted jobs (bunk, you're sunk!)
2. That you're a full-time resume writer (do you have the time or desire to rewrite your resume 5 times every week?)

If you buy their hooey, we have some waterfront property in western Kansas that we'll sell you cheap—and throw in a shrimp boat at no extra charge.

Granted, you may not be a wordsmith, but you CAN write a good resume. Whatever you do, we don't recommend that you hire someone to write your resume, because you now possess the keywords that a good cross-section of employers are looking for. More importantly, you know more about you, your industry, and your background than any resume writer could—or should.

re are many excellent sample resumes on the Internet that you can
⸻ ˪emplate. With what you've already assembled, we believe that no one
can tell the story of You, Inc. better than you. At least give it a try first, okay?

If it makes you feel better,
when you're successful you can send us a big fat check.

Early on we established that having a gap in your resume can do great harm to
your chances of getting a job. Recruiter.com has claimed that criminals have a
better chance of getting hired than the long-term unemployed[1,] and *Bloomberg
News* claimed that the average period of transition in the United States is more
than nine months, with those suffering from long-term unemployment
becoming viewed as pariahs.[2] One expert we quoted earlier said, in effect, that
you're *garbage* (our term) if you've been in transition longer than six months.[3]
Unfortunately, for anyone who's been out of a job for a while, each additional
month widens the gap from your most recent job to now (Red Flag!). Setting
that aside for the moment, let's discuss the three major resume types:
Chronological, Functional, and Hybrid. We'll start with the resume type you
should *never* use.

Functional Resume
A Functional Resume features your accomplishments and avoids detailing your
employment history. This is an immediate Red Flag to recruiters or talent
acquisition managers, who will think that you're trying to hide something (and
you probably are). We will admit that many longtime Hiring Managers love
Functional Resumes because they allow them to get to the meat of what the
candidate can do without having to plod through all the puffery. Still, we believe
that, no matter what your situation, you should not use a Functional Resume.
There are better options.

For a Functional Resume example please see:
http://jobsearch.about.com/library/samples/blresumefunct.htm

We suggest that you print examples of the resumes you're interested in using.

Chronological Resume
The Chronological Resume is what most HR professionals and recruiters want to
see. It's what they're used to reading and there are many ATS software systems

that pull information directly from a Chronological Resume and plug that information onto their forms. If you're not careful, though, a Chronological Resume can hurt your chances. If you're more comfortable with what's most familiar, fine. However, we want to show you how to produce a *better* Chronological Resume than you've known up to this point, improvements that should help you first get through the Black Hole and then give Hiring Managers more of what they want to see faster.

How to Construct a Chronological Resume:

Let's start at the beginning.

Your heading should contain the following:
- Your name (the name that you're known by professionally)
- City and State *where you want to work* (If you live in Denver and want a job in Los Angeles, you're less likely to get an interview if you put your Denver address.) For safety purposes, do NOT include a street address.
- Phone number (We suggest getting a Google Voice number to use for this)
- Email address
- Condensed LinkedIn URL Address (make it easy for them to find you)

Most recruiters believe you should NOT include an Objective. We disagree. This is the ONLY thing you should change when applying for a posted job. The only thing that should be stated in your objective is the job title and the job number (requisition number), if available. Restating the title of the available job will increase your keyword count by one AND show that you're not merely applying blindly with a generic resume. (An objective is unnecessary when sending a resume to a potential employer for which there is no posted job).

The best example of a specific Objective is from a resume I (Al) received many years ago. The stated Objective was simple: Sales Leading to Sales Management. The job I had available was for a field sales position. The applicant made it clear that he knew what the position was and that he wanted to earn a management position in the future. I could see that he understood the present position, and I also knew how to manage him later so that my managerial needs were met and his stated goal was obtained. He became an award-winning salesman who is now a top-notch sales manager.

Ironically, the worst stated objective I got was for the same position: pharmaceutical salesperson. The applicant's resume stated that he was interested in a grocery sales position. I almost never read the applicant's name, but I couldn't resist this time. As it turned out, he lived three houses down the street from me! (Joey, Joey, Joey.)

Your Career Summary comes next. It must be short and to the point, no longer than three sentences, never more than five lines, with a maximum goal of three. Why? In over 30 years as a Hiring Manager, I never looked at a Career Summary (with the above exception). Besides, that real estate is too valuable to waste.

Real Estate?

No, we didn't misspeak.

The average recruiter can "read" a resume in less than 10 seconds (some say that it's more like two to six seconds). *Your entire professional history is crammed into less than one-sixth of one minute!* And they can receive upwards of one thousand resumes for an opening. Recruiters DO NOT have time to waste. So if you don't get their attention fast, you'll be forever consigned to the the circular file—the Black Hole.

How much can you read in 10 seconds? Not much, right? Maybe 30-60 words if you're Evelyn Woods. If you could only read 60 words, what would you read in that ten seconds and what would you avoid? (It's time to think like a recruiter!)

What are the first 60 words of your present resume? Do a word count—seriously. Would your first 60 words make you want to read more or dump your resume into the trash? That's what recruiters do.

So the most important real estate on your resume is the first five inches after the heading. Neither a recruiter nor a Hiring Manager spends a single moment on your heading (never actually use the Header feature of your Word document because according to Ruthie Powell, long-time recruiter and founder of *The Ruthie List*, the scanning software does not read it[4]). They also don't read your name because you're not a real person to them yet. So what you put in that first five inches after your heading must be something that catches and holds their attention.

Your goal is to get the recruiter to spend more time on your resume than other people's resumes. You literally want to take time away from everyone else! As a former client put it, *"You want to suck all the oxygen out of the room."*

So what should you use?

Better than a lengthy Career Summary would be a set of bullet points of your Career Highlights.

Career Highlights

Your career highlights could be a series of accomplishments, credentials, certifications, etc. (Remember all that stuff we had you put together earlier in the book?) You'll be grabbing the reader by the throat and not letting go. These highlights should be filled with keywords. Every accomplishment should be described using the keywords you uncovered in your word cloud, the ones most likely to be scanned for by the ATS software. This will help you avoid the Black Hole and get in front of the eyes of a real person. (An example of Career Highlights appears in the section below).

The fewer the number of overall words the better. Remember, we live in a Twitter world of 140 characters. People don't read a lot these days! And if you don't give them a reason to keep reading right from the start, they'll simply stop reading your resume and move on to the next one.

Now, for the body of your Work History (Professional History, Career History):
- Name of company on the far left (in bold print)
- Dates on the far right of the same line
- Title or series of titles

- Accomplishment-based duties (Yes, you can and should reiterate what you had earlier, but now you can expand on them.) Whenever possible, use bullet points and sub-bullets. And all of this should be rife with your word cloud's keywords!

Don't forget to include pertinent volunteer activity, professional continuing education, and training, including current training. You want to fill in any gaps, if at all possible! This shows your future employer that you're keeping up with the times and not just sitting on your keister.

Education, awards, associations, additional languages, and specialized training should come next. Don't forget to include special skills. You wouldn't believe how many secretaries don't bother to put down that they're proficient in various software packages such as Word, Excel, PowerPoint, WordPerfect, etc., or how fast they type—or how *accurately!*

The goal of your resume, once it has crawled out of the Black Hole, is to give a recruiter just enough information so they'll want to learn more. But if you open the kimono too wide, they will have seen it all, and there would be no need to speak with you. They could also nitpick you to death.

Note: Your LinkedIn Profile should not be a regurgitation of your resume nor should you post your resume on LinkedIn. By doing so, there is no need for the recruiter to contact you. The Kimono showed too much.

For a Chronological Resume example, please see:
http://jobsearch.about.com/library/samples/blresumechronolog.htm

We suggest that you print examples of the resumes you're interested in using.

Hybrid Resume
A Hybrid Resume is a cross between a Chronological Resume and a Functional Resume. For many, this will be your best option, especially for those of you who have been in transition for a long time, people who have worn a lot of hats over the years, and folks who want to change professions. This type of resume features your current and transferrable skills.

A Hybrid Resume is largely accomplishment-based to showcase what you bring to the table, just like a Functional Resume does. But it clearly states your work history and dates similar to a Chronological Resume. A recruiter or HR executive will either love or hate a Hybrid Resume—there is no in-between. Hiring Managers, however, will almost surely love it since they, like us, won't have to wade through a lot of type to determine if you can actually do the job.

The beginning of a Hybrid Resume is exactly the same as the beginning of a Chronological Resume: Contact Information, Career Objective (if applicable), and Career Summary. What comes next is what makes the difference, and it begins with the first five inches.

As we said, you must capture the reader's attention immediately or you're likely to lose them—and the job. A couple ways to grab attention are with tables and bullet points—and if they extend beyond the normal margins, great! You don't want a monolithic column of type. As in a newspaper or magazine, anything that breaks up a column of type attracts the eye.

"White Space"

Focuses the eye on what you want them to see. (See what we mean?)

What goes in the table?

You did a lot of work assembling key elements from your employment history that should be attractive to your future employer. Those were the things your former employers paid and granted you raises for. That's a start. If you can segment them in a table, all the better. The more awards, dollars, percentages, and numbers you can include, the greater chance you'll get someone's attention. These past achievements are seen as predictors of your future at your new company.

If your resume will be sent electronically, you first have to get past the scanning software before your resume gets into the hands of a living, breathing human being. Remember all those keywords you found? Use them whenever possible to describe what you did.

Tables are easy to create. In Word, first click on **Insert** then choose the number of columns you desire and the the length of those columns. You can bold the titles of your columns and increase their font size. You can set the width of the table by dragging the cursor. You can add bullet points, as well. Try to have an equal number of points in each column.

Below is an example of what your table might look like:

Career Highlights

Training	Field Management	Executive Management
National Job-Coaching Trainer	President's Club Winner	National Sales Manager 3 Pharma Co's
National Pharma. Sales Trainer	8-State Regional Sales Mgr	Multiple Product Launches
Regional Sales Trainer (Pharma)	National Sales Manager	140-Person National Sales Force
National Sales Trainer (Consumer)	Last to 2nd Mgr. (2nd Year)	400% revenue increase (3 Years)
Creator Job-Coaching Methodology	#1 Area Sales Manager	300% increase 1st Year

Would something like that get *your* attention?

The table above would probably be even more effective if the candidate concentrated on various aspects of one major area and showed how those accomplishments fit the qualifications and requirements for the position he or she desired—again based on keywords from your word cloud. Are you beginning to see how a set of columns in a table stands out? If you were a Hiring Manager and saw only the table above, wouldn't you want to learn more?

For example, your Career Highlights table of columns (It could also be titled **Value Proposition** since you're presenting the value your Brand brings a company) could be displayed on the page with or without the borders. It could also include bullet points (highly recommended), doesn't need to be centered, and doesn't necessarily need headings. We suggest you play with it to see what you're most comfortable with and what you believe is most effective—keep in mind that this is YOUR resume.

The section immediately below your Career Highlights might be titled **Selected Accomplishments.** It should expand on the topics in the table above it. You'll want to add more specifics, but they should be in bullet point form, as well. To make things more remarkable, we suggest that you use a different style of bullets in each section. Remember, bullets and sub-bullets make it easier for the Hiring Manager to read.

Here's a small sample of what this section could look like:

Selected Accomplishments:

<u>Executive Management & Field Management</u>:
- Recruited as Director of Sales and Marketing of 140-person national sales force
  - 200% increase first year
- Provided leadership and direction to the creation of marketing collateral
  - Created company's 1st-ever ethical marketing materials
- Boosted key product sales 100+% utilizing superior sales talents
- Managed 36 field sales team and managers
  - Exceeded overall sales objectives 425%
  - Expanded customer base 25%
- Introduced strategic marketing plans that increased revenue levels 400+%
- Oversaw company expansion of over 300%
  - Represented multiple pharmaceutical and DME companies simultaneously
  - Sales results so remarkable, 4 client companies established own sales forces

Here you're giving them a little more meat to chew on, but note that there are no dates yet. You're taking accomplishments from any point from your career, the accomplishments that best showcase the talents you've discovered they're looking for. You can even include information from employers you're not listing in your employment history. (Many experts believe you shouldn't list more than 20 years of employment history. We are ambivalent on this subject.)

Grouping your accomplishments this way makes a bold statement about the value you'll bring to your new employer. You're also making it easy for the Hiring Manager to determine whether you'll be a asset to his or her team or a threat to his job.

Following your Selected Accomplishments section comes **Employment History,** or some similar title. We suggest that you name the company (far left) in bold print, your titles in the center, and dates to the far right.

Many of us have earned numerous promotions. If you've moved up within a company, we suggest that you name each title, one below the other, so it's immediately apparent that you played a variety of roles at that company during your tenure. It's impressive, and it shows that your accomplishments were recognized by your employer. Then briefly list a series of accomplishments at those companies (remember your keywords). Use THOSE keywords to describe what you did (yes, state your accomplishments again). Make sure that the terms you use are the currently used terms for the things you did, not necessarily what your employer called them, which may be outdated. Also, different companies may describe the same things differently.

Your education, training, certifications, reiteration of awards, languages, affiliations, etc. round out the document. If you have volunteer activity, it can go in this section or in your employment history section (or both), depending on whether you have employment gaps. Volunteer work is an outstanding way to fill in employment gaps—and possibly land a paying job!

Many people ask if a resume MUST be two pages or less. The answer is no, with a caveat. Two pages is still preferred by most Hiring Managers. It shows that you can get to the point. But two pages is an impossible limitation for some professions. In IT for instance, many people have a series of short-lived contract positions that preclude a two-page resume. In any case, make every effort to limit the word count on your resume without doing yourself a disservice. *Size doesn't matter.* As *The Daily Muse*'s Adrian Granzella Larssen puts it, "What's much more important than the length of your resume is that it tells a story to the Hiring Manager about why you're the right fit for the position."[5]

There's one other method you may want to employ to get people's attention with your resume, but it only works when you're sending your document to a real live person: using your former employer's company logo (LinkedIn often does this automatically). We first saw this tactic on the marketing plan of former Kraft Foods marketing executive and all around good guy, Rick Steinbrenner. We immediately knew we would have to ~~steal~~ borrow the idea. Thanks to social media and the pervasive use of images, most people would rather view images than read text. It's becoming the norm rather than an exception.

Imagine if an executive picked up your resume and saw the logo of one of his former employers staring him in the face? What an impression and instant connection you'll have made. And if you speak additional languages, using the appropriate country's flag effectively communicates that skill without writing a single word. The same goes for a volunteer organization's logo, an easy way to show that you volunteer your time, as well.

We had planned to have used the actual logos of a number of the companies Al worked for, or contracted with, over the years as an example of what this could look like for you, but copyright laws precluded their use. Instead, we're using the companies' names. Try it out for yourself and see if using logos makes sense for you. We've also included flags, though they're in black and white. (The language flags are mostly for effect since Al can barely speak English much less have fluency in *another* language, n'est-ce pas?)

Success

Brymill Cryogenics   Diabetic Products, Inc   Hi-Tech Pharmacal   Torino

Kimberly-Clark Corporation   Becton Dickenson   Well and Wise

GenDerm   Fujisawa   Cincinnati Sub-Zero   Warner Chilcott

Draxis Health   AstraZeneca   Bioglan Pharma   Dermatology Sales Specialists

Bradley Pharmaceuticals   Kingsport Thoroughbreds   Kenwood Therapeutics

Languages

Any Hiring Manager in the healthcare field would recognize a number of the listed companies (or their logos), as would many Hiring Managers in other fields. If you shared a bit of employment history or similar background with the reader of your resume this way, you would forge an instant connection through your common kinship—or competition. All this without a single word.

If you worked for any of those companies and were looking to hire, wouldn't you like to know more about this person, such as when he or she worked for that company and who they knew in the company? Wouldn't you be more likely to connect with someone who had a similar background? So, if a picture is worth a thousand words, what are logos worth? An interview?!?

Before we move on, let's reiterate that this method DOES NOT work for electronic submissions and is equally ineffective when sent to HR. The software will not read the logos. A resume that includes logos must only be sent to a specific person (executive or known Hiring Manager) within a company.

For a Hybrid Resume example, please see:
http://jobsearch.about.com/od/sampleresumes/l/blresume7.htm

We suggest that you print examples of the resumes you're interested in using. We also suggest that you save your resume in .pdf, .doc, .dox and .txt formats.

Infographic Resume
There's a new kid on the block: the Infographic Resume. Like a newspaper ad that's chocked full of stuff from top to bottom, an Infographic Resume can overwhelm a reader. Every one we've seen has too much going on to be effective. But as we said earlier, we want you to be aware of these things.

Don't get us wrong, the goal of an Infographic Resume is laudable: to make you stand out from other applicants. And we believe that practically every single element of this type of resume is excellent in its own right. But when so many of them are crammed onto a sheet of paper we believe they lose value.

Erica Swallow, owner of Southern Swallow Productions, where she creates compelling tech and lifestyle content, has an outstanding article at Mashable.com on this topic called, "4 Simple Tools for Creating an Infographic

Resume." [6] In it she suggests using maps, charts, graphs, and symbols (where have you heard that before?) and offers resources for the new apps you need to create one of these resumes on your own. If you follow her suggestions and limit the graphics to a handful, an Infographic Resume might be a good option to differentiate yourself from other candidates, especially for those of you in the graphic arts. One caveat, however: an HR department and its ATS might blow a gasket when one lands on their desk, and they may not be able to make heads or tails of it. They certainly can't take information directly from this type of resume and have it fit neatly into their little boxes. As such, this would need to be sent directly to a person who can assimilate its contents properly, which is always preferable to an HR department anyway.

Video Resume
If we weren't crazy about the benefits of an overloaded Infographic Resume, we're really cold to Video Resumes for the vast majority of us. All you have to do is take one look at photos of the two of us to see why! Still, a lot of smart people insist that a video resume is a good option.

In *Time's* 2011 article on the subject, Victor Luckerson wrote about a job candidate who wanted to land a spot with Google. The guy created an odd online video presentation to both display his skills and provide a glimpse of his personality—and it eventually landed him a job.[7] (Not at Google.) We do agree with Mr. Luckerson when he says, "Many job applicants feel that if they could get past the initial screening process and land a face-to-face interview with a Hiring Manager, they'd have their chance to shine.[7]"

But we have a few questions:
1. Will you be projecting the image you want a future employer to take away from your video?
2. How will you get the right people to see that video?
3. Are you comfortable enough in front of a camera and technically adept at making a video for it to be seen as representative of you?
4. Will it merely become another YouTube novelty?

As with any new technology, a cottage industry has cropped up around both Infographic and Video Resume creation. If you can afford it and feel it's to your advantage to use either form, please remember that this is YOUR Marketing Campaign. Do what you feel is in your best interest to differentiate yourself and land a job.

By the way, with LinkedIn you now have the ability to add all sorts of presentations, including video and PowerPoint, to multiple sections of your profile. This can help enhance it and differentiate you from others.

You don't have to take our word on resumes. Here's what professional resume writer, Tim Morrison, says in his article, "Miscellaneous Thoughts On Resumes...From One Who Writes Resumes as a Profession":

> Everyone has an opinion on what works and what doesn't work in a resume. They may have never written a resume. They may not have a resume, but they have an opinion. Ultimately, you for whom the resume is written has the final say on content and format. You have to feel comfortable with the document.
>
> 1. A one-size-fits-all resume fits nothing. You believe yourself to be qualified for three or four or maybe even five different kinds of positions. But do not try to craft one resume to fit all three, four, or five job titles. It forces the recruiter to figure out how (or if) you are qualified for the position, and the recruiter is not going to take the extra time to do that.
> 2. Always include a cover letter with your resume if it's directed to a person or if the job you seek is writing-intensive. You may have heard that "no one reads the cover letter." Some HR recruiters don't read cover letters, some HR recruiters do read them, and there are some who simply look to see if there is a cover letter. If they don't see a cover letter, they won't look at the resume. Do you want to take that risk?
> 3. Strong resumes contain bullet points. Unfortunately, those bullet points tend to be job descriptions—a list of what you were supposed to do. But you are looking for another job. Provide a three- to four-line, short and to the point job description using short, tight phrases—no long sentences. Then provide bullet points that list accomplishments, the impact you had where you worked. This conveys a clear message.

4. The most that a resume can do is get you get you noticed and contacted for an interview. A resume does not get you a job.
5. Use the cover letter to set up how you want your resume to be read. If you are making a career transition, indicate in your cover letter your transferable skills. If you have a gap in your work history, acknowledge it and explain why. If an HR person might not understand how you are qualified for the position, explain what makes you qualified.

Social Media Profiles and YOU

According to a CareerBuilder survey, much research happens PRIOR to a phone screen or interview[8] (see below):
- 48% of employers will use Google or other search engines to research candidates
- 44% will research the candidate on Facebook
- 27% will monitor the candidate's activity on Twitter
- 23% will review the candidate's posts or comments
- Some of the search activity happens before candidates are even called for a job interview

Gimme Whatcha Got

The starting point with LinkedIn, as well as with the positioning on all social media channels, involves looking at your Personal Brand, as discussed earlier. Ask yourself: *Who am I? What am I trying to represent? What strategy am I going to use?*

Once you've decided who you are, you then need to focus on how you're going to shape your identity so it attracts the type of potential employers you'd like to work for. What is your Value Proposition? How is it going to be communicated? These are things you want to articulate on LinkedIn. They should be consistent with what you did in your introspective look (See: Assessments).

Your goal should be to end up with a complete LinkedIn Profile. The last thing you want is a profile that looks like the lights are on but no one's at home, or something that's just a rehash of your resume, which may be sufficient in some occupations or for executives who already have esteemed careers. But for almost everyone else, it will reflect poorly on you. Potential employers may think that if you can't complete a professional-looking LinkedIn Profile, that's what you're going to be like as an employee. They're looking for 110%-ers, not people who aren't totally committed.

If you're having trouble getting started with your LinkedIn Profile, we suggest that you "borrow" from others in your profession. Simply do a search in quotation marks on LinkedIn for the position you're targeting and see the top five profiles that come up. (Look for ones that aren't 1st-level connections as previously instructed). Print them out and study them (can you say "word cloud"?). They'll give you insights on how to create a complete profile and position yourself well.

If you ever get stuck on anything in LinkedIn, remember that there's a great Help Center located at the bottom of your LinkedIn main profile page (look for it now so you don't forget). Simply click on it and you'll get all kinds of tips on how to use each and every feature. Surprisingly, this is something few users know about and avail themselves of. It also gives you a way to connect with LinkedIn should you ever encounter a problem.

LINKEDIN: Everything You Need to Know to _Get Started_

If you already have a LinkedIn Profile, we suggest that you print it out and save it as a PDF file titled "OriginalLinkedInProfile" before you get started. That way you'll have something you can readily reference that will also serve as a positive reminder of how far you've come once you've developed your new profiles. Notice that we said "profiles". You need to consider your LinkedIn Profile as a *work in progress* that you'll undoubtedly continue to modify to reflect changes in assignments, accomplishments, awards, and other things of note.

To save it as a PDF file, simply go to your profile in the profile mode. There's an edit button to the lower right of where your photo is. Click on the drop-down menu and you'll see an **Export to PDF** notation. Simply click on this to download it. Once it's downloaded, copy and save it to a LinkedIn directory that you've set up on your computer so that anything related to LinkedIn is easy to access. This will make life a lot easier.

Before you attempt anything further on LinkedIn, it's best to become familiar with the LinkedIn toolbar. You first want to get comfortable with the general overall LinkedIn Profile and the edit function, as these will be the two most important things moving forward after the settings described below.

Before you go any further, you need to appreciate the importance of LinkedIn Settings, which can be found in a drop-down menu that becomes visible when you run your cursor over your photo in the top right-hand corner. Focus first and foremost on the **Privacy and Settings** notation. If you haven't already done so, go to **Turn On/Off Your Activity Broadcasts**. This is extremely important because when you're making changes, you don't want to irritate the connections you already have by making them aware of each and every change you've made. (Any time you make a change to your profile your network is notified.) Not only will some of your connection find it distracting, but as you're modifying your profile you might make spelling mistakes, grammatical errors, and not finish what you set out to accomplish due to interruptions. You want to wait until you're reasonably satisfied that what you have on your profile is what a potential employer would be happy with before you go "live" (See: Prelaunch Checklist). Once you've completed the profile, have it reviewed by someone who will honestly critique it. You will turn the activity broadcast setting to ON when you're ready to "Light this Candle."

Activity Feed
In addition to the broadcast settings, you also want to pay attention to who can see your activity feeds. This is *critical* if you're currently employed. If so, you want to make sure that your search is being done as discreetly as possible. If you are currently employed and are enhancing and changing your profile to secure a new position, only make it visible to yourself. The last thing you want your employer to know is that you're seeking to leave.

There are four settings to choose from under the **Select Who Can See Your Activity Feed**:
1.   Everyone
2.   Your network
3.   Your connections
4.   Only you

PROFILE (TOP SECTION)

Once you're sure your connections aren't going to be updated with every one of your changes, you can begin updating your profile. There are a number of steps you'll want to take.

Start with the top section of your profile. There are a number of areas here that can enhance your profile. Click on **Edit Profile** on the toolbar. This will give you access to the edit function for the top section, as well as all the other sections on LinkedIn. To make edits, simply click on the pencil icon, which will lead you to the edit function for that section. Things you want to edit in the top section include:

1. PICTURE

By default, LinkedIn provides a simple avatar until you actually upload a photo. Get rid of this and replace it with a professional photo of yourself. We've heard many people say they're afraid to put a photo on LinkedIn because they may be perceived as too old or not attractive enough. *Get over it!* Without a photo, you're toast. Not only will the vast majority of recruiters and talent acquisition managers not review a profile without a photo, your credibility will be completely shot. (According to LinkedIn's own research, a photo increases by 7% the likelihood of your profile being read.) People want to hire *people*, not avatars.

Your profile picture should be as professional as possible—and recent. Perhaps you were better-looking years ago, but please don't post a photo from 10 years ago. It should be limited to just your head and shoulders, not the rest of your body.

Your photo should be used as a branding tool in each and every social media platform you participate in, including LinkedIn. It should not be a picture of you and your pet. (No matter how much you love your dog, Fido has no business being in your LinkedIn photo.) Go out and spend a few dollars or find some organization that will take a profile shot of you for free or at minimal cost. Dress the part of a professional and make sure you're carefully groomed. We suggest getting your photo taken a few days after a haircut, which will enhance your image. And no low-cut dresses, ladies. You want to be attractive in your photo but not look like you're out to win a beauty contest. You want to be seen as a serious candidate who can solve the employer's problems.

Make sure that the lighting is good and that there are no background distractions. Some experts suggest using a background that represents your industry, but we think that **YOU** should be the focal point. Lastly, when the photo is being taken, look slightly to your left. This will guide the reader's eye to the center of the screen where the meat of your profile is located.

2. NAME

Believe it or not, this is an area where a lot of people make a mistake. You want to make sure that the name you use here is the name that people will recognize you as—not a legal name that you seldom use or a nickname that may be cute but could be offensive to others. (Note: If you do use a nickname or are known by another name, you can add these to your summary or other sections, so if someone does a search for you using these names, you can be found.)

I (Jeff) experienced this when I first joined LinkedIn back in 2006. I wanted to be as proper as I could be, so for years I had used W. Jeffrey Sheehan on my business cards. My first name is William, but I've always been known as Jeff. When people who knew me started searching for me, they had a hard time finding me. After several colleagues told me this, I changed it to Jeff Sheehan, which made me much easier to find.

Another mistake we see people making is using degree designations, such as MBA, right after their name. In general, we don't think this is a good idea. Although obtaining an MBA is quite an accomplishment, most of the people who put MBA on their profile have not gone to a prestigious school, so it doesn't really carry much weight.

Something else people often do is list the number of connections they have—for example, John Doe 5,000+ or John Doe LION (LinkedIn Open

Networker). The problem is that you may be perceived as someone whose focus is "collecting" people, not developing true relationships with their contacts. This not only goes against the spirit of LinkedIn, but it may also be a violation of LinkedIn's terms and conditions. Although a large number of people do this, they're setting themselves up for potential disciplinary action by LinkedIn, which states the following:

LinkedIn requires use of true names rather than pseudonyms, business names, associations, groups, email addresses, or other characters when registering on our site. We believe that any information other than first and last names in the name fields undermines the professional nature of our site and services. For more information, see the LinkedIn User Agreement.

3. **LINKEDIN BADGES**
LinkedIn provides so-called badges people can display on their profile. These are:
   a. Premium Account
   b. Job Seeker
   c. OpenLink Network

The jury is still out on how effective these are as branding or job-search tools. We have Premium Accounts and we consult with people, groups, and companies on the use of LinkedIn, so we display this on our profiles. To be honest, we've never received one comment about it, except for the people who asked what it meant.

4. **HEADLINE**
The headline is one of the most critical components of your LinkedIn Profile. This is where the proverbial rubber meets the road. You really want to shine and position your brand with a substantive, value-added proposition in 120 characters or less.

What do you have to offer a potential employer?

Employers don't care that you're a detail-oriented accountant or an exceptional sales person. They want to see what you can do to help them solve their problems. Remember, you're selling yourself to a buyer who has a need to fill or a problem to solve. In this case, it's an employer who needs a human resource. If *you* can't fit the bill, it will be someone else.

By default, LinkedIn will fill in the headline with the job title of the job that you've listed as your latest position in the experience section of your profile. You need to be aware of this and change it by simply going into the **Edit** section of LinkedIn.

We also suggest that you separate the material in your headline with a | (divider) to make it clearer if your headline contains multiple points.

5. GEOGRAPHICAL/INDUSTRY AREA

If you're looking for a job in your own city, we suggest that you cast as wide a net as possible. The two of us live in the suburbs of Atlanta but chose "Greater Atlanta" as the geographical area to display on our LinkedIn Profiles. The reason is that few talent acquisition managers will be looking for someone in Marietta, which is the suburb where we both live. Instead, they'll be looking in Greater Atlanta.

If you're searching for a job in an area other than where you presently reside, we suggest you list that city or geographical area in your profile. The reason is that employers seeking candidates will first search locally and then cast a wider net. The last thing a company wants to do is have to pay for the cost of relocating someone if a suitable candidate can be found just a few miles away. One of our clients used this strategy to relocate to her hometown of Minneapolis. She simply changed the location information on her profile from Greater Atlanta to Minneapolis, and after several months of searching, this highly qualified person landed a great job there and is very happy with the way everything worked out.

In addition to geographical area, you also want to focus on a target industry. This is critical, as recruiters prefer sourcing from within industry groups. Very seldom, if ever, do they look for individuals outside that industry. Though not impossible, in the current economy few people have been able to move into positions outside their primary industry, even though they have skill sets that are readily transferable. There are just too many qualified candidates.

Although it may be challenging to change industries, you shouldn't completely discount the idea. If you have a real passion to do something different, do everything you can to position yourself accordingly. I (Jeff) was in the semiconductor/electronics industry for many years, but as most of the marketing and sales management jobs in that industry were being moved offshore, I decided to change my industry designation to Marketing. I had experience and education in this area and thought it would be a better fit for "rebranding" myself.

6. **CREATE A VANITY URL**
    When you initially set up a profile, LinkedIn uses a default URL to identify you. As part of your overall branding activities in social media, you want to change the URL so that it reflects your name, or something as close to your name as possible. With 300 million plus users, it's becoming more difficult to use common names as LinkedIn URLs, so you'll have to get a bit creative by using middle initials, area codes, or other characters to differentiate yourself. As something that will appear on your business cards, resumes, and other marketing tools, it's very important that you take this step. You want to be memorable, not *JohnDoe12abc*. If you aren't using your name in your URL, you'll be perceived as someone who doesn't pay attention to details.

MAKE SURE YOUR PROFILE IS PUBLIC
LinkedIn provides settings that will show you how you're seen when someone searches for you in the search engines. Make sure you're as visible as possible, so that you can be found on Google, Yahoo, Bing, and other search engines. Having your complete profile be visible isn't a bad idea because it will give you more reach. Although some people are afraid that they may be too visible, we believe that the positives far outweigh any perceived negatives.

IMPROVE YOUR PROFILE
Within the main upper body of your LinkedIn Profile, right below your picture, is an **Edit** mode button. Clicking on this allows you to fully edit your profile. We'll talk more about what you should be doing in this area in a moment. A very useful drop-down bar to the right of the edit mode displays five functions that will be of interest to you when using LinkedIn:

1. Ask to Be Recommended An easy way to get to the recommendation section to ask for recommendations. You can access it elsewhere, but this is just easier.
2. Create Profile in Another Language Useful if you're interested in working for a foreign company or working in a country where the language is different from your native tongue.
3. Share Profile A great way to publicize your profile on Facebook and Twitter or to facilitate views and additional connections.
4. Export to PDF You would not believe how handy this feature is. You can download your profile—and profiles of your connections—as a PDF and share it with others, even if they're not on LinkedIn. Great for three-way introductions where you introduce two people you know to one another. It's a real time-saver.
5. Manage Public Profile Settings By clicking on this you can immediately manage what others see when they do a search in Google, Yahoo, or Bing. You can make your profile visible to no one or everyone. (If you make it visible to everyone, you'll still be able to limit what can be seen by various criteria LinkedIn suggests for you).

CONTACT INFORMATION

This is another important section within the headline and photo section of LinkedIn. Make sure that you capitalize on it by displaying your email address, Skype number (if available), phone number for contact, and your main contact email address as your default address. Do not provide any home address information. You'd be surprised at the number of people who don't utilize this area and neglect to include their email address and phone number, which makes connecting with them very difficult. Make it easy for recruiters, talent acquisition managers, and others to contact you by having this information readily available.

Also in this area are prompts for listing your Twitter handles and websites. We strongly suggest that you include your handle if you have a Twitter account (you should!) and your website(s) or blog if you have them (less important than the people trying to sell you something would suggest). In the case of websites, list a name that ties in with your Personal Brand. Don't use the default LinkedIn provides. Remember, it's all about being found and being readily available.

Make it easy on people!

SUMMARY

After you've done the fine-tuning in the headline and photo section of your LinkedIn Profile, focus on the summary section. This is crucial for positioning yourself, enhancing your credibility, and being found, as you can insert multiple keywords associated with the job you're searching for and want to be discovered for.

Make sure that your summary is interesting and represents the professional you are. Show your passion. Don't make it sound as if it were written by a robot. Put some personality into it. Describe your expertise and use bullet points to make it an easy read. If you're in a highly competitive industry like social media, include rankings on various platforms that can help differentiate you. This is where, unlike in a resume, you can tell the story of your Personal Brand, the things you want them to know about you, without worrying about companies, conceit, or chronology.

SKILLS AND EXPERTISE

Clearly articulate your skills and expertise. Make sure that it's keyword-rich for the position you're seeking. Unlike for most resumes, the length of this section does not matter as much as proper keyword loading. This is how you get found.

EXPERIENCE

List all of the job titles and positions you've had for the last 20 years or so. In most cases, recruiters and talent acquisition managers don't care about what you did before that. They want to know what you've done most recently and how you can be of help to their firm.

On the other hand, if you once worked for a Fortune 500 company or prestigious institution long ago, add it. It will increase your credibility. In many cases, if you worked for one of these companies you'll be seen as someone special. For instance, managers who have worked for General Electric in the past are often deemed to be good candidates. The training programs and weeding out process at GE and other major corporations are well-regarded. If you were once employed by such a company or institution for a number of years, be proud of it and display it on your profile.

You might also want to list your experience from many years ago if you're trying to expand your networking reach. By actively displaying your former companies, those who have also worked for those companies might want to connect with you. It's really up to you.

RECOMMENDATIONS
We've spoken about recommendations and the need to acquire more of them. Again, we suggest you start with a minimum of 5-7 recommendations and add more as time goes on. Because they're so important, we've included an entire section on recommendations in Chapter 12: Advanced Social Media.

ENDORSEMENTS
We suggest you start with a maximum of 5-7 skills or talents you want to people to focus on. Endorsements are a part of the algorithm that moves you toward page one on LinkedIn, so their value cannot be overstated. We have an entire section on endorsements in Chapter 12: Advanced Social Media.

HONORS & AWARDS
LinkedIn has made it easy to toot your own horn without being a braggart. If you've been recognized for some outstanding contributions to your employer, former employers, volunteer organizations, various media outlets, or other entities, highlight them in this section. You did it, so claim it!

VOLUNTEER EXPERIENCE
You should list your volunteer experience because it contributes to your credibility. You'll be seen as someone who is a giver. But don't go overboard. Most companies like to see that people volunteer, but they don't want to see too many volunteer positions, as this might convey the impression that you won't have enough time to devote to the company.

EDUCATION
As with experience, add the educational institutions you attended, the degrees you earned, and any special accomplishments. You might also add courses you took that align with the position you're seeking. Don't forget certifications, honors, or any other formal training you've received.

ADDITIONAL INFO

This section can be used to reemphasize some of your core keywords and other information pertaining to how people can contact you. Study what others have done in this area and emulate their best practices.

Google+ Profile, About.me, Facebook, & Twitter
Having a Google+ profile is imperative due to the overall importance and market share dominance of Google. Yes, Yahoo and Bing are also used by a lot of people. But focus is key, so if you're going to focus on one search engine, you should use Google to be found (at least to begin with). There's much more on this in Chapter 12: Advanced Social Media.

About.me, Facebook, and Twitter can be important adjuncts to your search and are also addressed in detail in Chapter 12: Advanced Social Media.

Marketing Brochures

Marketing Brochures may be one of the most effective and least understood methods for securing a job.

What is a Marketing Brochure?

As opposed to only passively waiting for some company to come-a-callin', we believe that candidates should use *every* method—both passive and aggressive—to get a job. Back in the '60s, Dusty Springfield sang, *"Wishin' and hopin' and thinkin' and prayin'...won't get you into his arms."* Likewise, you must do more than wishin' and hopin' to win over your next employer. A Marketing Brochure in a job search is the purest method of proactively presenting your Personal Brand, "You, Inc." Marketing Brochures are an excellent way to stand out from other candidates, appealing to people who can create a job for you, showcasing your talents, and displaying your innate creativity.

There are three Marketing Brochures you will learn about in this book:
1. The Backgrounder
2. The Table Setter

3. The Clincher

Consider the Backgrounder as a cross between a Hybrid Resume and your LinkedIn Profile in the sense that you can tell your story in the manner that best suits your background and goals while giving the reader enough of what they're after to make them want to learn more. The Backgrounder introduces you to a potential employer and, ideally, gives them enough interesting and useful information so they'll accept your follow-up call and want to schedule an interview.

The Backgrounder is also a better setup for a face-to-face interview than a resume (we'll explain this in Chapter 13). The Table Setter expands on the Backgrounder by showcasing all the things you bring to the table—that is, it clearly states your Value Proposition. And the Clincher is aimed at helping you secure the position. We'll present only the Backgrounder in this section and cover the other two where they will work best for you, which is in the chapter on interviewing (Chapter 13).

At this moment, your future employer likely has never met you. The initial goal of the Backgrounder, as stated above, is to introduce you and your professional ability to a potential employer. It establishes the Holy Grail of job search, the 3 H's:

- ✓ Humanization
- ✓ Hirability
- ✓ Hunger

With a resume alone, your future employer most probably does not see you as a person. You're just another sheet of paper in the pile (alliteration intended). The Backgrounder offers parts of your biography in the form of a story that transforms you from being just another applicant into a real live person—it **Humanizes**. Listing key experiences and achievements based on what you know companies are seeking shows that you have the capabilities to do the job—you possess **Hireability**. The chutzpah of contacting an executive directly and the creativity with which you have done so eliminates all doubt that you have a real **Hunger** for working with that executive.

Your Backgrounder should include many of the following, in whatever order you feel makes sense for you:

1. Biography

2. Proof Sources
3. Accomplishments
4. Certifications & Credentials
5. Professional Attributes
6. Charts & Graphs
7. Value Proposition
8. Contact Informtion

1.   **Biography:** This is a must. As we've said before, your target executive doesn't know you yet.

Your biography can be written in the first person, but we strongly suggest that you write it in third person. That way it won't feel like you're bragging about yourself, AND the reader won't tend to feel that way either.

Think about the worst date you ever had. Your date probably talked incessantly about themselves (I, I, I, me, me, me…). By writing your biography in the third person you avoid being a *bad date*. For example, you use "He is known for…" rather than "I am known for." Or "Ms. Smith always…" rather than "I always." Or "Brad consistently brought projects in under budget....." Isn't that better than bragging? But while we can say whatever we want about ourselves in our biography, none of this holds as much sway as when someone else says you're better than sliced bread. Which brings us to #2.

2.   **Proof Sources:** One of the few demands I (Al) placed on my sales reps. as a manager, trainer and executive was that the representatives had to have and use a proof source binder. The salespeople could always point to third-party proof sources for every claim they made—they could *prove* that experts agreed with what they said!

A while back, my daughter needed a new car. With a bit of financial assistance from me, she bought a vehicle "on her own." Soon after the purchase, she called saying, "I hate salespeople. They always lie!" In response, I reminded her that I spent much of my life calling on the same clients month after month. I asked her, "What do you think would happen if I got caught lying even once?" She was taken aback and concluded that they probably would never buy anything from me again.

Many people believe that salespeople do nothing but lie (the good ones don't).

It's the same with job transition. Employers assume that candidates will—at minimum—exaggerate their experience (ask George O'Leary about inflating credentials; he might be Notre Dame's all-time winningest coach by now). If you make a claim about yourself, take a short phrase from a recommendation to back up your claim. Then you're neither bragging nor exaggerating. You're merely delivering a proven statement of fact.

Use the recommendations you've assembled. What you quote should be short phrases, and they don't even have to be full sentences. Always give attribution to the source you're citing. You can either use the person's title and company when they made the recommendation or you can use their present company and title. Some examples (names changed) of biographical statements with third-party proof sources:

Who is Sharon Whosis?

Sharon Whosis is a highly experienced Executive Assistant who is an exceptionally detail-oriented, well-organized, dynamic team player who has proven to be an asset to each of her employers.

> *"...I have employed four other secretaries. Sharon ranks at the top of that list..."*
> -James E. Whatsis, Esq.
> Dewey, Cheatum, & Howe
> Attorneys at Law

In her 15+ years as an executive legal assistant/legal secretary, Sharon has experience with firms ranging in size from 3 to 60+ attorneys. She possesses excellent oral and written communication skills. She is adept at proofreading, has exceptional organizational skills, and can manage multiple demands simultaneously.

Possibly her most outstanding attribute is that Sharon has the ability to anticipate potential "projects" on the horizon and, as opposed to so many of today's assistants, Sharon does not require *babysitting*. She actually looks for work when others remain idle.

"She constantly looked for work from us and reminded us of deadlines a few days ahead of time. She often anticipated and accomplished projects without being told."

-William D. Whynot
Whynot, Because, Assad
Attorneys at Law

In the first quote above, only a phrase was used. When there is text before or after the quoted section, just add dots to indicate a partial quotation. If you need to add or change a word, use [ ] to indicate a change from the original text.

The real-life Sharon got a 40% response rate from her Marketing Brochures. Twenty percent is considered great. Here's another example:

Conscientious budgeting and diligent cash management at the growing publishing company resulted in maintaining the brand health of two publications and their subsequent sale to a large publishing conglomerate at a price equivalent to 5 times earnings.

"Jack's reports and advice were invaluable in helping me and the rest of the management team guide the company, not only in weekly planning meetings but also in project- and budget-development meetings."

-Christine Bigg, VP Editorial,
Collins Media and Events
(Formerly Dir. Publications, Metropolitan Publishing)

In his actual brochures, Jack changed font color for each section, which made his material even more distinctive to his targeted executives.

Want some more?

"Marshall has the unique ability to bring out the best in his people."
-Frank Brisbaine,
COO, Cerson & Povey

In the last example on the previous page, the person's title when he recommended Marshall was Vice President of Sales. The corporation for which they both worked no longer exists. Frank is now the Chief Operations Officer (COO) at a company that is thriving (name changed). Which is more impressive? Those were his words about Marshall from the previous company. Nothing else has been altered. You decide what would work best for your needs.

3.   **Accomplishments:** Each of us should be able to name quite a few accomplishments at companies where we've worked. For some, it's easier to quantify accomplishments than it is for others. If you can, point to sales performance, marketing tools, designs, dollars saved/earned, improvements, ROI, etc. Even group accomplishments can, and should, be claimed. Present your accomplishments as bullet points and short phrases. Your goal is to get the person's attention and leave them wanting to know more. Some examples:

<u>ACCOMPLISHMENTS</u>

- Achieved $9,000,000 in net revenue gains nationwide for Cullins' metal scrap over the course of 15 years, or $600,000 per year.
- Worked directly with plant engineers to improve material handling and direct conveyance infrastructure, saving clients in annual freight cost and material handling in the hundreds of thousands of dollars.
- Sold aluminum directly from manufacturing plants to secondary smelters, significantly improving client revenue.
- Improved profitability 15%-20% for national accounts in a two-year period.
- Realized a net gain of $88,000 in scrap nickel/cobalt revenue for Smith & Jones for a six-month period by going to specialty alloy markets.

Anything that is quantifiable is considered an accomplishment. If the numbers are estimates, use the ~ symbol to denote approximations.

Here's another example:

Notable Accomplishments

❖ Designed, created, and implemented Web-based demand planning system
  - Trained over 150 sales & marketing personnel on the system.
  - 99% - 100% accuracy for 7 straight years
❖ Created and Implemented program that reduced finished goods inventory by $37 million.
❖ ~20% Inventory reductions at P&E
  - $400,000 Annual Savings
  - Earned 100% of the business—$4.5 million per year
❖ Turned Around European Inside Sales
  - On-time delivery increased from 20% to 80%,
  - Lead time reduced from 16 weeks to 10 weeks,
  - Expedited deliveries down from 75% of orders to less than 40%.
❖ 100% approved supplier status on over $300 million bids
❖ Improved new business quote time by 50%.
❖ Implemented process to collect and analyze competitive pricing data for new bids and quotes.
❖ Developed merger analysis
  - 1999 merger achieved at A Johnson
  - Became #2 North American Paper Machine Clothing company.

❖ Selected as a member of the 5-person Sales and Marketing Strategy Team
  ▪ Tasked with developing sales and marketing strategy for the newly merged A Johnson

This candidate distilled long-winded paragraphs into bullets and sub-bullets. The information is easier to read and can be expanded on during a follow-up conversation or interview.

Accomplishments

- Guided two magazines from purchase to sale at 5X earnings using diligent cash-management & proprietary sales-forecasting techniques.
- Implemented CRM solution to consolidate sales, marketing, and billing functions, saving company 24% in Admin expenses and providing CEO dependable sales-tracking metrics.
- Full project management of client's customer-appreciation program, producing a 60% profit margin—directed staff, finance, & IT needs.
- Increased bottom line by 29% at consulting firm by designing time & billing software solution to capture all billable hours.
- Created efficiencies in M&A accounting functions by expediting joint-venture, franchise, and earn-out tasks in-house.
- Achieved company-wide adoption of CRM system using training-plus-feedback methods with sales reps, marketing staff, and management team.

- Enabled production staff to meet deadlines and other staff to stay IT-current through careful infrastructure planning.

4.   **Certifications and Credentials:** Some of you may find it impossible to state what you've accomplished during your career. Okay, fine. Then let's state what you *do*. If you've used machinery, software, or material, state it! You're making no claim about you that isn't true.

Many of the qualifications that are required for jobs are never claimed by candidates, and that candidate is quickly disqualified. Remember that there are more candidates than there are jobs in today's world. Tell them what you've done! Give them reasons to *include* you, not exclude you. Here's an example of certifications and credentials:

Administrative Qualifications

- ProLaw
- LexisNexis File and Serve
- WordPerfect 8.0 (and earlier)
- MS Word 2010 (and earlier)
- PowerPoint
- PC Docs
- TimeSlips
- Orion
- Concordance
- Outlook
- PACER
- I-Manage
- Shorthand
- Dictaphone
- 75-85 WPM Typing *Accurately!*

Please note that last line. There is a tremendous difference between 85 words per minute and 85 WPM typed <u>accurately</u>. Be sure and make distinctions where applicable.

5.   **Professional Attributes:** What are the terms that describe you? Better yet, what are the attributes others say you possess? List five to seven of them. If

those terms are ones that are qualifications for a job (keywords), all the better. They can separate you from all the other candidates. Here's an example:

What to Expect

- Professionalism
- Exemplary Work Ethic
- Anticipates Projects Prior to Being Told
- Efficient
- Dependable
- Quick Study
- *No Babysitting Necessary!*

These attributes could be added to the back of your business card too. (More on that in a bit).

6.　　**Charts, Graphs & Logos:** The goal of your Marketing Brochure is to get attention and separate you from the crowd—to get more eyeball time. People LOVE graphs and charts. At a minimum, most people want to figure out what you're saying.

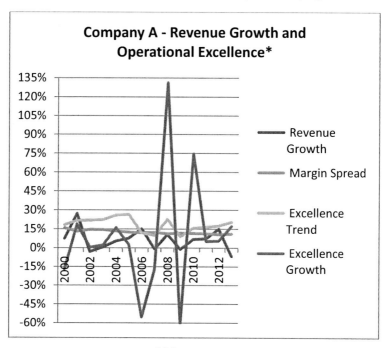

To avoid copyright infringement, we've adapted the brochure below from its original form to include the companies without using their corporate logos. Imagine the impact of seeing the logos of all the following:

Credentials

Financial Services	Manufacturing & Transportation	Technology & Consulting	Luxury Products	Educational Credentials
Citi	UPS	Deloitte	Hyatt	Indiana
Chase	Sunpower	KPMG	Georgia Pacific	Duke
American Express	Nucor	Snickleways	RTD	Harvard
UBS	Ford	AT&T	Mohawk	Princeton
Bank of America	HighMount	Oracle	Brown-Forman	
	Boart Longyear	SAP	Nestle	
	Cabot		Fauchon	

Here's another example of what might be included in your Marketing Brochure:

An interior designer showed a before and after example of her work. It doesn't have to be overly clear, it merely needs to get someone's attention. You will show more of your work (with companies blacked-out!) during your interviews.

7. **Value Proposition:** What do you bring to the table? What do you believe you can do for your target company and how do you believe those goals can be accomplished? Some of these can be assumptions, but most should be

derived from your knowledge of the company and your keyword research. Here's an example:

Value Proposition to Deliver Results

What I bring to the table ...	What I can do for Embraer ...	How I can do it at Embraer ...	Opportunities for Embraer ...
• Passion for Aviation and Manufacturing	• Drive Strategic Top- and Bottom-line Change Initiatives, Mitigate Risk	• Effective Leadership and Communication	• Global Enterprise of Excellence to Drive Business Growth, Increase Nimbleness, and Reduce Product Development Cycle
• Career dedicated to Excellence, Innovation, Superior Quality, and Outstanding Customer Service	• Strategize and Deliver Tactical Execution of Vision	• End-to-End Strategic Planning thru Tactical Execution	
• Executive Leadership	• Implement Operational and Communication Excellence	• Enterprise Alignment to Embrace Strategic Initiatives	• Increased Margins
• Global Experience, Languages, and Insight	• Eliminate Inefficiencies and Redundancies	• Collaborative Team Building and Leadership Alignment	• Increased EBITDA
• Big 4 ERP, Strategy, and Operations Consulting			• Successful Strategic Initiative Implementations
• Extensive Change Management	• Champion Executive Jet Value Proposition	• Current State Assessments; Future State Modeling, Roadmap Development	• Realized ROI
• Best Practices: Industry- and Enterprise-wide	• Develop Sound Business Cases	• Complex Problem Solving	• Increased ROA
• World-class Tools, Techniques and Methodologies	• Restructure Operating Models to Create a Global Approach	• Global Change Management Program Development and Implementation	• Decreased Margin Spread
			• Increased Enterprise Excellence

Most of us should develop our Value Proposition for—and present it during—our face-to-face interviews based on answers to our probing questions. We'll talk more about this tactic during the chapter on interviewing.

8.   **Contact Informtion:** As we said earlier, you can use symbols to add to your brand's identity. This is a good example, though we suggest adding your LinkedIn address:

Marvin Da'andy Nights
4720 Ownship Walk
Marietta, GA 30066

marvin.da@yahoo.com
(678)555-6286 (home office)
(843)555-4217 (cell)

*"Providing Innovative Solutions to Enable
the Gears of Business to Run More Smoothly."*

Marketing Brochure Formats

There are many formats you can use for your Marketing Brochures. You can also use a combination of formats for different situations. The choices are many and they're dictated only by your particular situation, creativity, and what you want to present. But the message of your Personal Brand should remain constant. Format choices include:

- Tri-Fold
- Bi-Fold
- Multi-Fold
- Portfolio
- Electronic

The **Tri-Fold** brochure will fit neatly into the breast pocket of your coat or a standard envelope. It's one sheet of paper printed on the front and back. It's a convenient way to present your Value Proposition since it's divided into thirds. It's more informal than a portfolio or electronic presentation and can be used by any level candidate.

The **Bi-Fold** and **Multi-Fold** are variations of each other. They're one or more sheets of paper folded in the center to make pages in multiples of four. A Bi-Fold might be a good idea for someone starting their career since they don't have much background to present yet. People in the graphic arts, sales, marketing, and others who need to present more information should use the Multi-Fold version especially when you want to show comparisons and examples. Templates are available on the Internet, or they can be easliy set up directly by you in a Word document.

Note: Never send any of the above Marketing Brochures via email. The layout makes no sense when sent electronically, firewalls often don't like attachments, and it's way too easy for the recipient to press Delete. Marketing Brochures are meant to be mailed or used as a presentation tool during a face-to-face interview.

We recommend a **Portfolio** for executives. These are extremely impressive documents that can be quite elaborate. They should only go to company presidents or other C-level officers. Lower-level employees will be intimidated by a properly formatted portfolio.

Mail or courier is the preferred delivery method for Portfolio Brochures, although they can be sent electronically.

Electronic Marketing Brochures are recommended for executives and can be used in conjunction with written materials. Tablets, laptops, and projectors are the preferred vehicles for this sort of presentation of your qualifications. The candidate is in control of the presentation, but it should be pre-planned with the interviewer(s). Few words should be used in deference to charts, graphs, and other representations whenever possible. This allows for the free flow of questions and answers as opposed to a lecture.

Marketing Plans

Businesses develop marketing plans to help them be more successful. When you're in the business of a job search, why wouldn't you take the time to develop a Personal Marketing Plan to help you be more successful? A carefully laid out Marketing Plan can help you (and others) understand who you are, what you have to offer, where you want to work, and how you will get there. The why in this equation is the reason for doing it in the first place—to get your next position! Nadine Walley is a former member of the Georgia Department of Labor and has many certifications in the job-search area. In her article, "Conducting the Business of Job Search Like a Business," she shares some of her thoughts:

> You probably spent countless hours on your résumé, carefully crafting it to make it your best. A marketing plan can be used to supplement your résumé so that it will help you get the word out about you. It can guide you in your networking meetings and provide structure and focus so that it is easier to communicate your message of WHO you are.

When people find out that you are not working, they usually say, "Let me know if I can help." When I follow up and meet with these people, I like to use my marketing plan rather than providing them with a résumé. Résumés tend to be overwhelming and job-specific; a marketing plan can help you focus more on your competencies and less on your history. The Marketing Plan helps people who want to help you. In the words from the movie *Jerry McGuire*, "Help me help you." People often don't know **how** they can help you. A marketing plan makes it easier for them to "see" what you can do and where you might fit.

Components of a Marketing Plan
There are no rules, but the key is to keep it simple and make sure that it does communicate your message clearly. I like to include my career goal in mine but do not put my geographic location target. Below are the seven topics that every marketing plan should include:

1. Positioning Statement
Your positioning statement is similar to a summary statement in that it needs to be clear and concise so that it is obvious to anyone who reads it. It needs to respond to the statement, "Tell me about yourself." It usually starts with a profession (e.g., I am a healthcare marketing leader). Your expertise usually focuses on competencies and skills. This will be a separate area in your Marketing Plan, but for purposes of developing a professional positioning statement, include some examples of what your skills and competencies are. You can also include what you love to do or what differentiates you from others in your field.

2. Competencies
When I developed my plan, I went to my résumé and detailed each of my accomplishments and put them into my competency categories. Look at your accomplishments and see what competency categories they are in and keep it to three or four areas.

3. Target Companies/Types of Companies
List the companies that you might be interested in working for and do research on those companies. Search on LinkedIn or through

other networks to find people who are already working there. Please do not forget that, according to the Bureau of Labor Statistics, 99.7% of businesses in the United States are considered small businesses (i.e., employ fewer than 500 employees). So do not only focus on big companies; look in Hoover's or ZoomInfo to find firms that are progressive and innovative.

4. Action Plan

A true Marketing Plan has an action plan and dates on when you will complete each task. I suggest that you develop a spreadsheet and include individuals you will contact, their phone numbers and email address, when you contacted them and when you will follow up. I also include a notes section.

Different formats can be used for your Marketing Plan. I have developed a trifold that communicates this same message in a nice presentable manner. Be creative and remember that your resume, brochures and marketing plans are a marketing piece so there are no rules, but they must be truthful, comprehensive, neat, and tell the story of who you are.

Business Cards

Your business card is another extension of your Marketing Campaign. It's the most obvious method of communication between you and any contact. It should state your name, city, state, phone number, email address, and LinkedIn address. It should also include your Branding Statement, similar to the symbols used in the Marketing Brochure examples above. You want it to make a lasting impression to set you apart from others. By the way, business cards have two sides. Does your present business card take advantage of that valuable real estate? We believe it should.

A list of 5-7 professional atributes (1-3 words each) is one way to get your message across. Another is to employ a QR Code (more on QR Codes next). Whatever the message you include, business cards should be given out like candy. We suggest that you buy a box of 500 and, if at all possible, design your business card so that it stands out in a stack. Thicker stock, a silk surface, non-standard size or folded are surefire ways to stand out in a pile.

Some experts suggest including your picture, but that always makes real estate agents come to mind. We don't suggest adding your picture—especially if you look like us. We do, however, recommend that you invest the extra bucks that it takes to make your business cards work harder than your competition. Cheaper isn't always better. Sometimes cheap is just cheap.

QR Codes

QR Codes are a Japanese invention that began with the automotive industry. QR stands for Quick Response and are similar to the barcodes used on products. The difference is that a QR code can hold a wealth of information, including symbols. They can be read by smartphones and generated free of charge by use of a QR Code generator. There are many QR Code generators on the Internet.

Parts of your Marketing Brochure or an infographic resume are the best choices to be included in a QR Code. It will tell your story right there with a business card and that's possibly the greatest benefit of using them. An ancillary effect is to make you seem more tech-savvy when you're not. But there are potential negatives about QR Codes, as well.

At this writing, QR Codes are not being widely used, though they are becoming more prevalent. They have been known to include viruses and for that reason, some people refuse to read QR Codes from people they don't know. If you choose to use a QR Code, we suggest that you put it on the back of your business card. (Make sure your printing company can handle QR Codes and that the information is readable before you pay for your order.)

Now let's put all the pieces of your puzzle together so your Marketing Campaign can be launched.

Chapter 9: Pre-Launch Checklist

> *"Simple checklists help eliminate 'stupid' mistakes."*
> -Jonathan Babcock

You're almost ready to launch your Marketing Campaign, but there are still a few more details to attend to first. Let's make certain that all your ducks are in a row.

Spelling & Grammar

One of the quickest ways to sabotage your Marketing Campaign is to have spelling or grammatical errors. It is sad, but recruiters and talent acquisition managers would rather see a picture of you with a cocktail in your hands than spelling or grammatical errors. They are indicators of your attention to detail—or lack thereof—and are seen as predictors of what you'd be like after you're hired.

I (Al) was once given a book written by a job coach. I have to admit that I never read it. But one day my wife opened it up and began randomly scanning it. She placed a skinny purple adhesive Post-it® Note on each page where she found a spelling or grammatical error. She didn't read every page, but when she handed the book to me later, Jeff and I thought the thing looked like a purple porcupine! She claimed that there was not a single page that didn't contain at least one error. While many of the things that coach has to say have validity, anyone who opens his book will quickly begin to question his credibility because of his clear lack of attention to detail.

These errors are easy to commit but equally easy to correct. Once your credibility is damaged, it can almost never be regained.

One commonly misspelled word is MANGER.

How did you read that word: "manager" or "manger"? Jesus was born in one and many of us have been the other.

Just before we began to write this section we did a LinkedIn advanced people search for the word "manger." We clicked on Advanced, then clicked on People, typed "manger" in the keyword box then clicked Enter. The search returned 10,628 hits. Searching only the people in my network, ten thousand, six hundred and twenty-eight individuals had the word "manger" instead of "manager" somewhere in their profile!

It's such an easy mistake. We know what it's *supposed to* say, so our eyes don't catch it. The spell-checker goes right past it because it's not spelled wrong. (We are STILL finding errors in this book.) This is why we suggest that you search for "wrong words" prior to launching your Marketing Campaign. You can conduct your search using the method described above if you already have a LinkedIn or Google+ profile in place. On the other hand, if you've followed our suggestion to write your resume and profiles in a Word document first, just use the Find function.

Look to the upper right-hand corner of your Word document for the binoculars. Click on Control F or the binoculars icon. A box will appear asking, Find What. Enter a word in that box then click on Find In. Finally, you will need to click on Main Document. If the word you *don't* want to use is present, you'll be made aware of it and can make the necessary changes prior to launch.

Editing & Proofreading

While we're on the subject of searching for errors, we suggest that you get someone you trust to proof your resume, Marketing Brochure, business card, LinkedIn Profile and other online material. Is what you're saying clear and readily understandable? Again, you want all your marketing material to be perfect before you get your Marketing Campaign under way.

Betsy Rhame-Minor, a business communication consultant, writing coach, and book editor, underlines our point in her article, "Want To Look Good In Social Media? Then Spell Words Correctly and Use Correct Grammar":

Recently a presidential candidate's campaign misspelled "America" when launching a mobile application. Word spread quickly via the Internet, and the misspelled word, "Amercia," was even trending on Twitter for a while. Though this mistake isn't likely to harm this candidate's credibility and professional reputation, it goes to show that even presidential candidates need a good editor.

You've probably seen misspelled words or grammatical errors all over the place: billboards, restaurant menus, corporate emails. They're everywhere quite simply because they're so easy to make.

While some errors are simply incorrect, other errors can embarrass your company, confuse or offend your potential clients, or provide misinformation. By the time you've realized your mistake those prospects may have moved on to do business with your competitor.

Mark Twain wrote, "The difference between the right word and the almost right word is the difference between lightning and a lightning bug."

A good editor or proofreader can help you make sure the words you've chosen work for what you're saying, are grammatically correct, and make sense while ensuring that every word is spelled correctly (you can't trust spell-check to catch everything).

You can maintain your professional reputation by having someone read over what you've written. An editor or proofreader has a trained eye to catch typos that go unnoticed by others: transposed letters, too many or not enough commas, homonyms such as "their, they're, and there," and claims that don't make sense. If you don't have an editor close at hand, finding a friend, staff member, or spouse to read over what you've written can help catch the mistakes you've missed.

There's no shortage of communications pieces your company should be sending out into the world. Email campaigns, the company website, news releases, a blog, and a solid social media campaign are a few of the ways you can engage your fans and followers. You'll be at your best when you're reaching your customers in these ways, with accurate content containing no errors. Chances are your customers might think that any company that takes the time to make sure, literally, that all the i's are dotted and t's crossed will take just as good care of them too while delivering the best product or service.

Although you should carefully review your resume, considerably more people will likely be reading your LinkedIn Profile. For that reason, we feel you should take special attention when you review this profile. You and your proofreader(s) should cast a dispassionate and critical eye on what you want to convey versus what you've actually written down.

Here are some questions you should ask yourself:
1. If you were a person hiring for the position you qualify for, after reading a few lines of your profile (title line, summary, interests), would you want to read more or go on to the next candidate?
2. Are you telling the story you want people to hear? (Are you telling a story at all?)
3. Is that story interesting or compelling?
4. Are you using the right keywords?
5. Are you providing enough or too much information?
6. Is your passion evident, or is reading your profile's summary like listening to Eeyore tell Christopher Robin and Winnie-the-Pooh that he's lost his tail again?
7. Is there anything you could add that might grab the reader's attention? (A presentation?)
8. Based on what you've read, would you want to get more information about you, much less hire you?

One last thing about your resume: Once you're happy with it, never ever go to another resume review!

Voicemail

You never get a second chance to make a first impression (sorry for the cliché), but we're talking about getting a job here. Your voice message may just be the initial interaction between you and your next employer. Don't let that impression be negative or unprofessional.

Cutesy voice messages are fine most of the time, but not during a job search. Hiring Managers don't want to hear your child's voice, your dog barking *Jingle Bells*, or something that has a hidden meaning only you and some of your buddies get. Your message should be short, to the point, and professional in nature. Go back to *Jingle Bark* after you're hired if you want.

Here's what we suggest:
> *"You have reached <u>Your Name</u> at <u>Your phone number (include area code)</u>. I am unavailable at the moment. Please leave your name, phone number, and a message at the tone and I will return your call as soon as possible."*

Email Signature

An email signature is an oft-forgotten element, but it's a simple and essential tool to include as part of your branding effort and to help others introduce you to people you'd like to connect with.

Let's say you send us an email request for an introduction to a Hiring Manager. Without a pre-set email signature at the bottom of your email text, we would have to search for and add your contact information. The chance of us (or anyone else) doing that is somewhere between slim and none—and Slim just walked out the door. Make it easy for us to help you by adding an email signature to your email and Smartphone. It's simple to do. Here are a couple of examples:

Gmail:
- Click on the little gear-looking icon directly below the small picture of you on the right-hand side of the screen. (Don't have your picture uploaded? Do it!). A drop-down box will appear.
- Click on Settings.
- About halfway down the page there is an area called Signature.

- Type what you want to say in that box. We suggest:
  - Name
  - What you do/want to do (Supply Chain Director, for example)
  - Phone number or phone numbers
  - Email address
  - Compressed LinkedIn Address
- Click Save Changes.

AOL:
- Click Options on the far right of the screen.
- Click Mail Settings.
- Click Compose (left-hand side of the new screen).
- Type your email signature (as seen above).
- Click Save Settings.

All providers have their own little quirks, but they're all similar and easy to navigate. You can add other things—like a quote—but we don't advise it. Use the K.I.S.S. System: Keep It Simple, Sucker!

Do the same with your Smartphone. You don't want the signature to read, *Sent from my Android or iPhone.* Any time you send a message, you want to be certain that the recipient can easily contact you in return or forward your information to other interested parties. Make it easier for them to do so, and you will increase your odds.

Online Reputation

You already know that every job offer is contingent on a background check and possibly other tests, including a drug-screening. (If you smoke pot, at least give it up until you secure your next job. The stuff stays in your system for a month or more. Even in states that have legalized it, your potential employer almost assuredly will not tolerate it.)

What you may not be aware of is that many companies vet you before you get an interview. It's quick and easy to research a candidate. If a potential employer researched your name, what would they find? If you don't know, you need to check it out. There are a lot of search engines out there—and you should search them all. It's fairly simple and should be done now, before you launch your Marketing Campaign. Google is the search platform that comes to mind first for most of us, but you should also do a check on Yahoo and Bing. You should check YouTube, as well. You don't want there to be anything negative about you on any of these platforms.

Here's how to check your online presence:
Go to each platform individually (Google, Yahoo, Bing, and YouTube).
Enter "Your Name" in quotation marks.
Click Enter.
Check other iterations of your name (Joe Schmoe, Joseph Schmoe, Joseph B. Schmoe).

Check which page you find yourself on, and don't forget to search for images of yourself. You'll want to remove any non-professional photos, blogs, or videos. While you're at it, we suggest that you adjust your privacy settings while in search mode to make your profiles visible to everyone. You WANT to get found.

Note: To ensure the most reliable results, make sure you are not signed in to an email account associated with the search engine where you are conducting the search. For example, sign out of Gmail when searching for yourself in Google.

The Internet is an amazing tool, and the information at our fingertips now is practically limitless. Unfortunately, there is no hiding. You've probably seen the scam companies out there that are just short of blackmailing you to have them *clean your record*—for a fee, of course. Don't use the S.O.B.s!

You should also remove any non-professional or negative postings that you can and ask others to take down material that does not show you in a favorable light. Unfortunately, there may be unflattering things that remain.

What did you do? Come on, you can tell us.

Recruiters are not very different from you or us; they will probably search no further than the third page. *When you do a search, how many pages do you look at before you move on?* You can't make everything go away, but there's only so much looking people will do. So force the bad stuff past the fourth or fifth page.

Here are some effective ways to move unflattering information away from most prying eyes:

- Add content (lots of it) with your name in it.
- Create a website (not the best advice, but it's one method).
- Write a blog post.
- Comment on other people's blog posts.
- Use industry material then comment on it.
- Add lots of keywords to your material so you get noticed even more.

An added benefit to becoming active on the Web through posting professional content is that you will become more visible and credible—and isn't that what we're trying to accomplish?

Contacts

Now is the time to prepare an email campaign for your existing contacts. Create a generic email that can be sent individually or via blind copy (Bcc) to your friends, relatives, former colleagues, vendors, clients, etc. These are the people who already know you and probably want to see you succeed. The body of your email could look something like this:

Wanted to give you an update,

I hate to have to report it, but my job went away. They say that when one door closes, another opens. Hopefully, that door will present itself soon and I will have a key that fits.

Here's what I'm seeking _____ (Be very specific and include such things as your preferred industry, geographic area, and title. Include a few companies by name as targets.) If you can think of somewhat similar companies or if you know someone you think I should contact, please let me know.

I'll keep you updated on my progress. And if there is anything you need from me, please don't hesitate to ask.

Let's chat when convenient. I'd love to hear from you and catch up.

Don't forget an enticing subject line. Something like: *Quick update from*_____ or *Wanted to let you know* or *Big news from* _____.

If you haven't done this already, schedule dates to contact these people. Schedule this in your Google or Yahoo Calendar and follow up on a regularly scheduled basis. More likely than not, it will be a more productive way to spend your time than searching job boards! And it will certainly be less frustrating.

Since this chapter is full of clichés, let's add one more: *Out of sight, out of mind.* Stay in contact with these people—and not just with emails like the one above.

Human contact is a GOOD thing!

Remember to take advantage of the LinkedIn contacts function you set up earlier. Having and using a Customer Relationship Manager (CRM) system of any type is critical. Since much of your Marketing Campaign is centered on LinkedIn, using that system is quite an efficient method for staying in touch. But even a binder with paper will work just fine as long as you stay with it.

Set up Google Alerts on the industry you're interested in and other alerts that you could share with your industry colleagues, LinkedIn connections, former clients, and vendors. That way you're not seen as a bother but a resource. And as a bonus, you aren't forgotten.

'Now Playing in Poughkeepsie'

There's an old saying in the theater that goes something like, "See how it plays in Poughkeepsie before taking it to Broadway." It basically means that it's better to correct the inevitable mistakes every play will make on a small stage rather than screw up on the big stage in New York. Here's a real-life example from Al:

Everyone was excited about an upcoming product launch. We had a national sales meeting where the new product was introduced to the field sales force. There was role play, then we had breakout sessions by region to talk about what our strategy was going to be. As with many new product launches, we had a sales force expansion, so there were newly hired reps.

I asked, "Who are you planning to take it to first?" The reply was, "To my biggest prescription writers!"

"No," I said, "I want you to go out to the boonies of your territory so you can work the kinks out of your presentation."

As a result, our region had far and away the highest sales of any region in the country, in large part because when our biggest writers had a question, were skeptical, or offered an objection, we had already encountered those situations and knew how to properly handle them.

You probably have companies you *want* to work for, right? You should have a list of twenty to twenty-five to start with. But you also need to begin with a handful of dirtbag companies (three to seven, remember?) that you do NOT want to work for.

We're going to *take the play to Poughkeepsie* first.

Let's get the kinks worked out of our sales pitch. Let's practice on companies you wouldn't work for if they were the last ones on earth—because you can't afford to screw-up when you get an interview with the ones you WANT to work for. Note: You'll be amazed how many of those companies will respond to you. Use them for practice. Who cares if you screw up with them? You don't want to make mistakes later.

Waddaya say you have your people call our people and let's do launch!

Chapter 10: Light This Candle!

"Why don't you fix your little problem and
light this candle!"
-Astronaut Alan Sheppard
After his Mercury 7 Flight was delayed 3 hours
Sheppard was America's 1st man in space

'Let's Do Launch'

Our bet is that you're as eager as Alan Sheppard to light the candle of your job search and get this flight into the history books. So let's do it. But let's do it methodically. Below is a checklist to follow. This list will be expanded in the following chapter to maximize your Marketing Campaign's effectiveness.

Launch	How to launch
Voicemail	Set up a professional-sounding voice message
Email Address	Set up an email address and use a major email provider such as Google
Email Signature	Set up a detailed email signature so you can be easily contacted
Resume	Have electronic and paper versions of your resume available for immediate response
LinkedIn	Post your updated **LinkedIn** Profile (note your average weekly profile views)
Google +	Post your new **Google+** profile
About.me	Post profile using information from LinkedIn
Twitter	Post profile similar to LinkedIn and Google+ on Twitter
Job Boards	Post your resume on the job boards of your choice, especially the aggregators **SimplyHired** and **Indeed**
Marketing Brochures	Choose 5 companies that you DO NOT want to work for and mail (Snail Mail) **Marketing Brochure** to the president of each company
Contacts	Send out a mass email to your contacts via blind copy (Bcc) that lets them know you've begun your Marketing Campaign and tell them you will keep them up to date on your progress

This is an in-depth chapter, a step-by-step primer on how to assemble the various pieces of your Marketing Campaign. It's not meant to be read all at once like a novel. Rather, it's a plan of action. Once you've accomplished each task, mark it off your launch checklist. We'll get into considerable detail on what should be done and why. We're certain you'll get the hang of it in short order.

Voice Mail, Email Address, & Email Signature
If you haven't already set these up as directed in the previous chapter, now is the time to do so.

Resume
You should have both electronic and paper versions of your resume available for immediate use from this point forward. (We'll discuss posting your resume on job boards later.)

Reminder: Save your resume in .pdf, .doc, .dox, and .txt formats.

Naming, Saving, & Sending Your Resume
It's important to name, save, and send your resume correctly. According to Nancy Curtin Morris, Vice President of Learning and People Development at Hotel Equities and formerly at Marriott International, your resume should be saved as First Name, Last Name, and the Title you're seeking (e.g., JoeSchmoeMarketingExecutiveResume). Nancy says DO NOT *begin* with the word "resume" because HR will be getting hundreds of resumes for each position. She warns that if your document reads "dot.3" (dot.number) HR will wonder what the previous Dots say that this one doesn't. For the same reason, she says, with dot.number versions you should make sure the year is current or non-existent in the file name (e.g., JoeSchmoeResumeCurrentYear).

Ms. Morris adds that you should save your resume as both a Word document and a PDF. She further suggests that you forward that resume in BOTH forms and let them open the one that fits the needs of the recipient, since different entities prefer resume submissions in different forms. Make it easy for them!

LinkedIn
Posting your new LinkedIn Profile is pretty straightforward.

You're well-prepared and you've accumulated all of the information you need to finalize and launch it. Once you've completed adding all of the relevant information, you'll want to save your profile and give it one last look. Please have someone else review it to make sure it presents a stellar image of you. Before you *strike the match*, be sure you have sufficient endorsements and recommendations for your profile (See below).

Endorsements
Want to further enhance your **"Social Proof"** and online credibility? Want to have your achievements and accomplishments validated by others and not simply viewed as just something you're boasting about? Want to have a virtual billboard on LinkedIn? Think endorsements!

LinkedIn now makes it a lot easier with the introduction of the Endorsement feature. Just as we predicted, endorsements have become part of the algorithm that helps move you toward page one, position one, which should be your goal.

We suggest that you launch your Marketing Campaign with a maximum of 7 endorsement choices. There's much more in-depth information about the Endorsements feature in Chapter 12: Advanced Social Media.

Recommendations
It's important that you have a minimum of 5-7 recommendations on LinkedIn to be seen as credible. You should certainly strive for more as time allows, but use this metric as the starting point before you "Light the Candle" with your profile. There's much more in-depth information about recommendations in Chapter 12: Advanced Social Media.

LinkedIn Groups
Being a member of and participating in LinkedIn Groups can be a very important part of your overall LinkedIn strategy. There are thousands of LinkedIn Groups you can join for various professions, interests, and geographical areas. If you find that one doesn't exist for your profession or specialization, you could always create one. But understand that they are a lot of work.

LinkedIn allows you to join up to 50 groups and another 25 subgroups. We don't think you can keep up with or stay active in that many, but you should plan to become a member of a diverse set of groups that include your desired industry, companies, job groups, and recruiter-based groups. When considering a group, check out the number of members. Stay away from smaller groups because few people are likely to see you there. Also, groups where there has been minimal discussion activity will be of little benefit to you. Be aware that some groups have become quite spammy, so take this into account if you get involved. There is much more in-depth information about LinkedIn Groups in Chapter 12: Advanced Social Media.

Note: Active participation in groups not only enhances your overall visibility and credibility but also increases your profile views and search ranking.

LinkedIn Connections
A small number of connections limits your ability to uncover many insiders at target companies. Make a concerted effort to surpass the 500+ connection level within three weeks. To quickly accomplish this goal, see our advice in Chapter 12: Advanced Social Media.

LinkedIn Views
Please note the number of LinkedIn views you're currently receiving and chart your progress on a weekly basis. There is a rule of thumb that says a candidate needs, on average, a minimum of 300 "good views" before he or she can expect to secure a job. One of the reasons we want your profiles and resumes keyword-rich is to vastly increase the number of views you receive.

There is much more in-depth information about LinkedIn Views in both Chapter 10: Maximizing your Effectiveness, and Chapter 12: Advanced Social Media.

Launching Your LinkedIn Profile
Once you believe that your profile is the best possible representation of yourself, you need to reverse an action we had you take earlier. Turn back ON your Activity **B**roadcast. Do this in the following manner:
1. Go to your **LinkedIn** Home Page.
2. Move your cursor to the small picture of you at the top right-hand side of the page. A drop-down box should appear.
3. Click on **Privacy & Settings.**
4. Enter your Password where prompted to do so.
5. Look for **Privacy Controls.**
6. Click **Turn On/Off your activity broadcasts.**
7. Click the box: **Let people know when you change your profile, make recommendations, or follow companies.**

8. Click **Save Changes.**

Once you've done this, everyone in your LinkedIn network will get an update that your profile has been changed.

Google+, Twitter, & About.me Profiles
Check to make certain that your profiles are prepared as explained in Chapter 7: Assembling the Puzzle. There is in-depth information on each of them in Chapter 12: Advanced Social Media

Job Boards
You've probably already posted a resume on a job board. If not, now is the time to do so, and the process is fairly straightforward. Just follow the board's directions. At the same time, you might be prompted to set up your search agent. If so, opt to have job postings sent to your email address on a daily basis. When you're prompted to upload your resume, be sure to check everything, because your information will almost always be pulled from your resume. These engines make plenty of mistakes, and your chances go down with every error.

Remember, you don't have to post your resume everywhere. We suggest that you post your resume on one of the aggregators (SimplyHired or Indeed) and maybe one of the big boards like Monster or CareerBuilder. Apply only for job postings where you meet or exceed all the requirements—and are actually interested in the job.

Note: If you're in a niche market, be certain to post your resume to those specialized job boards (e.g., Dice.com or Dentalpost.net).

Marketing Brochures
Now is the time to send out your initial week's Marketing Brochures to the companies you **do not** want to work for. You'll follow up with them with the same zeal you would a company you'd love to work for. You want and need practice handling questions and coming up with answers because you can't afford to screw up when you reach your target companies. Make your mistakes now with your throw-away group of companies. By the way, don't be at all surprised when they want to talk to you. (This has occurred for the majority of our clients.)

Do not send Marketing Brochures to your target group yet, and don't mail more than 3-5 per week. You can't follow-up with more than that, especially since you'll be using other methods of contacting companies and applying for posted positions simultaneously.

Contacts

The final stage of your launch is to inform all your contacts that you are actively looking for a new position. We suggest that you send a group email to your contacts, which can be done en masse or in small groups.

In the subject line, you have to get their attention with something like, *Big news to share....*

Then in the body, *I'm launching my new job search. I'm seeking a position as _____ targeting _____ (industries and/or companies).*

Ask your connections for their help: *I'd love to send some of my marketing material to you to get your feedback and share some specifics so that when you come across an opportunity that seems like a fit, you can recommend me. Can I count on you?*

Don't forget to include something like this: *As has always been the case, I'm here when you need my assistance. How can I help you?*

Note: When sending via LinkedIn you're limited to 50 connections at a time.

Other Necessities

If you haven't done so already, sign up now for both a Bitly account (go to bitly.com) and a HootSuite account (go to hootsuite.com). Both are free. You'll learn much more about both of them in Chapter 12: Advanced Social Media.

Chapter 11: Maximizing Your Effectiveness

"People with clear, written goals, accomplish far more in a shorter period of time than people without them could ever imagine."
-Brian Tracy

How to Maximize Your Efforts

In the previous chapter, we included a pre-launch checklist. We will now expand on that list to give you a strategy to fully implement your Marketing Campaign and maximize its effectiveness.

Launched	How to Maximize your Effort
Organize Files	Organize online and hard-copy files to ensure that you can easily find materials associated with your job search A. Set up a Word document folder to serve as a repository for your LinkedIn Profile B. Use Notepad to record and store your password information
Google Email	Establish a Google Email account for your job search
LinkedIn	A. Give and ask for Endorsements: goal 99+ on each B. Comment and work your Groups; minimum goal: daily updates C. Add Connections: minimum goal: 500+ D. Monitor views: minimum goal: of 20-30/week
Google+	Maintain your new **Google+** profile
About.me	Maintain profile similar to LinkedIn and Google+ on About.me
Twitter	Monitor profile; post and retweet
Job Boards	Update your resume weekly
HR Applications	Online applications, goal: 3-5 per week
Marketing Brochures	Mail 3-5 Marketing Brochures to target companies per week. Schedule follow-up calls.
Contacts	Send mass email to your **contacts** via blind copy (Bcc) on a regular basis with updates, alerts (see below), and other information of interest to your target executives, insiders, and contacts. Stay in touch on a scheduled basis.
Google Alerts	Create Google Alerts for: A. Industry news B. Company News C. Executive News
Networking	Look at networking from many angles, especially B-2-B
Blogs & Website	Post and comment; don't just "Like"

Job Fairs	Hiring, fishing, or advertising?
Targeting	Continue to expand your targets
Recruiters	Find 3-5
Career Coach	Consider hiring a Career Coach
Training	WIA and other training/certifications
Volunteerism	Doing for others can do much for you
Calendar	Plan your work and work your plan

Organizing Your Files

One of the more frustrating things in a job search is the inability to quickly find files in your file cabinet or online. We strongly suggest that you purchase hanging or manila folders, label them for various aspects of your job search, and put them in a readily accessible area of your file cabinet. This will make life a lot easier and save you a great deal of time.

In addition to organizing your hard-copy files, you should also set up an online file system that will allow you to easily find everything you do online that's related to your job search. Make sure to set up the appropriate subdirectories so you can "uncomplicate" your life and find things in a hurry. We also suggest that you take any inactive folders you have on your hard drive and archive them so the only things you have to contend with are "live" folders.

You should also consider using a service such as Carbonite or other cloud-based service to back up all of your files online (Windows 8 offers this service). When you least expect it, your hard drive could crash, causing either the loss of all of your records or a very expensive exercise—in both time and money—to recover them. The same holds true for notes and contact information you have on your smartphone. Also, if all these things are on the cloud, they're accessible to you anywhere in the world anytime you need them. So back them up!

Word Document Folder

You should also set up a Word Document file that will serve as a repository for everything you do on LinkedIn. This way you can easily spell-check anything you're planning to post. Once you've updated the file information and spell-checked it, you can simply cut and paste the material into LinkedIn, feeling confident that it's fairly accurate. Remember, however, that spelling and grammar checks are not perfect, so it's critical that you—and at least one friend—proofread whatever you do.

Notepad

To enhance your productivity and to keep you from playing hide-and-seek for your passwords, establish a Notepad file. Store your passwords in alphabetical order. This allows you to copy and paste your passwords when prompted. Multiple passwords minimize the chance for valuable information to be captured by third parties.

Google Email Account

It will help your job search tremendously if you have a Google email account. Not only is Google the de facto email standard and number 1 search engine, the tools you have access to with a Google account are extensive and include a cloud-based calendar and telephone (Google Voice). Furthermore, by having all of your contacts on Google, you'll be much better organized. All you need to do is have your current email service provider redirect your emails to Google so all your emails reside in one place.

LinkedIn

We believe you should go to your LinkedIn home page every day. A robust, complete LinkedIn Profile is the single most important tool you can have as part of your launch. It's the fuel that will propel you into the stratosphere of today's job market. Without it, you'll be pretty much grounded, with little chance of being found unless you're already a well-known senior executive whose phone is ringing off the hook, or a celebrity—and that ain't us! Actually, even well-connected executives and celebrities could benefit from having a proper LinkedIn Profile because it would further expand their universe of contacts and improve their odds of being found.

Mastering LinkedIn is not easy, but it can be done if you set your mind to it. In the next chapter, we'll go into detail about what you should be doing to maximize LinkedIn's potential from an altitude of 30,000 feet. To fully cover all the bases would require a separate book dedicated entirely to LinkedIn. And because LinkedIn is constantly changing and updating things, you shouldn't be surprised if you go to your profile one morning and things are not the same. Given the ever-changing nature of LinkedIn, it is very difficult to master. To gain greater insight into LinkedIn beyond what you will learn in our Advanced Social

Media chapter, we recommend two authors we consider to be among the world's foremost LinkedIn experts, Viveka Von Rosen and Neal Schaffer.

Endorsements

The Endorsement feature on LinkedIn is something we have never been fans of, but with multiple billions of endorsements being logged, it's not going away. It appears to be an attempt by LinkedIn to get people to log on to the site, increase overall traffic, expose people to their advertisers, and promote click-throughs, thereby boosting shareholders' returns.

Soon after their launch, we predicted that endorsements would become part of the algorithm that helps move you towards page one, position one. We were correct. As such, your goal with respect to endorsements is to get as many as you can. It's their game, so let's play.

Think we're kidding?

One of the more fascinating articles we've read while doing research for our coaching clients and this book, was a blog post by Donna Svie at AvidCareerist.com. In it she confirms what we suspected: that getting found is a *numbers game* and endorsements are an integral part of that game.[1] She did a keyword search (similar to what recruiters do to find you for a hidden job) and found that the connection who landed page one, position one had that particular keyword 116 times in his profile while the person who finished in position six had that same keyword appear only five times.

Haven't you guys been touting the importance of keyword-loading all along?

Yes! But the person in position six had a whopping 625 *endorsements* for that same word!

To our way of thinking, the person who landed page one, position one in this case was gaming the system—come on, the same flippin' word used 116 times in the same profile? (See e-book Bonus Chapter: Proceed with Caution, *Keyword Over-loading.*) And it seems to us that the other person is much more on the up-and-up since he used the specific keyword a mere five times. But even though he had far fewer occurrences of the keyword in question, his huge number of endorsements for that word gave him a significant boost. (Words in the body of the text are weighted more heavily than endorsements, but endorsements are effective nonetheless.)

Note: Depending on the keywords, we have no problem seeing those exact terms used multiple times in your profile or resume. In fact, we encourage it.

You should begin endorsing your first-level connections and asking them for endorsements in return. Be specific about the endorsements you want. If necessary, tell your connections why endorsements are necessary and ask for them to endorse you for the 5-7 skills you want to highlight.

The reason we want you to focus on an initial 5-7 key endorsements is because you want to reach the 99+ endorsements level as soon as possible. Giving your connections fewer endorsement options ensures that your most important skills will be featured. As you near your goal, you can slowly add to the initial list. As silly as it may seem, this will help you move toward the coveted first position on page one when a recruiter or talent acquisition manager does a search for candidates with your background.

Remember to give endorsements ONLY one or two at a time. Every time you give an endorsement, an alert goes out to your entire network and the endorser's network. Don't fire all of your bullets at once. Spread them out over time.

In that same blog, Ms. Svie writes, "If you want to drive traffic to your profile via your position in LinkedIn search results, it looks as though it's smart to grab every meaningful <u>and meaningless</u> endorsement you can."

Groups
As we said earlier, LinkedIn allows you to join up to 50 groups and another 25 sub-groups. We also said we don't believe you can keep up with or stay active in that many, but join a diverse set of groups that include your desired industry, companies, alumni, jobs, and recruiter-based groups. And we suggested that you shy away from smaller groups since few people are likely to find you there.

Actively participate in your industry groups by making comments and creating posts that might be of interest to its members. You can use the same post on multiple groups simultaneously to hit a broader cross-section of people. Spread those posts out over several hours since they would otherwise all appear at the same time. Spreading them out adds significantly to your visibility.

Adding links to your post will also help get you noticed and can show that what you're saying is not merely your opinion. (Note: By using Bitly, you can track the number of views to your posts.) Do these things and your views will increase dramatically. By the way, this isn't merely *our* opinion. LinkedIn reports that "group participants get four times the number of profile views."

Here's one client's example:

Starting from a low of 17 profile views per week in late October (not bad), he increased the number to 111 in early January, as is shown below. On top of that, he has received numerous connection requests, including some from the highest management levels of his target industry.

Week Ending / Views

10/26	17	
11/2	28	
11/9	31	
11/16	27	
11/23	25	
11/30	22	
12/2	36	(This is when he really got serious about commenting and posting)
12/14	81	
12/21	59	
12/28	33	(Christmas)
1/4	35	(New Year)
1/11	111	

He maintains a 65+ average and other clients have since followed suit achieving similar results.

What do I post?

Google Alerts and LinkedIn Pulse Articles (formerly LinkedIn Today) are great sources of information that are welcomed by both company and industry insiders. These are "Hot off the Press" items you can use to start a discussion. Some discussions can stay active for a long period of time and position you as an expert. Do this effectively and you WILL get noticed!

Oh, and avoid merely "liking" someone else's post. A "Like" doesn't get broadcast to the members of the group. But when someone likes one of your posts, send a note of thanks and invite them to connect with you. By doing this, you will quickly exceed the critical 500+ connection threshold that recruiters like to see (especially with Baby Boomers). In most instances, LinkedIn groups also give you direct access to their members. This means that if you uncover an executive or corporate insider at a target company, you should become a member of that person's group(s) to directly connect. This could facilitate a meeting or give you access to inside information.

Note: Multiple posts or comments in groups will quickly advance your status to Top Influencer in those groups and dramatically increase your overall visibility.

Connections
Make a concerted effort to surpass the 500+ connection level within a three-week period. This is easy to accomplish. Here are some ways:

- Thank and then ask people who "Like" your posts to connect with you
- Thank and then ask people who comment on your posts to connect with you
- Comment on posts you like and send connection requests to that person (Don't just click "Like")
- Send connection requests to all new contacts (i.e., everyone you meet)
- Seek connections with LIONs (LinkedIn Open Networkers), most of whom will accept
- Send connection requests to recruiters

Having a small number of connections limits your ability to uncover many insiders at target companies. If you have ever searched LinkedIn and gotten results containing just a first name and an initial or Out of Your Network, you've experienced the downside of a smallish network. As we stated in a previous chapter: The larger your network, the broader your access to the millions of members in LinkedIn's universe.

Another important reason to become a so-called **"networking sponge"** is that you can only be endorsed by first-level connections. And we've already demonstrated how important endorsements can be for getting you found in Boolean Searches for hidden jobs. Remember, the more search results you turn up in, the greater the chance you'll be contacted for an interview.

One more thing: When you send a connection request to someone, *never* use the default LinkedIn message, "I'd like to add you to my professional network." Instead, take the time to write a personal note.

An original note every time??? Argh!!!!

Don't have a cow. Your "personal" notes can be written in advance and saved in a Word document or Notepad (See the section on organizing your files and Word documents at the beginning of this chapter). Write a series of these notes that you can use not only for Let's Connect but also for Thank You for the Like, Great Comment, Endorsement, etc. Most LIONs (LinkedIn Open Networkers) don't care one way or the other, but don't you prefer receiving *personalized* notes. Adding where you met is a good idea too, but having something prepared can save you time without appearing impersonal or canned.

While we're at it, offering your help to the other person is always a good idea.

DAILY/WEEKLY ACTIVITIES

LinkedIn Views
Track your views weekly. We'd like to see you exceed 20-30 per week. If the rule of thumb holds, you should be hired within three months (as opposed to the national average of 9-plus months). You will have saved tens of thousands of dollars of personal wealth in the process.

Keeping a close watch on your views should also alert you to things you might want to adjust. For instance, you may need to become more active in the groups you've joined, or add or delete groups. You may also need to add or change the number or types of keywords you're using. Remember, the goal is to get noticed to get interviewed, because you can't get hired unless you get interviews. And the best way to get them is for hiring authorities to find you. (For more on this, see Chapter 12: Advanced Social Media.)

Your Updates
If at all possible, try to post an update to your LinkedIn Profile at least once a day, or a couple of times a day. These updates should appear at different times during the day, not at the same time every day. Also, share the updates with the groups you belong to if they're relevant to that group. However, do not (as

noted above) share them with multiple groups at one time because they will be posted as multiple entries on your activity feed and may be seen by your connections as spam (or not seen at all). This could prompt them to hide your activity feed broadcasts, or worse, disconnect from you. (For detailed instructions on what to post, see Chapter 12: Advanced Social Media.)

Your Activity Feed
Another little-known method for gaining maximum exposure and solidifying your connection with others is to review your activity feed a few minutes at least once a day. For detailed instruction on what you should be looking for, see Chapter 12: Advanced Social Media.

Network Contacts
Go to the LinkedIn "Toolbar" and click on Network Contacts. You'll see a stream of photos of people, announcements about new jobs, birthdays, job anniversaries, and other information. By reviewing this and commenting, you can solidify your relationship with individual contacts. You may also learn that one of your contacts has moved to one of your target companies, which could be a door-opener for you, but be careful. We've noticed that this material can be dated. So before you send a message, check the person's profile to make sure the information is current.

Google+
Given the fact that Google is the number one search engine companies rely on, anything you do to enhance your presence on Google can only benefit your Marketing Campaign. Therefore, as part of your overall preparation for launch, you should ensure that you have a Google+ profile. Once it's set up and looks professional you can then start circling (following) people and posting updates to it. Your Google+ profile can be a virtual duplicate of your LinkedIn Profile. The more often your Personal Brand is presented, the greater your visibility and likelihood of securing interviews.

About.me
A site that many people are not aware of is About.me (an AOL property). It's a great tool for further positioning yourself online without much effort. You simply set-up an account online and use some of the profile information from your LinkedIn Profile to complete it. Once it's up and running, there's very little that has to be done in the way of updating unless you make a major change to

your LinkedIn Profile, at which time you should update this, along with any other social media channels you're on.

Twitter
Although used by hundreds of millions of people globally, Twitter is still viewed by many as a difficult tool to use, one that many overlook in their job searches. Not only do *we* find it a very useful tool, recruiters are using it to find and vet candidates. Aside from that, it's a tremendous source of information that includes millions of job listings. Almost every company has Twitter accounts.

But the main benefit of Twitter is that it lets you follow people and companies to gain a sense of what they represent. It also gives you the ability to possibly interact with them and carry the "conversation" over to LinkedIn connections, email correspondence, phone calls, and face-to-face meetings.

With a little guidance and practice, you can become fairly proficient and realize the benefits of Twitter. In the next chapter, we'll give you some steps to help you get going. As with LinkedIn, mastering Twitter goes beyond the scope of this book. For an in-depth look at how to get the most out of Twitter, we recommend Mark Schaefer's book, *The Tao of Twitter*.

Throughout your social media platforms, be certain to keep your message and Brand consistent!

Job Boards

In case you haven't figured it out yet, we're not proponents of using job boards as the centerpiece of your job search, but they should be part of your overall strategy. Virtually every job-seeker spends an inordinate amount of time on job boards, so we want you to severely limit your activity there. On average, people in every age group spend more than 90% of their search time at online job boards, even though more than 80% of jobs are never posted. Of course, people do get jobs through job postings. And, despite what we tell you, you'll probably spend beaucoup time there, as well.

To maximize your efficiency, however, we believe you should use one of the leading job aggregators such as SimplyHired or Indeed, which are the largest. But we told you at the beginning of this book that we try to include *every* method for getting jobs, even when we are not advocates of a particular method. As such, we would be remiss if we didn't at least mention posting to major job boards such as Monster, CareerBuilder, Dice, and SixFigureJobs.

Because recruiters still use them and since some people get hired through them, you can make a case that you should post your resume on one or more of the traditional job boards. It would be yet another seed that you've planted. At minimum, you can gain exposure and—who knows?—you could land a job this way. Others have.

The number and types of job boards you choose to post your resume on is entirely up to you. But to minimize your time and maximize your effectiveness, we suggest the following approach:
1. Search Agents:
   a. Create a search agent that sends posted jobs to your inbox on a <u>daily</u> basis.
   b. If you're getting too many postings, narrow your focus slightly.
   c. If you're not getting enough postings, broaden your focus.
2. Scheduled Time:
   a. Start every day in front of your computer applying to the posted jobs of your choice.
   b. Limit yourself to a scheduled 1-2 hours per day maximum applying to the posted jobs sent to your inbox.
   c. Start *before* breakfast! We suggest that your Search Day begin at 6 a.m. Bodily needs (hunger, thirst, bathroom) will help you limit yourself to 2 hours.
   d. DO NOT WAIT to apply for a posted position. Some jobs are filled within hours, after which additional applicants are not considered. Don't wait until tomorrow or the end of the week. You could miss out.
   e. Shower and dress for your Search Day—that is, "Go to work."
3. Updates
   a. Schedule a weekly update to your posted resume every Friday before noon. But don't go crazy here!
   b. Change a comma to a semicolon this week and the semicolon back to a comma next week then click Update. It sounds silly (and it is),

but at present this is sufficient to qualify as an updated resume. Recruiters will see that you're active, and they'll be more likely to view your resume.

4. Research & Contact
   a. Once you've applied for a posted job, search your contacts for a company insider.
   b. Contact any insider as soon as possible and ask them to get your resume to the top of the stack or to the Hiring Manager. Do not waste time!

One other thing you should know, if you don't already, is that if you have any sales or marketing in your background, you're almost certain to be contacted by an insurance company, granted an interview, and receive a job offer. The same thing goes if you have any financial background whatsoever; you can expect the financial planning companies to come-a-calling. Some of these companies will require a financial investment on your part and have a track record of employment lasting until you have signed up your last living relative. One insurance company's average tenure is reportedly a whopping *four months*. Many of these jobs are commission-only—you invest your time and money while they reap the rewards.

Purple Squirrels
What are purple squirrels, and what the heck do they have to with a job search?

A Purple Squirrel is a term used by recruiters who have been asked to fill a position with a candidate that possesses *superhero qualifications*— requirements that are virtually impossible to meet. In effect, the company is asking the recruiter to uncover a candidate as rare as finding a purple squirrel in the park, having it eat a peanut from your hand, and hearing it say, "Thank you kindly." Even a superhero probably wouldn't qualify for some of these positions.

Because there are so many qualified candidates seeking a job, the talent pool seems bottomless to many employers. As a result, they often extend the hiring process while they seek the elusive Purple Squirrel. The *Daily Kos*, an American political blog that publishes news and opinion, reported that "...job vacancies are staying open an average of 23 business days, compared to a low of 15 in mid-2009."[2] The article goes on to quote Glassdoor.com—a U.S.-based job and career site where employees anonymously comment on the pros and cons of their companies and bosses—as saying that "the interview process at many major companies has just about doubled in three years."[2]

At some companies, the pressure to find the perfect candidate is so intense that some Hiring Managers make the task impossible to accomplish because they can't afford to hire the wrong person. With a Purple Squirrel, they can tell their superiors that no one in the pool of available candidates had the right combination of required skills. In short, many hiring authorities are so scared to make a wrong decision (and possibly lose their job) that they make no decision at all.

There are, of course, huge costs involved with hiring the wrong person: the manpower cost during the candidate-gathering period, the cost of taking the Hiring Manager away from his or her normal duties, lost productivity from the open position, and reduced productivity during the inevitable post-hire learning curve. The greatest potential cost, however, is that many companies are more likely to fire a scapegoat who made the "wrong" decision.

We have our pellet guns ready, and we're aimin' to bag us
a mess of Purple Squirrels so we can all get back to work!

Human Resources

Many companies and virtually all large corporations have a requirement that a candidate must apply for a posted job prior to being considered. Okay, fine. Apply. Human Resources is nothing to fear. Indeed, many HR professionals are highly skilled and know what the company is seeking better than a Hiring Manager does. Many HR people are well-trained in the nuances of the hiring process. They are truly talent acquisition professionals.

Our experience in working with them at various career ministries is that most of these people are caring individuals who want to help people find employment. The problem is that they, like so many others today, are doing the work that 2-3 people used to do. They simply don't have time to address the needs of each and every person who applies for a job. To give you a sense of the enormity of their task, consider this, as previously mentioned: a talent acquisition manager for a Fortune 150 company posted a position for an administrative assistant and received more than 1,200 applications. There was no way this individual could screen that number of resumes manually, so she had to rely on what she could glean from information posted to the company's system about candidates who might be suitable for the position.

As a result, they are increasingly relying on ATS software to find candidates.

Often, you will find the name of the Talent Acquisition Manager in a job posting. If so, you should send a note directly to that person, aside from your electronically submitted resume. This might help you avoid the Black Hole. The note should be no more than a few lines and to the point. It should include the job title and requisition number. State that you have already applied, that you meet or exceed all the requirements (don't bother them if you do not meet <u>all</u> the requirements), and that you're requesting that he or she flag your application. It doesn't always work, but then nothing does.

Continue to research and use your connections just as you would in any other instance, but you will at least have covered all the bases by having applied as the company required.

So apply already—then get to the real work.

Marketing Brochures

Marketing Brochures can be one of the most effective weapons in your arsenal. This is especially true for executives, for people with gaps in their resume, and for those who are changing professions. For one, they can demonstrate your creativity. They're usually short, to the point, and often don't include dates. They tell the story you want to be told. Can you say that about a resume?

We recommend that you send them via snail mail directly to an executive—*never* via email—because the formatting can get messed up. Besides, these days people get surprisingly little regular mail versus being swamped by emails. (In fact, the Maytag repairman has been replaced by the in-house mailroom manager as the loneliest person on the planet.) As a result, letters sent via the postal service stand out more now than they did in the past. People actually read more of their paper mail as opposed to pressing **DELETE** on an email.

The key to your Marketing Brochure's success is follow-up. You should schedule a follow-up call for the day AFTER it should have arrived at the company office. Inside tip: Call before hours, after hours, or during lunch because the executive's administrative assistant is more likely not to be available to pick up the phone while the executive *might*.

If you reach the assistant, reach out to him or her and *make nice*. Executive assistants are similar to ICU nurses—they typically are the best of the best. They usually have a keen eye for things the executive should see. But be warned: They also have a built-in BS meter! They can make sure that the executive sees your document—or doesn't.

Amateur athletes practice until they get it right.
Professionals practice until they don't get it wrong.

Earlier, we advised you to launch your Marketing Campaign by sending out 3-5 Marketing Brochures to executives at companies you don't want to work for. Remember to follow them up as you would normally do, with the same goal: to get an interview. These are for *practice*. The idea is to get through the inevitable mistakes you're certain to make so you won't make them when you're following up with a company where you want to work. Maintain a three-to-five brochure quota per week. Mailing more than that precludes proper follow-up. Fewer than that won't produce enough opportunities.

Note: Only about 20% of your Marketing Brochures will reach your target executive.

You WILL often be rebuffed. But keep plugging away. You only need one job.

Contacts

One of the most challenging aspects in the job-search process is keeping track of all of the people you come into contact with. It's daunting. If you start from the get-go to organize them, however, life will be much easier for you.

The first step should be to consolidate all of your email and LinkedIn contacts into your Google email account and eliminate duplicates. Assign your contacts to files or groups based on specific criteria. This can also be done with the Tag feature on LinkedIn, which will be discussed in depth in Chapter 12: Advanced Social Media. With all of your contact information in place, you'll be much more efficient. This will serve as a mini-CRM (Customer Relationship Management).

Plan to update your existing contacts on a regular basis. The best way to make sure that you're following up regularly is to schedule it in your online calendar (or Daytimer). Sending each set of contacts an update every six weeks is enough to keep you in their heads without being a pest. Remember, these people are on your side and should know you well enough to tell you when too much is too much. When sending an email update, a few lines should suffice. And a couple of minutes should be all it takes when you make a phone call. Include something meaningful to them (Google Alert, news item, joke). Keep the material fresh and don't make it always appear self-centered. Always strike a positive note. Never get into a pity party.

Ask what YOU can do for them and they'll be more likely to want to do something for you.

Google Alerts

As we previously mentioned, one of the reasons to get a Gmail account is that it opens the door to a lot of great features. One of the most useful is Google Alerts. Take advantage of them. With Google Alerts you can set yourself up to receive notifications on industry events, company events, notices pertaining to specific individuals, and all kinds of other information that might help you in your job search and beyond. It's a tremendous time-saver. The information comes to you in the form of a listing that's easy to review. You can share items you feel might interest others in your network or keep relevant items as part of the research you're doing for your job search.

The alerts you set up now may help position you for subsequent jobs in the years ahead.

Networking

It's widely claimed that 80% of all jobs are attained through networking. Although we question that "statistic," working your contacts and personal network can be a great help. But it's no guarantee. Forbes writer Susan Adams found the same non-scientific Right Management survey that everyone seems to quote and even those results were half of what is stated as fact at most networking events.[3]

Although we're in favor of traditional networking—including attending networking events on a limited basis—we believe that electronic networking offers great advantages. The term "networking" is, of course, a very broad one. But we see dramatic differences between traditional networking and "new networking". Let's see if we can break it down. (All of the following may not be available in your area.)

Traditional Networking

A. **Current contacts**   (this is the most common and should be done on a regularly scheduled basis as stated above)
   a. friends
   b. family
   c. acquaintances
   d. former colleagues
   e. former bosses
   f. vendors
   g. clients

B. **Career Events**
   These can be valuable, but often can be time-consuming and costly when you calculate the total expense:
   a. Career Ministries   Church-based career events (usually Christian-based), secular
   b. Career Mixers   Non-denominational, secular, or non-secular
   c. Accountability Groups   Supposed to keep you/them on target, but if they turn negative, run like a scalded dog!

d. Speaker Events   If you believe you can benefit from the speaker's topic, go; otherwise, consider the cost-benefit ratio

Non-Traditional Networking

A. **B-2-B Events**   In virtually every town there are Business-to-Business events that are open to the public. One example is a local Chamber of Commerce meeting. Some B-2-B events have a fee attached; many do not. These meetings are perfect for a "prepared" candidate (like you will soon be) since the attendees are people who have companies and maybe even have job openings! At minimum, they have contacts.

Socialize!

Meet people and share your BRIEF elevator pitch. Exchange business cards (no resumes!), ask if they will connect with you on LinkedIn, and for goodness sake, follow-up! You wouldn't believe how many people don't! Remind them who you are in a brief email and let them know that you've sent them a LinkedIn request.

As we mentioned earlier, the two of us speak on a weekly basis and encourage attendees to connect with us and each other so they can enhance their network reach. Few people, however, take us up on this offer. As a result, we've never experienced an overflow in our inboxes.

Like Rodney Dangerfield, *We get no respect, no respect at all…*

Asking how you can help those new contacts is a great way to have them think about and offer ways to help you.

If cocktails are available, we suggest you refrain.

In our opinion, attending B-2-B events is far superior to career events, which are attended mainly by others who are in job transition.

B. Associations   We already urged you to find an association in your profession, and we directed you to Weddles.com, which at last count listed 97 associations. Attending an association meeting is a great way to rub elbows with others in your chosen profession and explore who's hiring and what the overall atmosphere is in your area. Some association meetings require you to join and pay a fee. We suggest you explain your situation to the person in charge and tell him or her that when you land a job you will join the association. (Be sure to remember anyone who helps you.)

Often, speakers and attendees at these events will be open to having coffee or a brief meeting. These meetings, however, should NOT be used to overtly ask for a job. You're seeking ADVICE. This is, of course, are a perfect opportunity to share your Marketing Brochure or Marketing Plan.

Once again, we encourage you to ask how you can help THEM.

C. Conventions   If at all possible, try to attend a local, regional, or national convention. These events have the greatest concentration of your industry's companies in one place at the same time. Take advantage of this if you can. Seek a badge through your industry contacts, but if you can't get one just hang around outside the meeting area. More importantly, try to make appointments to meet with executives who are attending. The best way to do this is to mail them a formal invitation and ask for a "couple of moments" of their time (a moment is non-specific and can last many minutes!).

Again, this is an opportunity to use your Marketing Brochure or Marketing Plan. But be sure to have a resume ready in case they request one. Trade business cards and follow-up, follow-up, follow-up!

'Executive Cultivation' All of the above are ways to get executives into your network (and get admitted into theirs). Once you do, ask for suggestions, ask for advice, and—if the opportunity arises—ask to be considered for an available position. The executives you meet this way may not have a job for you today, but they may have one tomorrow or when *they* change companies.

Many Hiring Managers and executives keep a file of people around the country who—if a position were to become available—they would seek out first to fill that position. Try to get into as many executives' files as you can. Once you're connected, continue to contact them with information that might be useful, such as industry news, company happenings, or notes of personal interest to them (birthday greetings, marriage in the family, or a new position—can you say Google Alert?). This way, you'll be seen as an asset and not a pest.

Emile Paradis, an expert networker, puts people together. In "Networking to Best Effect," he shares his perspective on how to define and best utilize the time you spend networking with others:

Networking has become an integral part of the business scene, its place an assumed necessity for new business development success. But networking applications go far beyond acquiring new customers, playing a role in our personal lives as we make recommendations for restaurants, doctors, plumbers, schools, etc. And with so many people looking for employment opportunities, there is a renewed interest in networking in job search.

We all have our networks, but for most of us they work in a random way. By assessing who we know and the nature of our relationships, we can begin to see the numerous ways we can help each other. In business and in our personal lives, our relationships serve different needs. And our various networks serve different needs, as well. You can consider your business networks as providing you **Information, Support,** and **Referrals.** These same networks can serve to help you in your job search.

Ron left the military and was seeking to start his career. Armed with a great resume, he started attending various networking groups oriented toward providing job-seeking information and job fairs, how to interview, and how to market himself. This was part of his **Information Network.**

Ron was able to leverage his previous career through his **Support Network.** This included military veterans groups and former service members of his particular service, the Marine Corps in his case.

His **Support Network** (which also includes family and friends) provided connections to groups that would prove helpful in his search: social media, personal networking, and reaching out through his personal networks.

His **Support** and **Information Networks** led him to an effective **Referral Network**. Utilizing his resources, he identified a few opportunities that fit his skill set and he landed a job that supported his goals.

Knowing people is one thing, but knowing them well enough that they will take the time to help you is another. And with people being busier than ever, asking for time is a big "ask." Make it easy for people to help you:

- Be ready with a clear description of what you need them to do
- Offer to pay for any expenses
- Make it something they can do right now without a lot of preparation
- Offer examples of any writing you need them to do (write it for them)
- Set up easy ways for people to introduce you to those you would like to meet by attending events with them.

We all know many people and may even consider them and the groups we belong to as part of our network. But to really capitalize on the resources we've created, we need to evaluate the depth of the relationships we have, as well as the nature and context of those relationships. By realizing the roles played by the people and groups in our lives, we can better utilize the assets available to us.

Blogs & Personal Web sites

Establishing your own blog or personal Web site can be useful for your job search, but they are not things we'd recommend unless you're trying to obtain a position where having a blog is almost a must (such as Social or Traditional Media), or if you're trying to clearly demonstrate your expertise in an area, demonstrate a track record, and have valuable information to share with others.

In the case of Web sites, we believe it's overkill unless you're applying for a position where knowledge of Web sites is critical. They may help with SEO, but it has been our experience in talking with talent acquisition managers that they just don't have time to look at personal websites except as part of the *final* vetting process. They simply don't have time and neither do you. Instead, we suggest that you invest your time on LinkedIn and the other tools we've talked about throughout this book.

One final note on the subject: With regard to blogs and personal Web sites, if you're not adept you can appear inept—and that's not good for your Personal Brand! Commenting, retweeting, and posting, on the other hand, can serve the same purpose without the necessary commitment to maintaining your Web site or blog post.

In addition to LinkedIn, recruiters rely on other methods to discover candidates on the Internet. Jim Stroud teaches recruiters how to use many of these alternative tools. Jim is often amazed at how much information is out there on any one individual and how readily available it is. In "There's More to a Candidate Search than LinkedIn," he shares some of his thoughts:

> If you're a job-seeker you should not overlook the fact that recruiters have a myriad of tools at their disposal and don't necessarily rely on LinkedIn for all candidates, although it's their primary source. Oftentimes, the proverbial Purple Squirrel (hard-to-source candidate) will be found by recruiters due to the exposure that the individual has on the Internet via the various job boards. In addition, those who have set up a resume-based website on Google sites will also be at an advantage when these recruiters search for candidates, as Google seems to give search preference to content from Google sites.

> Regardless of what approach is used, it is imperative that all job candidates critically evaluate the keywords that they are using in their resume for the position that they're seeking. After all, like LinkedIn, keywords are what are being searched in the pursuit of the perfect candidate, not the overall resume. Without them you're toast, as the Boolean search strings being used for the searches are all based on them.

One of the other things that you can do, in addition to posting your resume, is to become an active participant on blogs related to your industry. You might be asking yourself why blogs would be critical for a search. Certainly blogs can play a role in establishing credibility for an individual, and a great way of being perceived as an expert is to contribute comments to blogs. For example, if I were trying to locate a mechanical engineer that I wanted to ensure had a great deal of expertise in a certain subject area, I would go to Google and insert a search string using the so-called "numrange" search string on Google. It would be similar to:

"25..300 comments" site:wordpress.com infile: mechanical engineering

This search string would then conduct a search of all of the blogs on WordPress, a very popular blogging platform, and would provide results on the main blogs focused in on this area with the largest number of comments posted to them. I would then review the comments and glean information regarding who was commenting on the subject matter that I was focusing my search on. It would enable me to quickly identify those individuals with the greatest expertise based on their contributions. If they had links to LinkedIn, Google+, or other sites, I would do further research on the individual and their suitability for the position. If there was a fit they'd be contacted; the Purple Squirrel is found.

Based on the above, as a job-seeker, you should consider focusing in on blogs that have a great number of comments in your respective discipline and start providing comments to them, which will help position you as an expert. The same holds true for responding to discussions in LinkedIn Groups that are related to your expertise, as this will also increase your chances of being discovered by recruiters.

As Jim confirmed, adding comments and posting about your respective discipline and reposting links can be as effective—perhaps more effective—than creating your own blog (and requires a smaller time investment). It's important to once again note that you must take great care with spelling and grammar when you post. As we said earlier, few things can sabotage your positioning as an expert than multiple spelling and grammatical errors.

Job Fairs

We promised to share with you every method we know of for getting a job, even the ones we're not in favor of. Job Fairs fit into that category. We're not alone in our assessment. Allison Green, in her blog, *Ask the Manager,* writes, "[T]hey're wasting the time of the employees they send, and they're wasting the time of job fair attendees like you."[4] Because so few people are hired through job fairs, it has long been our contention that some companies use job fairs as an inexpensive marketing ploy or public relations gimmick to get the company name in the headlines. Popular CareerDiva.net's Eve Tahmincioglu interview called Job Fairs, more or less, "A waste of time."[5]

Look how successful we are...we're at a job fair!

In our opinion, job fairs are as hollow as those mystery job ads that appear, disappear, then reappear on an ongoing basis. The Atlanta area has had huge job fairs in recent years with nightmarish results. Hundreds to more than a thousand people would stand in line to meet with company representatives who would take the candidate's resume. Few of these people got called back much less received a job offer. Some literally waited all day in the "Hotlanta" sun and went home with nothing but sweat-soaked clothes.

One of the local career ministries here in Atlanta has added mini-job fairs to their regular group of events. These seem to produce better results than the mega-job fairs, but some of the companies' jobs leave a lot to be desired considering the level of the regular attendees. (There is nothing wrong with taking one of these jobs as either a bridge or a stepping-stone.) For example, recent events have been populated largely by companies seeking people for:
- Call Centers
- Landscaping
- Security
- Cable Television
- Rental
- Retail
- Insurance
- Pest Control

It's commonplace to see telecommunications companies, retail stores, and insurance companies trolling for bodies at this type of event. So, if your life's ambition is to sell telephones at a kiosk in the mall, a job fair may be just the thing for you. But if you have higher desires, you may want to spend your time elsewhere.

Targeting

Targeting is so important to your job search that we dedicated an entire chapter to it. But *knowing how* to target and *doing it* are two distinctly different animals. Once again, we're not talking about targeting posted jobs on job boards (you don't need this book to tell you how to do that). No, we want you to target companies and/or executives you want to work for. Imagine working at a job you actually enjoy.

Question: What do you do for a living and how many companies have people who do that? Follow-up question: Why shouldn't that person be you?

Two of the best resources for finding companies is Hoover's and ZoomInfo.com. Both are available for free at your public library. Type in a company name and about halfway down the page you'll see a list of similar, competitive, and ancillary companies or their suppliers. Bingo, you now have 20-30 additional targets you had never thought of. Once you have these additional targets, research and prioritize them. Finding individuals and executives within those companies is fairly straightforward. This is where becoming a networking sponge by building an extensive network pays off. The more connections you have on LinkedIn, the greater your reach throughout the business community.

We suggest that you create a stable of roughly 200 potential employers. *Impossible, you say?*

Well, according to Manta.com,[6] the Atlanta area has approximately 165,000 businesses. A 200-company goal, if you live in the Atlanta area, equates to about one tenth of 1%. Just remember that there are a lot of companies other than multinationals. And all you need is one of them to hire you.

Resources available to you include:
- Your contacts
- LinkedIn
- Twitter
- Jigsaw
- Hoover's
- ZoomInfo.com

Recruiters

In this section, the recruiters we're referring to are people who get paid a commission when they fill a job requisition. They do not work for the candidate. They work for themselves, and while they want to make a placement, they don't care who the candidate is as long as it's *their* candidate. Remember, a recruiter can't help you if they don't have a requisition. They can't *create* a job for you.

Recruiting always was a difficult business, but it's considerably more so these days. Many recruiters rely solely on electronic means to find viable candidates (Boolean searches, LinkedIn, job boards). Others actually take the time to specialize in one area of expertise, build a deep relationship with both clients and candidates, and maintain a stable of qualified candidates. You can readily tell the difference between the two types.

The latter is the type of recruiter you should seek. Try to find 3-5 recruiters to work and stay in touch with. In his article "5 Signs of a Great Recruiter,"[7] Miles Jennings, former recruiter and now CEO of Recruiter.com, lists the key things to consider when you go shopping for one:
1. Past Success
2. Company Knowledge
3. Project Information
4. Technical Understanding
5. Personal Connections

Once you've established a relationship with your recruiters, do your best to help them. They will be much more inclined to go out of their way to help you.

Never, ever ask a recruiter what companies they have requisitions for. Instead, ask what *type* of positions they have available. On the flip side, you come in contact with many qualified individuals, so refer them to your recruiters. Remember, these folks want to place people, and they need the "paper" to put in front of their clients' eyes to make a placement—and a commission.

Career Coaches & Job Coaches

Unlike recruiters, job and career coaches work on behalf of their client: you. As we told you earlier, the average time in job transition in the United States is in excess of nine months, and the cost of you spending that *average* amount of time unemployed could be in the tens of thousands of dollars. Hiring a job coach should save you many months of search time, which translates into beaucoup thousands of dollars. Of course, we're prejudiced. But we sincerely believe that hiring a job coach is a smart investment.

Most career coaches charge by the session (hour or half-hour). Some offer a discount for a package of sessions then try to sell you additional sessions. Charging a client per session gives the coach a clear financial incentive to keep the client "on the string." The longer they have you as a client, the more money they make. This could take you from a perceived investment of a few hundred dollars to a couple of thousand. At Transition Sherpa, on the other hand, we believe that a coach should charge a single fee and coach you until you get your next position, with no hidden or additional costs. If you happen to need more time than the average client, so be it. This places the burden of helping you get a job more quickly on the shoulders of the coach, not on your wallet/purse.

No matter the ultimate cost of a career coach, however, you should expect to shave three to six months or more off the time it would otherwise take you to get a job. Your coach should accomplish this by keeping you focused on your goal—and kicking you in the butt (figuratively, of course), if necessary.

It should be clear by now that we believe our clients should learn every method for finding a job because each candidate has a different comfort level for undertaking various tasks. Every coach is different, too; like you, we all have different strengths. And while a good career coach can make you stronger in many areas, we cannot change your nature. In short, not everything works for everyone.

You must feel comfortable with the coach you choose and completely confident in the methods they espouse. If it doesn't feel like a fit, find someone else. As is the case in every industry, some coaches lack integrity. Our perspective isn't the only one you should consider. Just because we say something doesn't necessarily make it so. That's why, during talks, we offer to give attendees the contact information of other coaches who we respect, believe have integrity, and are more interested in their clients than their own bank accounts (like us).

One of the coaches we recommend is Chris Gilliam. She has worked with the outplacement company Right Management for many years and has her own coaching company, as well. We've listened to the advice she gives candidates and have heard her present her program. We volunteer at a number of the same career events, speak at other venues, and don't always agree—but that's okay. Like our clients, hers are successful too. In her article, "Why Hire a Career Coach?" she makes a strong case:

> **M**ost professionals going through career transition are anxious to find their next position. A career coach can assist in accelerating the job-search process by partnering with the client to deploy successful search strategies and tactics.
>
> **Coaches Know Current and Competitive Approaches**
> Job-search methods have changed drastically in recent years. A coach will have experience in the latest techniques that will competitively position the client in the market. Experts agree that an effective job search does not begin with a "one size fits all" resume and lengthy generic cover letter submitted to online job boards. A savvy coach will collaborate with the client to identify key abilities and strengths, prepare marketing collateral and strategize on pursuing the most effective networking resources to maximize exposure. Nor will the search end with a spectacular job offer if the interview is stiff and lacking spontaneity. A skilled coach can guide a client in researching an employer, anticipating questions, and preparing success stories as compelling examples of past performance.

Coaches Offer Objective Observations and Feedback

Have you ever heard that "feedback is the breakfast of champions"? A seasoned coach is a truth-teller. A recent study by the International Coach Federation[8] (ICF) revealed that people who work with coaches gained fresh perspective on their personal challenges. This self-awareness led to:

- Improved self-confidence by as much as 80%
- Improved relationships by as much as 73%
- Improved communication skills by as much as 72%

It is the coach's responsibility to provide honest and direct feedback, delivered with the utmost integrity and respect. Does the client have a significant gap in work history or experience? Could the client's communication style derail an interview? Once an issue is identified, improvement plans can begin. On the other hand, many clients are not accustomed to receiving positive feedback. I make a point of recognizing the great experience, skills, and talents with my clients. We celebrate successes and wins along the journey! A recent client told me that working with me rather than with a recruiter was far more beneficial because I listened, helped him define his key accomplishments, and provided encouragement and consistent feedback.

Coaches Assist in Exploring Alternative Career Options

We know the world of work is changing! Many people in transition are seeking other career directions—either because they dislike their current work or because the profession or industry has changed. Fortunately, there is no rule book that dictates people must remain in the same career for their entire work lives. However, shifting professional gears can be confusing and intimidating.

Working with a coach, an individual can take a variety of assessments to identify strengths, personality, skills, interests, and values. Based on the results, the client and coach can develop marketing and search strategies to align with the new direction, while capitalizing on relevant previous experience. This approach requires time for introspection and research, and also requires creativity in recalibrating the client's marketing message, in addition to persistence and patience in the process.

Tips for Finding the Right Coach

There is an abundance of career coaches in most major cities. Career coaches' methods and styles will differ, so you will want to feel comfortable that there is good synergy and open dialogue. The goal for employing a career coach is to decrease the time spent in the job search, although it is not a race! Be wary of guarantees for employment within X number of days. Working with the right coach will help you land the right position—but not necessarily the first or fastest offer. While professional credentials may vary, there are many ways to find the right coach. Here are a few:

- Ask current/past job seekers for referrals
- Attend an event where the coach is speaking
- Read the coach's LinkedIn Profile and website
- Research the coach's credentials and certifications
- Ask about coaching process and timeline

Volunteerism

Volunteering is not only something we recommend, it's something we both do. That's why we strongly suggest that candidates do it, too. If it comes down to a choice between two equally qualified candidates, many employers will choose the person who gives of their time over someone who merely shows up for work. Many of us who volunteer, however, fail to let potential employers know about it.

That stops now!

In addition to the "soft" attributes of volunteering in a soup kitchen or similar entity where your effort is just labor, there can be some significant practical advantages to volunteering:

1. **Hone your skills**: If you're volunteering your time performing a duty for which you're professionally qualified, employers can see that you have been actively working on your skill set and are staying up to date.

2. **Fill in resume gaps**: The longer you are without a job, the greater the gap in the resume. We've already established how much of a Red Flag that presents and how costly it can be. It can even disqualify you as a candidate with some companies. Volunteering can fill those gaps.
3. **Meet Potential Employers**: It's not just people in transition who volunteer; business owners and executives do, as well. And those who volunteer usually surround themselves with like-minded individuals. Many of them hire from this expanded network and are willing to help you even if they have no position for you at their company. At the very least, they may be good for a recommendation because they've gotten to know you as a person.

Still not convinced?

Greg Baldwin of VolunteerMatch quotes Dr. Chris Spera of the Corporation for National & Community Service, one of the co-authors of "Volunteering as a Pathway to Employment," which tracked the relationship between volunteering and employment for a group of 70,535 respondents over a ten-year period: "Active volunteers were 27% more likely to get a job than non-volunteers. And the relationship held stable across gender, race, ethnicity, age, location, and unemployment rate."[9] (Special thanks to Steve Naughton for starting the LinkedIn discussion that brought these statistics to our attention.)

Volunteerism has always been a necessary part of our society, and it's even more critical in tough economic times. People need your help. And while you're helping others in need, you just might find that the person most aided by your volunteerism is you.

Wwwwwwwwwwwwwwwwwwwwwwwwww!

The Workforce Investment Act (WIA) was enacted by Congress in 1998 to replace the Job Training Partnership Act and create a single source of job training and skills preparation. (It recently was extended through 2017). The WIA is a public-private partnership between business and government (federal, state and local) to help train the unemployed in order to gain the skills necessary to return to the workforce. The program varies somewhat by state and county/parish. Please contact your local unemployment office for specifics to your area or go directly to www.doleta.gov.

In short, this program can help you get technical certifications and other training, things that may be requirements for posted positions. Depending on your location, you may be able to apply for a training grant for things like CRM, Microsoft Office, SAP, etc.

If you need certain skills, cannot or prefer to NOT use a government program, (or one is not available in your State or Province) training on specific packages might be available through the companies themselves or commercially available through skills-training companies.

One of those tools is called the W3 Schools Certification Program. As we've said before, we're not omniscient. This resource was made known to us by a candidate at a recent career event who lauded the online tutorials. Acquiring these certifications may further your career and allow you to give a concrete answer—if you're asked—to the question: "What have you been doing while you've been in job transition?"

> **Caution:** We have not been able to verify the relative value of these tutorials. We have heard claims of numerous errors in the tutorials and questions about the value of the certificates. Please investigate carefully.

Calendar

Throughout this chapter, we've pressed you to schedule your time. "Plan your work then work your plan." We cannot emphasize enough the need for planning. Here are some examples of what you should be adding to your online calendar (Google or Yahoo):

A. Marketing Brochure mailings & follow-up dates
B. Job Board times
C. Exercise (people won't hire someone in poor health)
D. Friday resume updates (every Friday before noon)
E. Applications (online & in-person)
F. LinkedIn Group activity

G. Google Alert activity
H. Contact management
I. Networking events (including returning calls, connecting, & composing emails)
J. B-2-B Events
K. Associations & Conventions
L. Follow-up calls to executives
M. Schedule daily 6 a.m. job board applications (2-hour maximum)
N. Comments on LinkedIn group discussions, endorsements, daily meetings and interviews
O. Phone screenings & interviews
P. Volunteer work

Your calendar should become increasingly full. You'll soon find that the fuller your calendar, the more you'll accomplish.

Caron Atteberry is a Talent Acquisition Manager whose article, "10 Job Search Ideas from a Recruiter's Perspective," provides some additional insight:

1. Make sure your resume is free of mistakes and is in chronological order with the job descriptions below the company name/title/date.
2. An employer/recruiter takes 5-10 seconds to screen a resume, sometimes less. Make sure you have keywords that pertain to the job in your resume. Anything in a job description that you have experience with should be in the appropriate job description where you have that experience.
3. Your resume does not have to be one page! If you have the experience to back it up, it can be 5+ pages, just make sure the experience is applicable.
4. Do not include high school on your resume. This includes school activities, unless you are 2 years or under out of school.
5. Take the objective off your resume. Recruiters constantly see objectives that don't match up to the job. It's a given that your objective is to get the job you applied for.
6. Don't waste your time on a cover letter. They almost always get overlooked. Just focus on making sure your resume has the amount of detail to show you are a fit for the role.

7. Don't apply for jobs you're not a fit for. Companies will notice the pattern and think you don't know what you want in your career.
8. Utilize LinkedIn. When you apply for a job at a company where you don't have an internal contact/reference, find a person on LinkedIn who may be the Hiring Manager for the role you applied for. Connect with that person and ask if you can email them your resume.
9. Make sure you have a professional picture on LinkedIn. If you have accounts with Facebook, Google+, Twitter, etc. , make sure potential employers can only see appropriate pictures. Make your page private when possible.
10. Always answer your phone in a friendly manner. You never know when it is a future employer calling.

Chapter 12: Advanced Social Media

Disclaimer: *Although this chapter is titled Advanced Social Media, each section below could fill an entire book. This chapter attempts to give you, the job candidate, more in-depth information than we've offered so far. But keep in mind that elements of social media are constantly changing. What is written today might not be true tomorrow.*

Today, it really doesn't matter *what* you know. The question is, *Can people find you?* You could be the next Albert Einstein, but if people can't find you in this Internet search-dominated society, you might never be discovered.

It's also the era of hyper-connectivity. Online connections are becoming increasingly important to your success, especially in marketing and sales. Your online Rolodex is your new gold mine, whether you're a job-seeker or not. The key to success, however, is how you mine it and how you utilize your connections in your job search.

The tool that has profoundly changed the job-search process is social media. Although it can be confusing at times, the reality is that social media is playing a much greater role in job searches, which means that your efforts in this area need to be properly managed. If you do decide to immerse yourself in social media, remember that a job search, as with all business, is still a contact sport. You can't nail the job if you don't meet with people face-to-face. It just doesn't happen. So do your best to master social media, but don't rely on it completely for your job search. Also, don't forget that there's this thing called a *phone*. Pick it up and call people. Don't just connect through social media. And be careful not to get so wrapped up in social media that you begin to feel overwhelmed by it. It can easily become more of a burden than a blessing in your job search.

Also, as we've tried to emphasize throughout this book, although a lot has changed, a lot of things remain the same. In almost every case, a new job will not magically appear as a result of a single strategy or magical method. Instead, finding a new job still requires a concerted effort on a variety of fronts.

In fact, according to a study we conducted at Transition Sherpa in the first quarter of 2013, the majority of people are still finding jobs via personal connections and networking. Despite all the hoopla about social media and its usefulness as a job-search tool, it wasn't the most important factor in most cases. Here are the responses to the question: *How Did You Find Your Current Job*[1]:

- Recruiters 7.7%
- Personal Contact 43.5%
- Networking 21.5%
- Job Boards 20%
- LinkedIn 4.6%
- Twitter 2.3%
- Other .8%

Although our research sample was too small to be considered statistically significant, the responses were nonetheless surprising.

Still, the growing importance of social media can't be understated or ignored. In fact, many major companies now rely heavily on it as a source of potential candidates. It makes the job of recruiters, talent acquisition managers, and Hiring Managers much easier and is becoming a much more important part of their candidate-search toolbox. Using social media also saves companies a great deal of money because they don't have to rely as much on expensive search firms or job boards for candidates. In a lot of cases they can search for and find candidates themselves. Search firms are now used more for finding the Purple Squirrels. Search firms are also used as a backup by overworked staff who have to outsource some searches because they don't have the time to do them themselves.

Here's what a representative of Accenture, a management consulting, tech services, and outsourcing company, said in a *Wall Street Journal* article: "Recruiting candidates is based in part on their activity and influence on social sites."[2] In essence, Accenture is "mining" LinkedIn Groups looking for comments by so-called thought leaders who might be good candidates and perusing connections these individuals might have at Accenture. They have also expanded their referral program and are utilizing social media to tap into and reward people who send them referrals.

In addition to finding potential employees, companies are using social media to vet candidates. This presents a challenge for candidates to keep their social media profiles as clean and middle-of-the-road as possible. So it's best to not discuss politics, sex, or religion on social media unless you're in one of these businesses.

A recent study by the Social Science Research Network lends support to this contention. In *An Experiment in Hiring via Online Networks*, researchers tried to determine if there was a link between hiring and a person's religion or sexual preference as indicated on his or her social media profile. The study found "...evidence of discrimination against Muslim candidates compared to Christian candidates among employers...." On the other hand, they found no evidence of discrimination against the gay candidate relative to the straight candidate.[3] Unless you're a politician, a preacher, or work in an industry or profession where such comments are not seen as out of the ordinary, these kinds of discussions are best left to your own inner circle.

Note: This study was not based on a randomly selected population, so you should take the conclusions with a grain of salt. All we're saying is that it's better to err on the side of caution here.

Social Media Footprint

Without a social media footprint, it is very difficult for you to be found, noticed, and contacted. In this era, not having one may shed a negative light on you as someone who is not keeping up with the times and, therefore, not a viable candidate. Realize that those who are competing for the job you're after most likely have a footprint. You're doing yourself a disservice by not being at least at the same level as they are. On LinkedIn alone, with its 300 million plus members, you create instant visibility and credibility for yourself. You're able to network with more people than you can imagine and do it from the comfort of your home or office. You can generate unimaginable opportunities.

Expand your reach!

A word of caution about using any of the social media channels: Proofread, proofread, proofread. There is nothing that will destroy your credibility faster than profiles with misspelled words, grammatical errors, or typos. Have someone look over everything you plan to post *before* you post it. (Yes, we know we've said this before, but we can't emphasize it enough.)

And please, for your own sake, make sure that whatever you present on social media is an honest depiction of who you really are. There is no longer any place to hide. The last thing you want to do is embellish your profile with information that's not true. It wouldn't be long before someone would call you on the carpet for an inaccurate profile. In addition, a potential employer might discover inaccuracies in your profile after vetting you, which would not only be embarrassing but could cost you the job.

Another thing to keep in mind is that anything posted on social media rarely disappears. Once it's posted, it's hard—if not impossible—to take it back. So keep everything positive, and never appear desperate.

The social media toolbox you could use is huge, but you need to be strategic in using it and not overdo it. You certainly don't want to be perceived as someone who has too much time on his or her hands and not focused. Besides, your ultimate objective is a job, not aimlessly posting.

ONLINE AUDIT

We discussed this in an earlier chapter, but it deserves repeating: Before you get started with social media, you should conduct an online audit of yourself. This will allow you to see how you actually appear on the Internet when someone does a search for you. Go to Google first. If you have a Gmail account, log out of it to ensure that there's no impact from Google's automated search tools biasing your results. Insert your name in quotation marks and start searching. Don't limit yourself to a general Web search. Go through and look at News, Photos, and Videos. Note anything that reflects negatively on you, especially items on the first three pages of the search, since this is where most recruiters will look when vetting a candidate. If you find something negative, you need to come up with a way to explain it to a prospective employer because you want to be able to discuss it logically and defuse the issue. In fact, if you already know of something that will immediately pop up if someone does a search for you, think about how you would address it during an interview (Remember Red Flags?). At the very least, you will show that you're honest and open and won't be caught off guard, which could knock you out of the game. Once you've done this on Google, do the same on Yahoo, Bing, and YouTube.

Another thing you can do if there are any negative references about you in Google is to start posting articles to your Google+ account. (Hopefully, you've already set this up as we recommended.) The articles should be related to your industry and/or profession. By posting a significant number of articles, you'll not only enhance your awareness and credibility within Google+, but you'll likely drive any negative references about you from the first and second pages of a search about you to pages 3, 4, and beyond. As with most Internet searches, it's unlikely that those vetting you will go beyond Google page 2.

In addition to the search engines, you should conduct a search in the social media channels to gauge your standing. One of the tools you can use is Reppler, a free service that will show you how you're perceived across the social media networks and the makeup of your connections. It will also notify you of any potential issues and risks.

Another tool you might consider using is BrandYourself.com, which is similar to Reppler. It lets you submit your most positive profiles and links—the ones you want people to see on Google—and uses an algorithm that helps these profiles and links rank higher. So, if someone does a search for you, these profiles and links will be the ones that come up first. It also allows you to track your progress and notifies you if someone has searched for you online and found your BrandYourself profile. This might help you after an interview by giving you a sense of where you stand based on people searching for you.

The Age of Aquarius?

Only after you've conducted an audit, have a clear sense of who you are and what your objectives are regarding a job search, should you get started on social media. You want all of your "stars" to align. The last thing you want to do is provide an inconsistent image and appear to have no sense of direction. If that happens, you're wasting your time and everyone else's.

Your starting point with social media should be LinkedIn. According to a recent study done by JobVite, a software platform that helps companies recruit talent, LinkedIn is used by 93% of talent acquisition people looking for candidates.[4]

LINKEDIN

As with every other social media channel, LinkedIn requires work. Like anything else in life, you only get out of social media what you put in. As Neal Schaffer, said in his book, *Maximizing LinkedIn for Sales and Social Media Marketing,* "LinkedIn is only valuable if you decide to be an active member."[5]

We touched on LinkedIn in the Assembling the Puzzle chapter, but now we need to expand on it so you can get as much value from it as possible. It would take an entire book to tell you everything there is to know about LinkedIn, so we're going to focus here on the things we believe will deliver the greatest return on your investment (redundancies intended).

Recommendations

It's important that you have a minimum of 5-7 recommendations on LinkedIn to be seen as credible. You should certainly strive for more, but you should have at least this many before you go "live" with your profile. If you haven't been working long, consider asking for recommendations from your professors, high school teachers, volunteer or community group leaders, or any other source that can attest to your capabilities.

How do I get people to recommend me?

Simply ask them. But do them a favor by offering to write it for them. Make sure you stress accomplishments he or she would be familiar with, use keywords related to the position you're seeking, and be certain that whatever is said reflects favorably on you and fits with what you're trying to accomplish. Just having someone say you're an awesome person doesn't cut it.

Once you've written the recommendation request in LinkedIn, send it to the people you've asked to recommend you and wait for a response. This might take a few days—people are busy and may be juggling a lot of projects. If you don't get a response within a week, follow up with a phone call and ask them if they received it. If they say they did and indicate that they'll respond when time allows and you never hear from them, don't take it personally. Move on to someone else who might be a good reference, and do the same thing.

In addition to asking for recommendations, you should also recommend people you feel deserve it. Target giving one recommendation a week, if you can. This helps create goodwill with people, and they'll be more likely to be on the lookout for opportunities to help you. But don't expect a quid pro quo—i.e., a recommendation from them.

Finally, you are free to display whichever recommendations you choose on your profile. If you get some that don't have much meat, hide them from view. Also, if you have some recommendations that don't mesh with the position you're seeking, consider hiding them.

Endorsements

Similar in many respects to a Facebook "Like" and a "+K" on Klout, an endorsement makes it easier for people to recommend you without having to go through the trouble of producing a full-fledged recommendation. Although an endorsement isn't as powerful as a recommendation, it still goes a long way toward validating that the claims you made on your profile are accurate and genuine.

Remember, endorsements are now part of the algorithm that moves you toward the top of any search done on LinkedIn for the keywords reflected in the endorsements. Of course, there are ways of gaming this, so like everything else in social media, you need to peel back the onion and carefully review all aspects of a profile to determine if the person is genuine and has the experience, education, and background to support the skills and expertise they claim to have.

We can't overstate the importance of accumulating a large number of endorsements. Without them, you won't be taken seriously as someone who has the skills and experience you list. Although this may not apply to some industries due to regulatory compliance issues, in most cases a blank slate of endorsements will have a negative impact on how you're perceived.

Six Tips For Using LinkedIn's Endorsements

1. Make sure that the LinkedIn Skills & Expertise section is displayed on your profile and that your top skills are listed in descending order of importance for the position you have or are seeking.

2. Move the LinkedIn Skills & Expertise section to the top of your LinkedIn Profile so that it's right below the Summary section. This will position it in a clearly visible area of the profile, what newspapers call "above the fold." This can be moved by going into the edit mode of LinkedIn and clicking on the top of the Skills & Expertise section and dragging it into position.

3. Check out the profiles of your key contacts. If they don't have the Skills & Expertise section displayed on their profiles, make sure that they adjust it. Send an email or call them. Explain the added exposure, the ability to be more readily found via a LinkedIn search, and the enhanced credibility they'll achieve by using it. This is an important development!

4. Review your LinkedIn contacts. Start endorsing the ones who are key contacts and those with whom you want to rekindle a relationship. Be selective about what you endorse them for and limit the number of skills. Only endorse them for skills and expertise you know they possess. After all, your reputation is on the line, so you don't want to endorse someone arbitrarily for skills you're not familiar with.

    a. Also, limit the number of skills you endorse them for at any one time to no more than two. The reason is that anytime you endorse someone, your endorsement will appear on their LinkedIn feed, creating awareness of your name and capabilities. Additionally, if someone notices the endorsement, they might click on your photo to see who you are. If you're already a 1st-level connection of theirs it might lead to an endorsement from them; if you're not a connection, you may receive a connection request from them. In either case, it's a great way to gain exposure and rapidly grow your network. Use this tool strategically and you can get a lot of mileage out of it.

5. Send your contacts an email indicating that you've endorsed them for a skill and ask them to reciprocate. Remember to identify the skill(s) you want them to endorse, the ones you're trying to be recognized for. Do this one at a time, not through a blast email to all of your contacts requesting endorsements. Sending a blast, if you're lucky, might produce some endorsements, but viewers of your feed may see this as spam. You might also be perceived as someone who has "bought" their endorsements. This is not much different than the bogus Likes that

were vetted a while back on Facebook. Finally, if you space the requests out, it will buy you considerable exposure since endorsements are posted on LinkedIn feeds and will provide you with an easy way to maintain the connection.

6. Thank the people who give you an endorsement. Either send them an email or endorse them for one of the skills you know they possess. Also, consider thanking them via Twitter similar to how you would thank someone for providing you with a +K on Klout (to be discussed later in this chapter).

Getting Rid of Unwanted Endorsements

Although we're firm believers in the overall benefits of endorsements, there are some inherent problems a user might need to address. These could include you inadvertently endorsing someone for a skill they may not be qualified for. Or an individual endorsing you for something that isn't one of your showcased strengths. You might consider deleting or hiding these endorsements.

If you made a mistake and endorsed someone for a skill that you didn't intend to, you can remove the endorsement by going to your connection's profile. Next, go to their Skills & Expertise section and move your cursor over the name of the skill. It will prompt you to undo the skill (Click on the plus symbol). Once you've clicked on it, your endorsement will be removed.

If an individual has given you an endorsement you don't want, here's how LinkedIn says you can get rid of it:

1. Move your cursor over **Profile** at the top of your homepage and select **Edit Profile**.
2. Scroll down to the **Skills & Expertise** section and click the Edit icon.
3. Click the **Manage Endorsements** link. This is next to Add & Remove.
4. Click on a skill in the left column to reveal the connections who endorsed you for that skill. You may need to use the scroll bar on the left side of the box to view skills further down in the list.
5. Uncheck the box next to any people whose endorsements you want to hide. Or, check the box next to any you want to unhide.

Note: You may check or uncheck the box next to **show/hide all endorsements** to take action on all endorsements under one skill at once.
6. Click **Save**.
7. Click **Done editing** in the top section of your profile.

Be aware, however, that according to LinkedIn, there is currently no way to *undo* this process. So please give this some thought before you choose to hide an endorsement. (You can permanently or temporarily remove sets of skills from your profile in a similar manner.)

Groups

As we mentioned in a prior chapter, LinkedIn allows you to join up to 50 groups and another 25 subgroups. We doubt that you can keep up with nor stay active in that many, but we do suggest that you become a member of a diverse set of groups that include your desired industry, companies, job groups, and recruiter-based groups. Stay away from smaller groups since few people are likely to see you, and don't join groups where there is little discussion activity. These groups are of little benefit to you.

Actively participate in your industry groups by making comments and creating posts that might be of interest to other members. You can use the same post on multiple groups simultaneously to hit a broader cross-section of people, but remember to space this out or turn off your activity broadcasts in the settings sections so you don't annoy people. Adding links to a post also helps get you noticed since they show that what you've written is not just your opinion.

Avoid merely "liking" someone else's post. A "Like" doesn't get broadcast to the members of the group. On the other hand, when someone likes one of your posts, send a note of thanks and invite them to connect with you. By doing this, you will quickly exceed the critical 500+ connection threshold that recruiters like to see.

Finally, don't forget to schedule a specific amount of time for participating in groups. Otherwise, you could find yourself doing nothing but posting comments and not getting anything else done. Yes, you will improve your visibility, but at what cost? Also, make sure that you're geographically and industry relevant.

There's no significant ROI in being well-known in Bangalore, India, when you're seeking a job in Springfield, Illinois.

As we mentioned, you can start your own group if one doesn't exist for your area of expertise. It will not only help you attract like-minded people, but it can also position you as an authority in your profession. And it will allow you to provide group and email updates to the members of your group.

But don't establish a group to try to position yourself as the President or C-level executive of something. The reason we're against starting a group for the sake of positioning yourself as an executive is that recruiters and talent acquisition managers will quickly spot you as a fraud. It may temporarily help you get viewed if someone is doing a search for a high-level candidate and you have President or CEO listed as part of your profile. But eventually you will be found out and will be discounted immediately.

There are some so-called LinkedIn experts, however, who favor employing this as one of your tactics (they have the secret you should take advantage of, for a fee, of course). But you might wind up being the moderator of a group with only one member, such as the Basket Weavers of Pondoland (this is an actual group on LinkedIn). We're totally against this practice.

If you do decide to establish a group, make sure it contributes positively to your Personal Brand.

Connections
Several years ago at a career event, former advertising executive Tom Berry recommended becoming a networking sponge and connecting with as many people as possible. The reason is now obvious: the more people you're connected to, the greater your ability to find people and for people to find you. But make sure these people are credible. Connecting with a nefarious character could damage your reputation. If you ever find yourself in a position where a connection of yours has been convicted of a crime or has received negative publicity, you should immediately drop him or her as a connection.

You should also consider disconnecting from obvious spammers. Yes, they're on LinkedIn, and we all receive spam periodically. If you find this to be a problem and feel that the connection isn't valuable to you, delete them. If it's a matter of someone posting a large number of updates to their profile, yet they have large networks, you can hide them from your feed by clicking on the top right-hand corner of one of their posts. That way you maintain the network reach but are not inundated with frivolous messages.

Once your LinkedIn Profile is maximized and is a clear representation of who you are—and you have the requisite minimum of 5-7 recommendations—start aggressively reaching out. If your profile is incomplete and lacks a sufficient number of recommendations, your credibility will be compromised.

As we've said before, you should make a serious effort to surpass the 500+ connection level. You can get this done in less than three weeks, and it will be a tremendous benefit. Here's how to do it:

- Connect with your current email connections by using the LinkedIn command under the network icon on the LinkedIn toolbar that prompts you to add connections. LinkedIn will then import your address book and suggest people on LinkedIn you should connect with. You choose who you want to connect with. Just check the box next to their name and a connection request will be sent to them.
- Thank, then ask, people who "Like" your posts or comments to connect with you. Given the fact that they've already "engaged' with you, the likelihood of them agreeing to connect with you is quite high.
- Use the Share button located in the drop-down bar right below your photo. This will provide a comment about you having a profile and invite people to view it and connect.
- Check out who's viewed your profile. If you find someone of interest or someone who might be of help to you, send them a connection request. Please note that you probably won't be able to see everyone who has viewed your profile. At this writing, you have to pay for a Premium account to get this feature. Also, a number of people wish to remain anonymous when they view profiles. If you elect to try to connect, simply indicate that they've done business with you (in the drop-down menu). They've looked at your profile and are probably familiar with you. More than likely, they will not give you an "IDK" or "I Don't Know" notation.
- Send connection requests to all new contacts you meet. Follow up your meetings with personalized messages indicating what a pleasure it was to meet them and that you look forward to talking to them again. DO NOT send them a canned LinkedIn connection request or tell them how badly you need a job.

- Seek connections with LIONs (LinkedIn Open Networkers). Most will agree to connect carte blanche. These are people who recognize the value of having a large network and will almost always connect without hesitation. You'd be surprised at how large your network reach will become by connecting with these people.
- Join TopLinked and LIONs groups on LinkedIn. These are groups for people whose main purpose is to connect with others to expand their own networks. By joining these groups and participating in some of the discussions, you'll immediately avail yourself of like-minded people.
- If you're on Twitter, periodically post a Tweet indicating that you'd love to connect with your followers on LinkedIn. You'd be surprised how many will take you up on the offer. Also, if someone mentions you, re-tweets one of your posts, or engages with you, reach out to them on LinkedIn and ask for a connection. Tell them you appreciate the communication on Twitter and that you'd like to carry the connection further through a relationship on LinkedIn. (We've seen this work quite well in our own networking.)

Conventional wisdom says the best way to use your LinkedIn connections is to request direct introductions to their connections within your target companies. We beg to differ. Don't get us wrong, you should feel free to ask for introductions, which can be effective. But you will quickly discover that most people don't actually know most of their connections. On top of that, you never know how your connection is thought of by the person you'd like to reach. Your connection might be the nicest person in the world, but what if the person you want them to introduce you to sees them as irritating—or worse? You could wind up being painted with the same negative brush. We believe the best way to utilize your LinkedIn connections is to let them help you uncover individuals in companies that you can then contact on your own.

We recommend that whenever you meet someone new, immediately add them to your Google contacts list and connect with them on LinkedIn. The reason for the redundancy is that each platform serves different functions and LinkedIn has a limit of 50 emails that you can send out in a single group delivery.

For example, if you meet or talk to a recruiter, add their contact information and add them to a group called Recruiters in your Gmail account. This will allow you to conduct a mass email campaign to all or some of the members of the group to announce a significant development with your search or to share information that might be of interest to them. Other groups might be clients, vendors, colleagues, friends, etc. In the case of LinkedIn, capture their contact information and start tagging them. With the new LinkedIn Contacts feature, you no longer have to be connected with someone to set them up as a contact, enter information about them, or Tag them. We suggest, however, that if you do engage with them, you should also connect.

Plan Your Work and Work Your Plan

Some elements of your Marketing Campaign must be scheduled daily or weekly. This section will address several of the social media-based ones.

LinkedIn Updates
Post an update to your LinkedIn Profile at least once a day—a couple of times, if possible. Note that your updates should be sent out at different times during the day, not at the same time every day. Also, share relevant updates with the groups you belong to. Do not share them with multiple groups at once because this will be posted as multiple entries on your activity feed and may be perceived as spam by your connections, which could result in them hiding your activity feed broadcasts or disconnecting from you.

What do I post?

This is easy if you've followed what we outlined earlier and know your target audience for the job you're seeking, the industry, and the skill set you're focusing on. Simply go to Google, Bing, or Yahoo and do a search on these platforms for relevant information. For instance, if you're a marketing person, you might search for items that pertain to marketing trends. This would show that you're keeping up with what's going on in that field. You could search for "marketing trends" under **news**. How many results you get will depend on the platform you use and the time-frame you specify. If you find an article you feel would be of interest to Hiring Managers (in this case Chief Marketing Officers or Marketing Managers)—an article that has some meat to it—then you should consider posting it. Doing this can position you as someone who does his or her homework. Here's how:
    1. Copy the URL.

2. Go to the Bitly account you should have set up by now and copy the link into the Bitly paste a link section. This will generate a shortened link for you.

3. Paste this link directly to the share an update section on the home page of LinkedIn. This will "populate" the area and provide you with a headline and summary below it while displaying the bit.ly link in the update section. You should then go into the summary section, add a similar headline or other comments, delete the bit.ly link, and then hit the share button. If you've followed our advice and set up a Twitter account and have LinkedIn connected to Twitter, you should then share it with Twitter. It will be posted simultaneously in your Twitter stream as a Tweet, which helps you maximize your exposure

4. If you want to share the information at a later time, you can go into the HootSuite account we also asked you to set up and simply paste it into the HootSuite **compose a message** field and schedule the message for an appropriate time. HootSuite will then prompt you to select the channels you want to share this with. Select both Twitter and LinkedIn.

LinkedIn Pulse (Formerly LinkedIn Today)
This will prove to be a very helpful section for you in locating content you might want to post as part of your daily updates. It could save you a lot of time when you're having to find articles on the Internet that might be appropriate for you to Like, comment on, and share as an update with your network. Essentially, you receive your own personalized daily newspaper or magazine from LinkedIn based on your profile and interests and artfully curated by LinkedIn. In addition to news, it provides you with postings by a number of so-called "influencers" that LinkedIn has identified. It basically consists of 5 tabs:

1. Your News
   As indicated above, this provides you with a myriad of information specifically tailored to you. It makes for great reading and is a superb way to stay up to date on industry events and news.

2. Influencer Posts
   These are posts from all of the people LinkedIn has deemed to be worth listening to. You might see posts from Richard Branson, Jack Welch, Barak Obama, Bill Gates, Tony Robbins, or almost any leading authority in a particular field. LinkedIn has done a great job of aggregating this information.

3. All Influencers
   In this section, LinkedIn gives you the ability to follow these influencers and avail yourself of their daily postings, which will show up as an update in your activity feed.
4. All Channels
   This enables you to follow areas and topics of interest to you. It features articles from influencers and news sources you might have an interest in. It includes such areas as accounting, banking and finance, recruiting and hiring, and a host of others.
5. All Publishers
   This section provides you with timely information from various news sources and well-known publications such as the *Wall Street Journal*, *Time*, *USA Today*, and much more. You can add or delete publications as you see fit.

Network Contacts

If you don't already have the updated LinkedIn Contacts section, it's important that you get it so you can take advantage of one of the best tools LinkedIn offers its users. You can do this by going to www.contacts.linkedin.com and requesting that they update your profile to reflect this function. Note that it might take some time for LinkedIn to actually provide you with the update.

Once you have the update, go to the LinkedIn "Toolbar" and click on Network Contacts. You'll see a stream of photos of people, announcements about new jobs, birthdays, job anniversaries, and other information. By reviewing this and commenting, you can solidify your relationship with individual contacts. You may also learn that one of your contacts has moved to one of your target companies, which could be a door-opener for you.

Your Activity Feed

Another way to gain maximum exposure and solidify your connections with others is to go to your activity feed and review it for a few minutes at least once a day.

What should I be on the lookout for?

1. Updates from your connections.

   This can provide a wealth of information about people's interests, what they're up to, etc. More importantly, it gives you an opportunity to engage with them by "Liking," commenting, or sharing their update with others. This could include the general public, your Twitter audience, your connections, or specific individuals

2. New connections that your connections have connected with

By perusing the new connections of your contacts, you might come across someone who could be valuable in your job search or a potential referral or strategic partner. If you see a potential valuable connection, LinkedIn will prompt you to connect with them. Simply click the **connect** button and it will bring you to a photo of the person and a brief description. You then proceed with the connection process. We strongly suggest that you send a personalized message. After all, you want to make a great 1st impression and there's nothing more impersonal than getting a canned invitation message. Show your would-be connections that you've done your homework, and let them know how they'll benefit by connecting with you.

GOOGLE+

As we've said before, having a Google+ profile is critical due to the market share dominance of Google. Yes, Yahoo, and Bing are also popular, but focus is key. So if you're going to focus on one search engine, focus on Google.

Setting up a Google+ profile is fairly easy from your Gmail account. If you don't have a Gmail account, you can sign up for one by using this URL: https://accounts.google.com/SignUp. Once you're on it, you can simply use the information and LinkedIn photo as a basis for creating your Google+ profile. Just copy and paste.

You can then decide whether or not you want to be an active or passive participant on Google+ circles. Being active by posting articles and commenting on people's posts will likely enhance your ability to be found in a Google search. Just having a Google+ profile to begin with is a giant step toward being found.

The second thing you might consider is setting up a resume Web page on Google. By going to the following link—https://sites.google.com/?pli=1—you can easily set up a Web site to display your resume. This will give you added search engine "juice" for being found. But don't share too much personal information because this will be readily searchable by billions of people. This will not take the place of a more sophisticated Web site or blog, but it's a fairly convenient way to position yourself.

In addition to having a Google+ profile, a Gmail email account, and basic Google Web site, you should make sure to use Google Chrome as your de facto Internet search tool. The reason is that Chrome has a great number of tools that will enhance your online experience and make you more productive. You can easily check out what applications may be appropriate for you by going to the Google Chrome Web Store. You can add what you want and remove them later if you find you're not benefitting from some of these so-called extensions.

It's All About.me
Once you've set up your LinkedIn Profile and Google properties, we recommend that you establish a profile on About.me. It's very easy to do. Use the information you've compiled for your resume, LinkedIn, and Google accounts to populate the site. What's great about it is that it's readily searchable yet doesn't require much work. Once it's set up, you can pretty much leave it alone unless you add social media channels to your portfolio or significantly change your career direction. Just as with everything else you're doing, make sure you make it keyword-rich for the position you're seeking.

TWITTER
Once you're done with the above, the next step in the positioning process should be with Twitter. Although it's a bit more difficult to use, Twitter has hundreds of millions of users (and counting) and thousands of jobs listed, which makes it a great tool for anyone looking for a job, trying to develop a Personal Brand, and countless other purposes. As Dan Schawbel, managing partner of Millennial Branding, a Gen Y research and consulting firm, says in his book, *Me 2.0*, "When it comes to your career, Twitter is extremely important because it levels the playing field. Also, the main difference between Twitter and the

Facebook and LinkedIn duo is that people can start following you and you can start following them without having to accept a friend request, you can directly communicate without interference with Hiring Managers and people whom you're genuinely interested in and network with them."[6]

Of course, Twitter can become time-consuming, so you need to limit the time you spend on it. But do get on and start using it. Even if you're not overly active, just having a listing and using it as a search tool will be of tremendous benefit. You'd be surprised at the amount of information at your fingertips via Twitter.

PROFILE

The first thing you have to do with Twitter is set up a profile. The profile, like everything else on Twitter, is character- limited, so you have to be creative. Use the same professional photo you have on LinkedIn and make sure your bio is keyword-rich for the position you're seeking. Again, as with all other platforms, recruiters will be searching for you on Twitter, and you want to be found. To help facilitate an easy connection once someone finds you on Twitter, make sure to add your LinkedIn Profile URL as the Web site listing. Also, be sure to list your geographical area so people can see if you're geographically relevant. You'd be surprised how many people neglect to do this and how frustrating it is for those seeking to connect with you.

ADDING FOLLOWERS

As you begin the setup process, Twitter, like so many other social media channels, will ask to find people you might want to connect with by utilizing your address book and other connections. You might want to use this to build your "follower" numbers. After all, the larger your following, the more likely you are to be seen as credible. So take advantage of this feature.

Twitter will also prompt you with the names of people it thinks you should follow. Take advantage of this and focus on those you think might be most relevant for you—i.e., individuals, target companies, celebrities, news sources, sports teams, and a myriad of other possibilities.

One of the best tools available for following are the Twitter Lists. To find them, go to some of the main job-related sites on Twitter. As you start to follow people, you should put them in Twitter Lists, which are very easy to set up and will help you become better organized. For instance, if you live in Los Angeles, you could set up a list of recruiters or HR people in L.A. that you're following.

Once you've established the list, you can just click on the list to see what they're talking about. Without having lists set up, all of the postings will appear in the general stream, and it will be difficult to catch them as they're only there for a nanosecond.

We also recommend that you "mine" others' lists and see who has listed them. A great starting point for mining would be to go to TweetMyJobs, which is the leading social and media job-distribution network. Not only is it a worthwhile site to follow, the lists that are on its profile could prove quite beneficial. One of the sites TweetMyJobs subscribes to is Forbes Top Career Sites, which is a great one. Clicking on this listing takes you directly to the list itself, where you'll be able to glean the names of many other sites that might be worth following on an individual basis or are part of the list itself, if you're a subscriber. We suggest you subscribe to the list and peruse it daily to see if there's anything there that might be of help in your search.

Following lists instead of people is a good idea because of the limitations Twitter places on the numbers and ways you can follow individuals. One thing you should be aware of is that this process continues to change. For instance, Twitter has for years blocked users from following more than 2,000 people without having ~1,900+ followers of their own. The exact ratio is Twitter's secret sauce. We don't know why, but they probably do this to prevent users from being overly aggressive following other users.

As a result, a Twitter user has to follow up to the limit, wait a few days to see who followed back, and then stop following those who didn't satisfy the ratio. In the past, a large percentage of people you followed would follow in return, but this has dropped considerably as Twitter has grown so large. There are a number of ways to "unfollow" non-followers. We recommend a tool called ManageFlitter. (Note: Twitter recently became more aggressive with its follower ratio, expanding it beyond the 2,000-follower threshold.)

Another thing Twitter has done is prevent you from seeing who's following certain other people. It's not pervasive, but you might encounter this as you try to see who is following someone with a very large following count.

To further your ability to be found on Twitter, you should register yourself on Twellow.com and Wefollow.com, the two main directories on Twitter that people refer to when searching for people with expertise in certain subject area. These tools are free and they're straightforward.

The above applications, like so many others within social media, will ask you to connect your account, which we recommend. As a member of these directories, you can also search for people or companies of interest and start following them.

Note: Some of these apps have paid subscription platforms that offer additional features that may be of benefit to you.

POSTING INFORMATION
You won't attract people or become visible on Twitter unless you start commenting or posting articles related to the company and/or industry of interest (use Bitly to do this). Tweet like you're an expert in your subject matter area by providing articles that reflect it.

ENGAGE WITH PEOPLE
To be successful on Twitter or any social media channel, you need to engage with people. One of the more effective ways to engage people is to comment on postings they've made or by retweeting or reposting material they've posted to their Twitter feeds. They may notice that you're doing this and follow back, thank you for the retweet, or take other actions that could enhance your visibility.

IRL MEETINGS
Like other social networks, Twitter is a great tool for facilitating IRL meetings— that is, meetings In Real Life. We believe it's one of the top tools for making connections that will lead to a new job. This is in line with what many other job-search pundits are advocating.

In her recent book, *Social Networking for Career Success*, social media strategist Miriam Salpeter says, "Remember, just because you meet someone on Twitter does not mean that you can't network in person! If someone seems like a good contact, and they're accessible, invite him or her to meet for coffee or lunch. If not, set up a time to speak on the phone and see how you can help one another. Never forget to make personal connections."[7]

FINDING JOBS, COMPANIES, INFORMATION

In addition to TweetMyJobs, there are multiple job sources on Twitter. By utilizing the search toolbar and putting search items within quotation marks to narrow the results, you'll be surprised what you'll be able to find. Look for opportunities such as "sales manager jobs." Focus on a specific geographical area by using "sales manager jobs in Boston," for instance. You can further refine your search by using the advanced search capabilities, which is readily accessible through search.twitter.com.

Also, take a look at TwitJobSearch.com, a great resource for jobs, recruiters, and other things associated with job search.

One of our favorite tools is the # symbol, the so-called Twitter hashtag. By placing a hashtag before a word, you can find all kinds of information on almost anything when you conduct a search. You should also incorporate these in your postings to ensure that people find you. Limit the number of hashtags to no more than two—maybe three on occasion—so you won't be perceived as a spammer or a Twitter novice.

FACEBOOK

Another social media tool in your arsenal is Facebook. With well over a billion people on it globally, it's a great resource for your job search. What's good about it is that it doesn't involve a great deal of daily activity from you like some of the other platforms.

The first thing you want to do as a job-seeker on Facebook is update your profile to reflect most of the information and keywords you have on your other profiles by going to the **Edit profile** section and then **About** on your Facebook page. Use the information you've compiled for LinkedIn and your resume to "populate" the section. Also, make sure that your profile is "clean" and that there's nothing on it that might alarm a potential employer. You can also change your privacy settings so people only see certain things about you. You can also set up Groups so that only members of those groups see what you post.

Once you've done this, you can let your Facebook following know that you're looking for a job by posting it as an update on your wall. Be very specific about the kind of position you want. You want people focused on the lookout for you.

Also, check out the many companies who have Facebook pages devoted to career opportunities. Do this by inserting the company's name in quotation marks in the search bar at the top of your wall. Some of the best we've found include UPS, Intel, and Cisco. There are thousands more. The job listings and resources companies provide candidates are outstanding. In addition, most of the job boards such as Indeed, Monster, CareerBuilder, SimplyHired, and others also have pages, so you can review their listings and job-search tips, as well.

We suggest that you "Like" the Facebook pages of the companies you're interested in and post relevant comments. This will enhance your visibility at those companies. More importantly, by following the pages, you'll be privy to the latest and greatest job opportunities that companies have at their disposal before they've been posted to other sites.

By reviewing the company sites on Facebook, you'll also gain a better understanding of the corporate cultures of companies. For instance, if you're 50-something and you see a company on Facebook that only has pictures of 25-year-olds you can essentially rule out getting a job with that company unless you have a very unique skill set that they absolutely can't live without. Otherwise, your chances are about as good as holding a $1 million winning lottery ticket.

In addition to Facebook itself, you might want to take advantage of a couple of job-related apps in Facebook, such as BranchOut, and BeKnown (by Monster). You can find both by using the search bar on Facebook.

BranchOut is the largest professional community on Facebook, with more than 30 million users. It allows people to build their professional brands by sharing photos and posts that dynamically showcase their professional skills, expertise, and accomplishments.

BeKnown also contains a large number of job listings and other job-search-related information.

OTHER DIRECTIONS

There are many other social media channels to address such as Pinterest, YouTube, Slideshare, and Instagram, with more emerging almost weekly that you could also develop platforms on. But unless you're seeking a position in digital marketing, there will be a diminishing rate of return in using most of these, so you need to be sure you're not getting involved with something that's more of a hobby than something that's going to position you for a job. Yes, you will expand your reach, but at what cost? You're better off spending the time connecting with people in real life by attending industry events rather than frittering your time away on every new channel that comes along.

We do recommend, however, that you use Slideshare and YouTube for research. There is a wealth of information available on each one that can be an asset for your search. For instance, by posing a question within quotation marks in YouTube such as "How To...?" you can almost always find a solution to a problem.

We should point out, however, that the success we're seeing with positioning yourself on these other social media channels is more the exception than the rule and is somewhat limited to the marketing and graphic arts areas. But in the future, it's likely to become the rule for most hires, so, you'd better start preparing yourself now.

If you're involved in the digital marketing area, you'd best be prepared to use the online world as fully as possible in your job search. If you're not, understand that your competitors will be, which will put you at a definite disadvantage. Marketing recruiter Raegan Hill explains why this is so necessary in her article, "Digital Marketers: Learning How to Use Their Online World to Job Search":

> Recruiters pay close attention to what job-seekers do, and don't do online. Both can have a positive or negative effect on the success of a candidate's likelihood of landing a job.
>
> Digital Marketers are especially scrutinized. After all, they are marketers. However, trying to find your dream job at the precise time

you're looking is a lot like trying to win the lottery. In other words, it's not easy! But marketers have an advantage over the average job-seeker. They already know how to use social media and online tools to promote a product. The difference this time is that the product is *them*. Yet in spite of this knowledge, many marketers overlook the obvious.

Here are some online techniques that marketers, as well as others who have an affinity for marketing, should tap into if they are looking for a job online:

A. **Listening Strategy**
They should create a "listening" strategy to find conversations relevant to their job search. Hiring Managers, recruiters, and even employees who want to tap into their company's referral bonus program will post tweets about open positions. On Twitter, a marketer can create queries that return tweets with keywords and phrases like "Looking for" or "We're hiring" and save these queries as lists that they can monitor live. They can narrow the results to show only tweets in a geographical area which contain "marketing" or "digital," for example. I tweet about job openings before I even get off the phone with the client! I use hashtags such as #JOBALERT and #HOUSTON and include "marketing" in the tweet. Professionals who follow me will usually know about an open position before anyone else. I also have a Twitter query that looks for tweets that include "I'm looking", "seeking new opportunity", "currently looking", "available immediately", etc.

B. **Inbound Strategy**
No matter how great a marketer you are, you'll never be able to reach out to everyone online to introduce yourself one-on-one. It would take forever! And why do all the work promoting yourself when there are other people who can do it for you? You need an inbound marketing strategy that increases the number of times you show up in search results and the number of times your profile is clicked on.

The more "important" or relevant you appear to be to others in your network, the higher the odds that you'll show up in searches on the first page or two.

Learning how to optimize your profile is a must.

C. **Piggyback Strategy**

Leverage social media in job search by associating your online persona with well-known industry thought leaders or high-profile organizations. How to do this:

1. When you connect with successful people and organizations online, other members who are searching for those thought leaders and organizations will inevitably see your profile in their search results.

   I volunteered as a local spokesperson for a global CMO group called The CMO Club. I then asked for the founder's permission to add The CMO Club to my LinkedIn Profile and link it to their company page. Now, when a marketer searches for "CMO", "The CMO Club," or "Pete Krainik," I'm usually the first, second, or third name to appear in the search results. So find thought leaders and connect with them. Don't ask for anything; simply let them know that you'd love to have their expertise in your network.

2. Look for high-profile associations, pay the member dues, and volunteer. This will allow you to add them to your LinkedIn Profile as a company that you volunteer for. When someone searches for that association, you're going to show up.

D. **The Chess Game Strategy**

Use social media to find the peripheral influencers within a company. This could be an executive administrative assistant, those in the department you want to work in, employees in the finance and accounting department, sales people.

Anyone at the target company who has a large network and is actively on LinkedIn is a good person to connect with. Move these peripheral chess pieces to first-level connection and interact with them through likes, status updates, etc. Other employees at that company will log in and see you listed to the right of your home page where it says "People you may know."

Employees you connect with might mention a job they saw posted on the company Intranet.

E. Peek-A-Boo Method

We are all just children at heart. On LinkedIn, when you click "Who's Viewed My Profile," what do you instinctively do? You view *their* profile! Your curiosity takes the wheel and hot coals under your feet couldn't stop you from clicking their link to see who they are. Now reverse this.

Find decision makers on sites like LinkedIn who have posted a position on their company Web site. View their profile, wait a day or two and check to see if they viewed you. Be ready!

Your profile needs to hit all the key aspects of the open position. If they don't reach out to you, view them again.

I won a new client using this method. They had sent out an open marketing position to over 20 staffing firms. The job was not properly written and no one was allowed to call the Hiring Manager directly. Everyone was submitting candidates, but they were mismatched to what the client actually needed.

Instead, I ensured that my profile hit all the key points in the job description, found the Hiring Manager online, and viewed his profile. Then he viewed mine. We did this back and forth for several days followed by a LinkedIn InMail from him asking if I could help him fill his marketing position. I agreed to represent them, but only if we met in person. We filled the position. This method requires a little patience, but it works.

F. Peek-And-Read Method

Let's say you're looking for Directors of Marketing within the Chicago area. You run your search and discover 100 in your network (LinkedIn). Before you click on them, post a meaningful status update that would appeal to a Director of Marketing. Perhaps post a link to a recent marketing article that touches on a modern marketing challenge that Marketing Directors are dealing with.

Add your comment in the status update area above the link. Then, click their profile. Keep clicking. Get through them all and don't post another status update for a couple of days. Check to see who's viewed your profile. Follow up with an invite and mention something about a recent status update they made or recent company blog, or just find something to say that is meaningful and industry-specific. Don't ask for a job. Everyone does this.

Hiring Managers are desensitized to professionals asking for a job. It triggers the "I feel bad" emotion if they don't have anything open. No one likes to have to reject someone, so they just avoid responding to you.

G. Push the Help Button

Use social media to build real rapport and establish common ground before you inquire about open positions. Do this right and it will trigger the "help" button vs. the "gimme, gimme" or "I need, I need" button.

Start real conversations. Follow their updates, comment on their status updates, share useful information then go dark for several days, resurface and mention a strategic networking event that they or those on their team may want to attend. You could even find an intern opportunity and mention it. They may have children of post-college-intern age.

The point is to add value first. It generates an "I want to help this person" atmosphere and this is when you are more likely to get a positive response. Then you can ask if their company is hiring.

H. Create Multiple Online Profiles

If you can create an online profile for free, do it!
Local associations and meet-up groups often allow you to add a profile about yourself on their platform.

Recruiters use Google Boolean search strings to find profiles and hidden resumes on the Internet. The more online *stickiness* you create, the higher your chances of being front and center when a recruiter is searching for keywords via Google. Below are things that recruiters pay close attention to when searching online:

1. **Online Consistency**: Simple yet often ignored is the value of a consistent personal brand across all online social media channels. If your Facebook is public and you have a Twitter account, a Google+ account and a LinkedIn Profile, make sure that all the social media channels that you're on consistently send out the same professional message. Recruiters pay close attention to a candidate's ability to build a cohesive online persona across all online channels.

This goes for your cell and home phone voice-mail, as well. Lose your favorite hip hop song or voicemail of you, your children, and your dog barking and replace it with a professional message that goes with the online profile.

I have opted not to move forward with a candidate after listening to their unprofessional voicemail.

2. **'Find-ability', Reach-ability, Availability**: Recruiters are constantly working what we call "closest to the dollar." We look for candidates that are
   - Easy to find
   - Easy to contact and
   - Available NOW.

Make sure you're fully out there on all the popular online channels so we can find you. Place your contact information (phone and email) into the summary area of your profiles. Please don't make me have to send you an InMail and wait for a reply. Two days in a recruiter's world can be the difference between filling a position and losing it to a competitor!

If I can't get a hold of you in that moment, I'll email you, but will keep looking until I find a candidate that I can contact immediately.

If you just left your last job, show the end date! I'll call you before I call an equally qualified candidate who is working and might get a counteroffer or take months to negotiate and woo away from their current employer.

3. **Outdated Links**: Many job-seekers forget to update the URL Links they added to their LinkedIn Profile. These links go to previous company Web pages or an old blog that they no longer update. Even worse is when a link goes to your Twitter page and you have 10 followers and 4 tweets—posted last year. This implies you're not good at keeping material relevant and updated. If you can't keep up with your personal online brand, how would you be able to keep with a company's online brand?

4. **Outdated or meaningless Headline on LinkedIn**: The first thing I read when I find you in a search is your headline. Many marketers forget to update it when they leave a company. Even worse, they type something like "Account Manager" or "Actively looking—will take anything"—please don't do this! The Headline should be to you what a tagline is to a company's brand. What's your tagline? If you're a marketer, this should come easy.

5. **Do you walk the walk**: I place Digital Marketers for a living. If I'm going to consider you for a digital marketing job and you're out there on the World Wide Web in all the usual places, you need to walk the walk.

   - Are you actively tweeting?
   - What's your follow-to-follower ratio (especially if you're applying to my open Social Media Strategist job)?
   - Are you retweeting relevant content?
   - Is your LinkedIn 100% complete?
   - Do you have followers?
   - Do followers comment on your status updates?
   - What about Google+?
   - Do you blog?
   - Are you interactive with your online network or just out there on the surface?

Never has there been a time like we have today where professionals with no direct social media or online marketing experience have the potential to land a great digital marketing role if they just take the time to leverage online marketing tools to promote and brand themselves. There are tons of online tutorials that dig into the tactical "how to" of the various online social media channels, but if you're not using social communication strategies like the ones above to achieve your desired result, you're just looking at a fancy Web site with a lot of shiny new toys to play with. Always be learning and updating your knowledge because nothing social stays still for very long.

This pertains to all job-seekers because one of the three jobs you have in job transition is that of a Marketing Brand Manager. Are you marketing your brand to the fullest extent?

Websites & Blogs

We've already shared our opinion on the establishment of personal websites and blogs. If, however, you're inclined to set up your own website on the Internet for your job search, this can be done fairly easily by using the Google website tool. You might also consider using Wix and Weebly.

Yes, you can also blog if you're so inclined, but remember that you'll have to commit the time and energy to become effective at it. Only you can make the decision if it will be something that will be beneficial for you. If you're professionally involved in social media or trying to position yourself as an expert in a certain discipline, go for it. Our recommended platform is WordPress. As blogging expert Melissa Galt explains in her article, "Blogging: The Inside Scoop on How to Mesmerize Your Potential Employer with Your Expertise," there are a number of benefits you can realize:

You are an expert; you are a thought leader. You have a unique history, education, experience, talent, and point of view that your market (audience) wants to hear, read, and consume. Blogging is one of the most effective ways to share that content and to be noticed by potential employers.

Blog posts, like all content, are simply a form of information, nothing more. In order to make the most effective use of your time, create a blogging strategy before jumping in. The number one question to ask yourself is, "What is my purpose in blogging?"

What is it you want to achieve by blogging? Why is this an activity that will enhance your job search?

Beyond doing this because you simply enjoy writing, there are three primary reasons to blog:

1. Blogging increases your visibility in your industry and niche.
    a. It allows you a format for getting your experience and education into the marketplace on a consistent and persistent basis.
    b. It is a great way for industry associations, publications, and potential Hiring Managers at corporations to find you for speaking opportunities, consulting, job opportunities, and much more.
2. Blogging is an excellent avenue for enhancing your credibility. Regardless of the format you choose, it provides a powerful way to share your point of view, your expertise, and your unique talents with your market.
3. Blogging gives your target audience a chance to know, like, and trust you. It builds your KLT (know, like, and trust) factor, all important when it comes to expanding your reach, your impact, and your potential for being hired.

If you're limited by time, or a bit reluctant to blog, something you can do instead of developing a full-fledged blog is to find prominent blogs in your area and start commenting on them.

Demonstrate your expertise!

One of the sites that will help you locate them is http://alltop.com. As Jim Stroud advised in his discussion earlier in this book, make sure that they are blogs that have a sufficient number of comments, as this is where recruiters and talent acquisition managers will be searching for candidates.

You've Got KLOUT!
If you're serious about social media and are competing for a position in it or something marketing-related, you need to consider becoming involved in one or more of the so-called "influencer sites." These include:

- ➤ Klout
- ➤ Kred
- ➤ PeerINdex
- ➤ Empire Avenue

Although not necessarily true outside the marketing arena, more and more individuals and companies are judging people by their influencer scores. Of the four we just listed, perhaps the most recognized and used right now is Klout.

Klout uses an algorithm to develop a so-called Klout score for an individual based on his or her social media activity, engagement, and following. It tends to fluctuate without reason, and a person's score can change dramatically overnight. Nevertheless, it's a benchmark that's being used to "rank" people, and it should be something you take into consideration.

In their book, *Klout Matters*, social media strategists Gina Carr and Terry Brock concur: "Increasingly more decisions are being made on who to hire for full-time employment or for a specific contract across different industries. For instance, we know that many actors are being rejected or accepted by directors and producers based on their Klout scores."[8]

If you're active on social media, you should at least register for Klout to determine what your score is and take the necessary steps to improve it. You can try the other platforms as time allows.

THE FUTURE

Vala Afshar is the CMO and the Chief Customer Officer for Enterasys Networks and is considered a pioneer in cloud computing. In his article, "The Now & Future of Social Media's Role in the Hiring Process," he gives us a hint of things to come:

> For most companies, the use of social media in the hiring process has been limited to finding candidates primarily through LinkedIn and to a lesser extent via Twitter and Facebook. We are currently the exception to the rule and are using social media more thoroughly in the candidate selection process and are migrating away from the use of traditional hiring practices such as reviewing resumes in the process itself.
>
> We still currently look at paper resumes and LinkedIn Profiles. What we've found, however, is that these documents really don't tell you the

whole story about a person. In most cases, they are always positive representations of potential candidates but don't reveal who they "really" are and whether or not the information being shared regarding accomplishments hasn't been overly embellished to shed the most positive light possible.

To ensure that we get a sense of the "true" candidate, we will Google the person's name to review their Internet footprint and spend time reviewing it. It really tells you an awful lot more about who the person is, how they communicate, how they interact with others, and if they're going to be a good cultural fit for the company.

In addition, in March of 2013, we embarked on what was a true paradigm shift in the way that we hire by writing a blog post explaining that we were hiring a person for a six-figure digital marketing position that would be based on the social media footprint of the individual. We had hundreds of candidates apply who clearly demonstrated their overall breadth of knowledge in digital marketing as was reflected in the social media footprint. It was so much more inclusive than what could be shown on a resume. I like to refer to a digital footprint as digital exhaust. We ended up hiring an extremely qualified candidate with extensive experience in working with one of the world's largest corporations.

Given our success with this position, we are currently finalizing the candidate selection process for a new CIO. This search was done entirely through social media with a campaign via Twitter. We had numerous responses and found a true thought leader who is a blogger and someone with a great footprint. Oftentimes, the best candidates are not seeking to change position, so their positioning on social media can assist in helping you to find the best possible candidates.

It is our intent to accelerate the hiring of candidates for almost all positions within our company based on how they present themselves on Social Media. It just tells you so much more about the person and whether or not they are going to be a cultural fit. Will they be an influencer, or a thought leader who can contribute to our success?

Although we have been at the forefront in the use of social media for hiring, we look for more and more companies to aggressively move in this direction and for it to become the norm within not too many years. We look at tools such as Radian 6 to enable us to more clearly vet candidates based on social media and hire the ones that will truly be the best possible fit. Hiring is an expensive proposition and having a full insight into an individual via this process will be in the best possible interest of all involved.

As a job-seeker you should recognize that this is the new trend and make sure that you put yourself out there. You're no longer in an isolated room looking for a job. The Web is now the room and you need to use it to your advantage.

Chapter 13: Interviewing

> *"In the modern world of business, it is useless to be a creative, original thinker unless you can also sell what you create."*
> -David Ogilvy

Interview Overview

Interviewing is either a buying process or a selling process, depending on your perspective. Each candidate wants the Hiring Manager to "buy them." The Hiring Manager, on the other hand, needs to "buy a product" but, like you, never wants to be "sold."

Quite the conundrum!

Hiring the right person for any position can be crucial for companies. And the cost of hiring the wrong person is exponentially greater for all involved. Can you feel the pressure mounting?

The costs include: creating a *necessary* position, seeking qualified candidates, the interviewing process, assessing the candidates, coming to a decision, training the chosen candidate, ramp-up costs, and numerous others. These all pale in comparison to hiring the *wrong* person. As a result, the hiring process can be intimidating and uncomfortable.

Speaking of comfort, are you comfortable in interview situations? Most of us are not—but neither are they.

Would it make you feel better to know that the vast majority of Hiring Managers have never had interview training? It's true. Few companies invest a dime on training its Hiring Managers how to interview, although companies are willing to dump good managers who are untrained at hiring if they hire the wrong people. So we'll ask again, *Do you feel the pressure mounting?*

Here's a secret: Most Hiring Managers don't like the hiring process any more than you do. It's time to heave a huge sigh of relief—*go ahead and breathe deeply*. By the time you finish this chapter, you will have vastly superior interviewing skills than the majority of Hiring Managers.

Aha! Now we finally hear a sigh of relief!

There are dozens of interview types and we'll attempt to introduce you to most of them while giving you strategies for becoming better at them. Though interview styles vary, the objective is always the same: to find the best fit for a position. And that fit is a two-way street. It has to be a fit for you, as well as them, or both you and your employer will be miserable. And who needs that?

Keep in mind that if you get an interview (any interview), *they* already know you're qualified for the job.

Questions, Questions, Questions   **?   ?   ?**

We've heard it said that the best listeners are good trial lawyers. Some of them are so intent on the questions of the opposing attorney or the testimony of the witness that they break out in a sweat.

Al: Most of my life has been spent in various areas of sales. Unfortunately, it's been my experience that the majority of salespeople are terrible listeners. They are so intent on presenting features and benefits that they never bother to find out the needs of their clients or customers—the "Show-up and Throw-up" method of sales. The same is true with how candidates present themselves in interviews, which is another type of sales situation.

When I was a young salesperson, I was pretty good, but I was intent on MY needs, MY goals, MY quota, My bonuses. One day I stumbled onto a book that unfortunately is no longer in print, **From the Buyer's Side**. *I have no idea who the author was, but it changed my life.*

From that point forward, I asked many more questions and made it a point of finding out the needs of my clients because if I knew what their needs were, I might be able to satisfy them—and my needs in the process. I was also known to tell a client if I thought a competitor could better satisfy their needs (sometimes to the chagrin of my managers). *In so doing, however, I positioned myself as a trusted resource, as opposed to just another schlepper only looking out for himself.*

Thus the power of questions.

You need to learn to ask questions during your interviews. Lots of questions! By asking the right kinds of questions, you can uncover the needs and hidden objections that others can only guess at.

Ready?

There are two general types of questions: Closed and Open probes.

A closed probe is a question that elicits only a yes or no answer. The person feels no compelling need to offer any further explanation because none is required. Another variation of this type question is when you give someone a choice, such as, "Would you prefer to meet on Monday, or would Tuesday be better?"

A closed probe should be used only when trying to confirm information. A couple examples are:
- Will you be forwarding my resume to the next interviewer?
- Will my next interview be with the Hiring Manager or with the talent acquisition manager?

Open-ended questions, on the other hand, tend to produce more in-depth answers. Often you can uncover information the interviewer never intended to share with a candidate. This is what you want. Open probes include any of the following words:
- Who?
- What?
- When?
- How?
- Where?
- Why?

Examples:
- Who will I be interviewing with next?

- ➢ What are the 3-5 most important tasks you'll want me to accomplish when I get started?
- ➢ When will our next interview take place?
- ➢ How many rounds of interviews will there be before you hire me?
- ➢ Where will I be seated in this office?
- ➢ Why do you enjoy working here?

As you can tell, you'll learn much more from an open probe than you can from a closed probe. You should work at asking this type of question long before your first interview so the questions flow naturally.

Develop a well-thought-out list of questions:
- Know your stories and their key points
- Be clear on the value you bring to the company
- Research (if possible)
  - the company
  - its position in the market
  - its competition
  - its challenges
  - its opportunities
- Research the person you'll be talking with: look them up on LinkedIn, Google, etc.

Some of your research may have to be done *after* your initial (phone) interview, especially if you've been contacted for a hidden, non-posted job—and those are the majority of the jobs out there, remember?

Research alone, however, won't give you a clear enough picture of what's going on with the Hiring Manager or the company. And just like any good salesperson would, you MUST ask questions so you can properly position your "product" (you) in the most favorable light.

- How did this position come open?
  - o Is it a newly created position?
  - o Was the person promoted?
  - o Was the person fired?
  - o Did the person retire or otherwise move on (voluntarily)?
- How long has this position been open?

- How quickly do you want to have the position filled?
- How effective was the person I'll be replacing?
- What are some of the key traits of your most effective employees?
- What will I need to do to be more effective—i.e., live up to your standards?
- What landmines will we need to avoid?

Can you see how answers to the above questions would elicit more information than you would otherwise find out? Might the direction of your presentation take a different path, depending on what you learned from these types of probing questions?

Note: One thing you must remember is to resist the temptation to break a silence after you've asked a question. Wait for as long as necessary for the interviewer to answer.

Sales 101: Ask a Question then...

SHUT UP!!!

You MUST let the other person speak next. There's an old adage in sales that goes, "The person who speaks next loses." You want to win!

Phone Script

Each of us can anticipate a number of questions that we're likely to get. Current "hot" questions are available on the Internet. Earlier in this book, we pointed you to star recruiter Abby Kohut's pamphlet, *Top 12 Interview Questions Exposed*,[1] as an excellent source for these questions, such as *Tell me about yourself*, *Name a challenge you overcame*, and *Give me an example of a time when you...*.

We also asked you to assemble a list of STAR Stories and Red Flags. Phone screeners are the place where these can first come into play. We also suggest that you assemble a list of anticipated questions from your screener and answers for them. All of this should be in bullet-point form to use only as a reminder during your call. Most of your "script" will be used during every screening call.

That's not the end of the story. As Lisa Quast, a Seattle-based career coach and consultant, notes in her excellent *Forbes* article, "Job Seekers: Don't Forget To Interview the Company (And Hiring Manager)," this is a two-way street. YOU need to be asking THEM questions throughout this process, as well.[2]

As with any script, a phone script must be practiced but never read (during the interview). You'll want to be able to ad lib, which is why your script should be no more than bullet points that can remind you what you want to present and get you back on track if you wander off it.

In addition to your script, you should be asking questions from the beginning. Make a list of probing questions, and write down the answers so you can use them as a base for subsequent interviews.

NOTE: Use a large font size when assembling your bullet points. Normal font sizes may be too difficult to read in an already nerve-racking interview situation.

Phone Screen Interviews

Let's start with what's bound to be the initial contact you'll have with your future employer: a Phone Interview or Phone Screen. The task of initial screening calls at most companies is often handled by the lowest-level person on the Human Resources totem pole. Some of these people barely have a pulse, much less know anything about the job, the company's products/services, or the needs of the Hiring Manager. It's not entirely their fault, though, because they've probably never been given that information.

One of the things that ticks us off the about virtually all interview courses and interview trainers we've listened to is that they neglect to talk about phone interviews or screening interviews. This angers us so much because you almost certainly will have to get past this person to speak or meet with a decision-maker. If you don't handle the phone screen properly, it could lead to you losing a job before you've even gotten to first base.

Being prepared is the key tenet of a successful interview. We know what you're thinking: *Okay, smart guys, how do I prepare for a call I don't know is coming?* The answer is, *You can't—so don't!*

Has the following ever happened to you?
> The phone rings and on the other end of the line you hear something that sounds like, "This is #^@&(*&^%$!)* with ONWHDTK Corporation. Is this a good time?"

Remember the old Charlie Brown shows on TV? The voice you hear when you get one of those calls is like what Charlie Brown would hear whenever an adult was talking to him: *Whah, whah, whah, whah-whah-whah.* The worst mistake you could make is to take the interview right then. If you're anything like us, you wouldn't have caught either the person's name or the company!

What we suggest you do—after you get over the initial shock of actually getting a call from a company—is to ask them to repeat their name and company (*I'm sorry, I didn't catch your name*). Then write their name and company! Explain that you're expecting a call from another company and you thought this was the call from that company. Then ask if the person could reschedule their call for the following day 2 p.m. or the day after that at 11. (These are made-up times, of course).

This accomplishes several things:
- Gives you time to prepare yourself for the interview
- Lets you properly research the company and possibly even the interviewer
- Enables you to prepare questions targeted to their stated or perceived needs (based on your research)
- Gives you a chance to rehearse your answers for anticipated questions in the form of your STAR stories
- Gives the interviewer the impression that you're in demand

Before you let the screener go, you might want to ask him or her to email you the job description *just in case anything was added since you applied.* Certainly, if this is a call for a hidden job (a job you didn't apply for), you have not seen a job description or the position's requirements, so asking for a current job description is a legitimate request. Besides, it's a subtle way to get the screener's email address! (It also allows you to verify the person's correct name and title so you can research them, as well.)

You'll then have the tools at hand that other candidates probably do not. You'll be considerably more prepared and relaxed than your rival candidates who accepted the impromptu phone call. AND you have a way to send a note of thanks to your phone interviewer. That's something your competitors can't do.

Because an interview can be somewhat confrontational in nature, you're much better off if you can defuse any tension and convert it to a more relaxed, conversational exchange.

When your interviewer calls back, thank her or him for rescheduling and try to make nice. Ask where they're calling from and show interest. Ask about their day or how their week is going and empathize with their busy work schedule. Try to make a personal connection. Remember that your phone screener is a person too and will certainly appreciate being treated like a human being.

We believe that as a candidate you should attempt to take control of your interview from the beginning. Maybe "control" is too harsh a term. But you should at least attempt to *guide* your interviewer in the direction you want the exchange to go. You can do this by asking the first couple of questions after your initial discussion. We suggest that you ask permission to ask a question, then ask your first probing question. For example:

Before we get started, do you mind if I ask a question?

(We've never known anyone to say no.)

You could go on to ask something like this: *Hopefully, you've had a chance to review my background and compare it with the job's requirements. What key qualities do you feel that I bring to the table?*

(If this was a job you had not applied for, this question is especially important since they found YOU. In either case, the answers will give you some clues you can pick up on, because there are only three possible answers to that question:

1. They can tell you the things that they liked best about you. When they finish, you should thank them for recognizing so many of your positive traits and how you believe that those traits will help you hit the ground running after you're hired. (You're already planting the seeds for you to be the chosen candidate by assuming that they're going to hire you.)
2. They can say that they don't know why they are speaking to you. Maybe they were told to do the screening (if so, they'll have a set of questions they are required to get answers for). We suggest you offer a few reasons why their superiors might have wanted you to be interviewed in the first place. (The answers you give would be based on the keywords in the job description.)
3. They could also say that they have a gazillion questions to ask in the allotted time and that if there's any time left at the end, you can ask any question you want. (If this happens, answer their question in the form of a STAR story, if possible, then ask them what attracted them to the company, what they like best about the company, or something similar in an attempt to steer the interview toward being conversational in nature.)

The information above is similar to the interview training tips you would find in transition coach Bruce Dreyfus' book *Personal Marketing Strategies Program*.[3] The interview section of the book is quite strong. In fact, the best interviewee question we've ever heard is attributed to him, "What is it about my background that made you want to speak with me today." He says it in virtually all of his public seminars and presentations. Jay Litton's, the *WOW! Interview*[4] is highly effective and is similar in many ways.

Answer number 3 above is much more likely to occur during an initial phone screening than in face-to-face interviews, although it can also occur then. Do not press during the phone screening. You're probably speaking with a low-level member of the company who has been asked to seek answers to specific questions. The best way to get positive results is to begin your answers with a yes or no then tell an abbreviated version of the appropriate STAR story.

Another key to any interview is to sound excited about the position. A great way to sound excited is to stand during the phone call. We suggest that you have your research notes and questions spread out on your desk or a counter for quick reference. And be certain to take notes when the caller is answering your questions! If there is a delay when they finish, simply state that what they said was important and that you were jotting down a note about it. They'll understand. Another method for displaying excitement during a phone interview is to speak into a mirror during the interview.

An additional thing to remember during a phone screening is that they can't see you. So you must be vocally expressive—*Uh Huh, Yes, Absolutely, Exactly, You're so right....*

> *Many years ago I (Al) was terrible at being interviewed over the phone. I am a reader of body language and am very expressive with my body language. At one point I realized why I was having so little success: I was nodding my head during* phone *interviews! There were long, silent pauses while I was nodding in agreement with what was being said, but they couldn't see that. I would lose out at interviews I would have otherwise aced.*

Your goal in virtually all phone screens is, pure and simple, to get to the next interview. Ask for it! Ask often without being a pest. We believe you must ask at least three times to fully express the proper degree of interest in the job. This can and should be done using a tool all decent sales people use: Assumptive Closes. You have read some of these earlier in this section and will continue to do so throughout.

Some additional examples:
- Who will my next interview be with?
- What's my next step in the hiring process?
- When will I be interviewing next?
- Will my next interview be face-to-face, phone, panel, Skype?
- Will I be interviewing here or at the home office?
- I hope I'll meet you after I get hired. (Okay, that's not a question.)
- Have you met the person I will be interviewing with next?
- Is there anything you can share about my next interviewer that could give me some insight into what he or she is looking for from me?
- Is there something I could or should prepare for the next interview?

These questions can and should be asked during the course of the interview, if at all possible, and certainly at the end of the screening since you're almost certain to be asked if you have any questions. Never say you don't have any or that the person has already answered them. You MUST ask a question if offered the opportunity. Any of the above will suffice.

Try your best to get the name and location of your next interviewer and let your research continue. You have a fish on the line. Don't let it slip off the hook. Keep reeling!

Develop a MORE-well-thought-out list of questions based on what you've learned during the screening:
- Know your stories and their key points
- Be clear on the value you bring to the company
- Research
  - the company
  - its position in the market
  - its competition
  - its challenges
  - its opportunities
- Research the person you will be talking with; look them up on LinkedIn, Google, etc.
  (Are you experiencing déjà vu? Yes, you have read this before.)

Finally, if at all possible, send an email thank-you note the same day. The subject line should read, *Thank You!* The body should read something like, *(Insert Name), it was great to speak with you today. I hope I get to meet you when we're officially working together.* Add a postscript that includes the job title, requisition number (if available), city, and state.

'Planned Spontaniety'

Don't you wish you could come up with the snappy retorts we hear in movies and on television? Much thought, time, and planning goes into those witty and insightful seemingly impromptu replies. Ah, but your research and pre-planned questions can accomplish the same goals. We call it *Planned Spontaneity*.

We had a client whose research was so extensive that he greeted each of his interviewers by name and was able to compliment them on a particular part of their background. He totally blew away his competition.

Another way to take advantage of your planning and research is to pause before you answer your interviewer's question, or repeat the question. It gives you a moment to think of what parts of which story best apply to that question—even if you already know what you want to say.

- It's funny you asked that question...
- Something similar to that happened to me...
- Although it's not exactly the same situation...
- When I was with XYZ, we had this problem...
- I encountered a challenge like that once...

Your stories should be practiced so they flow naturally. They shouldn't feel forced like Dennis Miller's jokes often did during his dreadful two years on Monday Night Football. They should take less than a minute to draw a picture of the SITUATION, what TASKS/TACTICS were necessary, the ACTIONS you took, and their RESULTS.

Salary Prep

Everyone seems to have problems when addressing the question of salary. Actually, there are two very different questions that can be asked about salary and they require totally different answers:
1. What did you make?
2. What do you want to make?

How much you made is a historical fact. You can add to it or state any bonuses and benefits, but your compensation was what it was. Some exceptions:
- If you took a bridge job, you can spell out the circumstances (you had to pay the bills, after all)
- If you made considerably more than you will be making, state that you are aware of the difference in salary and you have no expectations of earning what you did before

- You can also say that what you made at the last position is similar to the one you've applied for

"What do you *want* to make?" Is a bit more tricky.

Very often that question about your salary requirements is a screening tool (that's why we positioned this topic here). We advise that you tap dance around the subject, if at all possible. A few suggestions:
- If possible, can we set aside the salary issue for now?
- I'm confident that if we feel we're right for each other, we can come to a compensation package that is within your range and fits my needs.
- I'm sure there is a range for this position. Can you share that range with me?
- I'm sure that a company like this offers a salary commensurate with someone of experience.

If, however, they insist on what you want to make, tell them. This can also be a range—they have a range, so should you. Don't be afraid to ask for what you want to make. You're not doing yourself any favors by low-balling. As a matter of fact, you can underprice yourself out of a job as quickly as you can overprice yourself out of one.

You need to come up with your desired salary range. What would you love to make? What is your lowest acceptable amount? What is your "Goldilocks" number—not too high and not too low? These numbers need to be realistic, not pie-in-the-sky But we think you should lean high and build in some wiggle room. Then ask what the range is.

Research is again an essential element for a salary range. There are numerous salary calculators available on the Internet, although we've found that they tend to be lower than they should be. We suggest that you research salary ranges for your position and geographic area using Internet tools such as PayScale.com or Salary.com.

We stress, however, to avoid telling them what you want to make early in the process, if at all possible.

Face-to-Face Interviews (Initial)

Because of your research and preparation, you should enter most every interview with confidence...not to mention that you will, most likely, have more interview training than your interviewer.

Look, you already qualify for the job because you were contacted initially AND you successfully made it through the screening process. Now it's time to look at interviewing from the Hiring Manager's point of view. It's not what you might expect. Hiring Managers tend to like the interview process about as much as you do: not at all. They have a job that they are being judged on, and the interview process takes valuable time away from those duties. Also, there are a lot of things that can happen with a new hire, and few of them are beneficial to the manager's career.

First, no Hiring Manager cares one bit that YOU need a job. He only cares about HIS job. Will the new hire work out? Will the new hire stay? Will the new hire make her look good or bad? Will the new hire be a risk or a reward to his career? We're not exaggerating when we say that at many companies, one bad hire can cost the manager her job. So you're seen as a risk. Looking at it from this perspective, your task is to mitigate that risk and make him believe that it is to his advantage to hire you over the other candidates.

Think about it this way: Your interviews can be compared to your best or worst date ever. If you focus your presentation on what YOU want, it will probably turn out like the worst date you ever had. On the other hand, if you focus your attention on THEIR needs, you'll have a better chance of getting what you're after. You do this simply by asking questions to find out what the Hiring Manager's needs are. What headaches does she have that you can be the aspirin for? Additional examples:

- What are the top five things I should concentrate on after I start?
- If I could wave a magic wand, what would you want me to get done for you?
- Based on what you've shared with me today about your needs from this position, the overall needs of the company, and the list of tasks necessary

to be successful, may I put together a short presentation for our next interview?

- What traits do your best _____(sales reps, managers, software engineers, etc.) have and why are those traits vital for the success of your next hire—me?

One mistake many people make is leading with their resume. Because so few Hiring Managers have had interview training, they will typically stick their nose in the resume and you've lost them. You want to get them talking, so don't offer up your resume in the beginning of the interview unless they ask for it. Many is the time when an interview is ending before the interviewer realizes that he doesn't have it yet. That's a winner!

If you do hand them your resume, be certain that it features what you bring to the table, with lots of examples of what you accomplished. You don't want them to have to dig to find your strengths. If they do, you will most likely lose them.

This is where a hybrid is better than a chronological resume. It even gives you a chance to explain why the resume is set up the way it is.

I reformatted my resume so you could quickly find some key things I can do for you rather than have you wade through a couple of pages of text.

Even better is to hand the hiring authority a Marketing Brochure that establishes your value proposition. We suggest you make a value statement right up front based on what you learned from your initial interview, your research, and/or assumptions based on your knowledge of the company, industry, competition, etc. Most importantly, your positioning statement should be based on your initial questions to the Hiring Manager. We recommend that you include the hiring authority's name and the company logo in the brochure, if possible. It can really get their attention. No one else will have done any of this!

Compare the statement above with the one below:
I reformatted my resume so you could quickly find many of the key things I can do for you rather than have you wade through a couple of pages of text.

I've also taken the liberty to put together a Marketing Brochure based on some of the initial research I've done. May I share with you a couple of the highlights?

By doing this, you have an opportunity to guide your interviewer to where you want to go. There should be give and take here as opposed to a barrage of questions from the Hiring Manager alone. This will increase your confidence level as you present your STAR stories. And your level of excitement about the position (planned spontaneity) will become evident to your interviewer. That excitement will be shared by the Hiring Manager—and excitement sells!

This would also be a good time to ask permission to put together a little presentation on what you hope to accomplish within the first 90 to 100 days after you're hired. Your presentation must be based on what you've learned the Hiring Manager's greatest needs are. A few caveats:

- You may choose NOT to explain the form your presentation will take so as not to let the potential "pet candidates" (internal candidates) do the same. Just leave it at *a short presentation.*
- Ask if the interviewer would prefer it to be on paper or on your tablet/notebook. (If you choose to make an electronic presentation, be sure to create a paper version you can leave behind.)
- If you'll be presenting to a group or panel, you may ask if a projector might be available.

From the very beginning, you should be making mental notes. Do the walls or desk give you any insight into the hiring authority's personality or interests? They WANT you to notice these things, even though they might not be conscious of it. After all, this is THEM.

Find out as much as you can about them, and be sure to let your personality come through. Humor is good. If it fits, use it.

Al: My best interview ever was at a brand new 5-Star hotel in New Orleans. When I arrived, I called the Hiring Manager, who told me what suite he was in. I went upstairs and knocked on the door. He opened the door and joked that if I had known that the brass thing in the middle of the door was a doorbell, I would have gotten the job without the need to interview. I promptly slammed the door in his face and beat on the doorbell like crazy. I could hear Mike laughing through the door. He opened it and said, "No, no, no, it's too late. You have to go through the interview."

Obviously, I had broken the ice.

The interview went so well that he said he had something to show me. I followed him into the suite's bathroom, where there was a bidet. He stepped on the foot pedal. Me being me, I said in my best southern drawl, "Hot damn! They even got a water fountain in the bathroom!"

Not only did I get the job, but Mike later named me regional trainer and helped me become regional manager. We later became business partners and have been friends for more than twenty-five years.

Again, interviews are like first dates. Be yourself. You're about to enter into a relationship that will hopefully last many years. So you don't want to "tie the knot" with someone if the fit isn't right.

At the end of your interview, as with every interview, you will likely be asked if you have any other questions for them. As we said before, never let this opportunity pass without a question. Here's one of the final questions we like best:

"I am really excited about working with you, and I can see myself thriving in this position and being an asset to you and the company. Do YOU see me as a perfect fit?"

This is another attempt to judge where you stand and uncover any hidden objections. You might even joke that you can make his or her life easier right now—no need to waste time with further interviews: *The best choice is right in front of you.*

No matter what happens in an interview, be sure to ask for the job a minimum of three times during your interview. It's even more important now than during the phone interview because the person you're speaking with is likely to be making the hiring decision. *Do you want me to start Monday or would Tuesday be better?* Be sure that you say this with a smile on your face so you're seen as confident rather than arrogant

Note: Never smoke or have a cocktail during an interview, even if the interviewer does. Oh, and taste your food *before* you add any salt or pepper. (It sounds crazy, but I (Al) know a company president who would not hire someone for those sins). No talk about religion or politics either.

Panel Interviews

One of the latest darlings in the corporate world is the panel Interview. They can take the form of the illustration above where a number of people from different parts of the company gang-tackle you, or there can be a series of one-on-one or a-few-on-one interviews at a time. In either case, you should treat them as individuals since each person has his or her own needs and goals. In our opinion, panel interviews are designed to be a C.Y.A. method of shared blame. If the panel makes a bad hire, no one can be singled out as responsible— or take the fall.

> *Al: I had a client who we dubbed the Panel Interview King. The first time he had a panel interview, it took an entire day with twelve people, and it was with one of the companies he DID NOT want to work for! He was offered the job, but I advised him to turn it down. A couple of years later he became a client again. He outdid himself the next time, with 14 people on the panel! He's once again our favorite kind of client: a former client.*

One thing to remember about most panel interviews is that practically none of the participants wants to be there. They have more pressing things to do and being on this panel is keeping them from those tasks. Panel interviews almost always follow a script that you can anticipate. The participants are likely to pose questions or offer scenarios that test how you're likely to react to those situations. Just take your time and use your STAR stories as examples.

They are also there to test you in THEIR area of expertise. Someone from accounting or accounts receivable, for example, is only interested in your "fiscal fitness." The person from HR is likely to want to determine if you will fit the company's culture. And your future boss will certainly ask more pertinent questions about the job itself and how well you can do it.

As in any interview, focusing on the needs of the interviewer(s) will help them want to add you to the team. You should be asking questions about what they feel the person in your position can do to help THEM or make life easier for THEM, then adapt your STAR stories to those needs.

Interviewing 101

Here are some basics for every face-to-face interview:

- ✓ Relax
- ✓ Smile
- ✓ Give a firm handshake (If you are hyperhydrotic, wipe your hands on your pants leg or skirt before you shake.)
- ✓ Make lots of eye contact
- ✓ Offer your business card (try to get one of theirs)
- ✓ Wear appropriate attire (it's better to overdress—see section below on Interview Attire)
- ✓ Sit slightly forward in your chair
- ✓ Use a portfolio of some kind for note-taking. It's a convenient place to store resumes, brochures, and other material you may want to refer to
- ✓ Have a list of questions you want to ask
- ✓ Take LOTS of notes
- ✓ Create a list of words that will remind you of your STAR Stories
- ✓ If you carry a briefcase, have it organized and open to be able to quickly reach for necessary documents, computer, or other electronic devices
- ✓ Leave your cell phone in your car or turn it off prior to arrival at the meeting place
- ✓ Don't glance at your watch (take it off)
- ✓ Have Thank You cards with you (leave one THAT DAY!)
- ✓ Send an electronic thank-you after business hours the same day
- ✓ Exude confidence. You're better than the other candidates, so show it!
- ✓ Be exceptionally nice to the receptionist, these people are often asked how you acted and reacted

800-lb. Gorillas

What is that in the middle of the room no one wants to talk about? Could it be an 800-lb. gorilla? You see a gorilla? I don't see a gorilla. Oh, you mean THAT gorilla!

The vast majority of interviewers have had zero interview training, and, as a result, will more likely than not answer any questions you posed. Some of these questions are intended to uncover what we call the "800- lb. gorillas"—that is, hidden objections. We said earlier that we can't ignore the 800-lb. gorillas; we need to take them on, even if we lose a battle or two.

We believe that uncovering hidden objections is best done by asking probing questions. We can also directly address potential objections <u>in an offhanded way</u>. We advise using both methods. Let's start by handling some of the prejudices younger Hiring Managers tend to have against older candidates:

Prejudice: Older people won't work for a younger manager, or with a younger team

Suggestion(s):

- *I have thrived working for younger managers. It's been my experience that their energy level is contagious. I can sense your intensity and look forward to working closely with you. Don't you love the dynamic of a diverse team?*
- *I have both lead and worked on teams with members younger and older than I am. In every case, we have been successful. You can expect exactly that when you hire me.*

Prejudice: Older people lack energy

Suggestion(s):

- Always sit forward and toward the edge of your chair.
- Be animated!
- Display "Controlled Excitement."
- Ask about their activities and talk about yours.

Prejudice: Older workers have health problems

Suggestion(s):
- DO NOT talk about your health problems; instead, mention how energetic you're.
- *Many of my friends both young and old have health issues; I on the other hand, can't even remember the last time I had a cold! I bet you're fit as a thoroughbred, too.*
- *You can always count on me to be there. I almost never take a sick day.*

Prejudice: Older people are not mentally agile
Suggestion(s):
- Talk about what you have done *recently*.
- Mention something you've blogged, tweeted, commented on, etc.

Prejudice: Older workers can't deal with change
Suggestion(s):
- *You know, one of the few things you can count on is change. I feel sorry for people who don't relish change, or can't run with the new technology, don't you?*
- *What are your thoughts about...[this or that new thing]???*
- *I believe that people who aren't moving forward with or ahead of the technology curve are missing the boat.*
- *I tend to be a change agent.*

Prejudice: Older people are often overqualified (and might threaten my job)

Suggestion(s):
- *As you can tell (have said), I am highly qualified. I want to bring my qualifications to your team.*
- *I no longer feel the need to "rule the world." Use my qualifications to hasten your rise through the ranks.*
- *When I was a young manager, I hired an older, highly qualified person. I didn't realize it at the time, but upper management was impressed that I was confident enough in my own ability to hire that person. This person also helped me avoid mistakes I might have otherwise made.*

- *For me, it's pay it forward time for all the blessings I've received.*

Heidi Holmes of Adage, a job-search Web site for mature workers, states that older people have a lot to offer and that businesses should be looking at the benefits older workers can bring to the table. "Employers are becoming increasingly aware of the power of reflecting your customer base in your workforce," she says. "The mature market is a very important consumer segment, holding over 50 percent of household wealth in Australia. Older workers are often customer-centric and have an ability to empathize with customer needs. Having employees who understand and resonate with the Boomer consumer will become increasingly important for employers going forward."[4]

No matter your age group—Boomer, Generation-X, Millennial—present your strengths! Let your interviewer know what you bring to the table and how your "place-setting" is of benefit to them. Clearly state your value proposition! Practice your value proposition so it flows naturally in response to any sort of question, whether they're ones you anticipated or completely off-the-wall.

Al: Speaking of questions that are easily anticipated, we've cited "Absolutely Abby" Kohut a number of times, in part because she and I jokingly "stalked" each other the last time she was in the Atlanta area, but mostly because she surprised the hell out of us. Frankly we had no interest in hearing yet another "expert" spew the same nonsense about resumes, cover letters, and the rest, but our wives forced us to go. We were standing in the back of a packed room when we heard a purple-haired lady from Brooklyn making many of the same points we do. We've mentioned her book and interview question pamphlet previously, and she has graciously offered to share more of her thoughts in an article entitled, "How do you answer the standard interview question: 'What is your greatest weakness?'"

We all have weaknesses, yet only some of them affect our job performance. Although you may believe that recruiters ask the weakness question to intimidate you, in the majority of cases, these are the actual reasons:

- ❖ To determine whether your weaknesses are detrimental to the position in question
- ❖ To determine whether you are an honest person
- ❖ To determine whether you are willing to admit you're not perfect
- ❖ To determine whether you are coachable
- ❖ To determine your long-term potential at their company based on your weaknesses

The key to answering this question is to describe the weakness and then follow up with an explanation of how you are overcoming it or working around it. Here is an example of a strong answer: "I am a perfectionist. While this is a strength for me in my editing work, it causes me to put off finishing projects until they are "perfect." To overcome this, I impose deadlines on myself because when I have a deadline, I am always able to finish my work on time."

If your interviewer doesn't think you are being genuine, he or she will continue to press you until you reveal a weakness that is more believable. Here are some examples of answers that will likely cause more questioning:

- ❖ "I am a workaholic. I need to achieve more balance in my life."
- ❖ "I can't say no. I continue to take on more responsibilities until I'm about to burst!"
- ❖ "I was always rated highly on my performance reviews, so I can't think of any."

If you truly can't think of a current weakness, perhaps you can remember one that you overcame in the past with the help of a manager, which can serve as a great example of your being coachable. This also proves to the interviewer that you are willing to hear negative feedback and then take deliberate action to improve your behavior. For example, you can say, "A few years ago, I was told by my manager that my presentation skills needed some work. I asked her to provide more opportunities to speak in front of groups so as time went on, I was able to improve in that area. On my own, I also signed up for a Toastmasters class to develop my skills."

Remember that there are no perfect employees. Companies want to hire honest, coachable ones. The key is to know yourself, know what makes you a strong performer, and also know what areas you will need your manager's help with.

If this is still difficult for you to come up with a couple weaknesses, we stress that you take a formal assessment like DISC. You should be able to build from those results.

Face-to-Face Interviews (Final)

A final interview is your ultimate moment to shine. If you're following the program laid out in this book, you should blow the competition away. The answers to the questions you asked earlier will have set the foundation for the presentation you will make here. It's time to seal the deal.

We highly recommend that you create presentation materials. No matter what form you choose—Tri-Fold, Bi-Fold, Multi-Fold, Portfolio, Flip-Chart, Infographic, PowerPoint or other—you can and should present your qualifications based on a combination of information gleaned from questions asked in previous interview(s), logical assumptions from your research, and innate knowledge of the position, company, and industry.

Now, more than ever, your final interview must be an exchange of ideas between you and the interviewer(s). It is crucial that you to do the following:
1. Discover any previously unspoken needs
2. Determine if they are considering internal candidates (see below)
3. Uncover any hidden objections (revisit 800-lb. Gorilla above)

Let's focus on uncovering needs here. As you did in your initial face-to-face interview, you'll use open probes to draw out more information from the interviewer. You can use variations of the same questions you used in your first interview. Another method is to paraphrase what was stated and ask if there were other things that could benefit him or her and make you both more successful.

When you're satisfied that you've learned as much as possible, remind the interviewer that you had asked if it would be all right to create a brief presentation. This is the time to ask if he or she would like to look at what you put together. Your presentation should be a two-way street. You want interaction. If you get interaction, you'll most likely also get buy-in. (When they talk, you'll be seen as brilliant.)

We suggest that you begin your presentation with a caveat (the same goes for the written version you'll leave with the Hiring Manager) that everything you're about to present is subject to change based on the needs of the Hiring Manager (name him or her) and the company. You don't want anyone to think that you want to run the show unless that is the position you're seeking. Make it abundantly clear that these were their stated needs and that you're offering possible ways to satisfy those needs as effectively as possible.

Start with your value statement, something like, "Based on what we discussed previously, I believe that these are some of the things I bring to your team, some of the things I believe I can do to meet your needs (and those of the company/district/office/division), and how I believe I can do it. (This is where a tri-fold brochure or other type of three-page presentation works to your benefit). Here's a specific example:

Based on our last conversation, I put together a possible Plan-of-Action to achieve the goals you mentioned then. It's not perfect by any means, but it might be a starting point—with your input and approval, of course.

I have broken it down into X Months for benchmarking purposes. It might be ambitious, but then again, I tend to set my goals higher than most. Here are some of my initial thoughts. What are your thoughts about...?

You should be asking for their approval throughout. Questioning whether something is the best option or if they would suggest an alternative method is an excellent way to discover what they really think. Even if they disagree with a point you've made, that's a good sign. Take notes on the spot and mark through the original text. Display your willingness to work with and for THEM.

Excellent point. I see what you mean...That shines a different light on the situation...I hadn't looked at it from that perspective...That changes things...

A timeline helps show how you plan to execute your initiatives. It could offer benchmarks to determine your effectiveness (those benchmarks could also be used to negotiate early pay increases). It can be divided into an additional three-part plan:

- 30-60-90 days
- 100-day plan, which includes work done prior to your start date
- Six-month or 1-year plan

This is an aggressive positioning statement. Virtually no Hiring Manager will have ever seen such a presentation, nor will other candidates take this approach.

You will immediately differentiate yourself from the other candidates.

Throughout this process, we've wanted you to take advantage of every opportunity to nose out your competition. Positioning your final interview is no exception. One of those opportunities is your interview time. If at all possible, we suggest you take the latest possible interview appointment of the day. The theory behind this is that "the person seen last is the person remembered best." Despite your excellent interview presentation material and leave-behind, it's difficult for a Hiring Manager to remember everything about a candidate because he or she is probably interviewing four or five impressive individuals over a period of a few days. We want you to be foremost in their mind.

Overcoming Internal Candidates

One of the toughest obstacles to overcome is the internal candidate. There are tactics you need to take to combat them. If you've ever finished second, an internal candidate is probably the reason why. In any case, if there is an internal candidate, you will need to address this competitor during your final interview.

Generally speaking, companies would rather promote from within than hire an outsider. The reasons are simple:

1. It is a corporate downer (negative motivation) for internal candidates who apply:

a. *So I wasn't good enough for them? Maybe I should be looking elsewhere.*
b. *You mean to tell me that we didn't have a current employee good enough for the job?*
2. The internal candidate is a known quantity:
    a. Both the strengths and weaknesses are known (you, on the other hand, are an unknown).
    b. Thus, they are perceived as less of a risk to hire than you are.

It can be tough to beat out the internal candidate, but it's <u>not</u> impossible. The first step toward supplanting an internal candidate is to find out if one or more are being considered. You have to ask.

Are you considering internal candidates? How many?

You know, in most cases, I'm sure you would prefer to hire from within, but sometimes the better choice is the external candidate. They can bring new blood and some fresh ideas.

Sometimes things are done a certain way because they have always been done that way. It's like the term we learned in college "Groupthink." I'm not saying that My Way is right, but because I come in with no preconceived notions, I promise to keep us from Groupthink!

You might also want to cite one of Virgin Group founder Sir Richard Branson's *3 Tips on How to Hire the Right Person*: "A person who has multiple degrees in your field isn't always better than someone who has broad experience and a great personality."[5]

Skype & Video Interviews

Video interviews are becoming increasingly popular and shouldn't frighten you. They are less expensive for the company and faster to complete. This is especially attractive when the company is global or there is a large expansion with a corresponding need to quickly place a large number of new hires.

A video interview is merely a face-to-face interview where the participants are not in the same room, or even in the same country. Frankly, we prefer a video interview to a phone interview because there is an opportunity to read some body language, which is impossible to do over a standard phone. In addition, a computer's microphone is usually much more sensitive so you're likely to be heard more clearly than you would be over a cell or speaker phone. And there seldom is any feedback, reverb, or echo. What's more, you can adjust your speaker's volume.

Some companies conduct video interviews at a corporate office. If this is the case, arrive early and ask someone to help you get the hang of the equipment you're going to be using. Be sure to use the picture-in-picture feature so your interviewer isn't just viewing the top of your head. Just as proper business attire is required with an onsite video interview, you should dress just professionally even if you're doing the interview from home.

Skype, which is now owned by Microsoft, has become the generic term for remote interviews using your computer. A few hints about Skype interviews:
- Your computer must have a camera and microphone. (External cameras with a mic can be purchased at your local office supply store for less than $100)
- You should practice your interview skills
- Remove all clutter from the camera's view:
  o Make sure you're centered in the screen without being too close
  o Do not move excessively, drink, or eat during the interview
- Conduct the interview where there is no background noise
- Do not tap or shuffle papers; the microphone will pick up every sound

Business attire is required for a Skype interview—at least from the waist up

Cocktail Umbrella Questions[6]

Al: I'm not sure if it's merely "because they can" or because some *genius* came up with this brilliant idea, but some companies are asking seemingly crazy questions toward the end of interviews. A few years ago, a former client was flown to the company's headquarters on the opposite side of the country, breezed through this interview (final) and just before wrapping-up was asked, "How many cocktail umbrellas are sold worldwide on a daily basis?" He was dumbfounded and stumbled badly. He didn't get the job.

When we heard about this, we were incredulous, did some research and found that this wasn't as rare as we thought. If you're curious, Google "Cocktail Umbrella Questions" and discover the reasoning behind this bizarre type of questioning. Some companies simply want to see how you'll react to the unexpected and believe they can gain some insight into your deductive reasoning ability. We don't buy cocktail umbrella questions as a legitimate interview tactic because we don't think it should be the way a company goes about making hiring decisions.

On the other side of the coin, we had a client who was interviewing with a large three-letter telecommunications company that gave the candidates a series of questions in advance that they wanted answers for. This method of questioning seems vastly superior to us because the client and other candidates had a chance to think the issues through in a logical manner. In our client's case, he created a PowerPoint that he presented to a panel of employees during the interview.

But be aware that both extremes—the logical and the ridiculous—exist, so be prepared.

Negotiation

Congratulations, you've received a job offer! They like you, they really, really like you. Now, let's take full advantage. It's time to negotiate your package.

Yes, we said negotiate.

In almost every case, companies have wiggle room regarding salary, location, time, hours, and benefits. Virtually nothing is off the table. In some instances, companies expect you to negotiate. Granted, CareerBuilder reports that 18% of companies may disqualify a candidate if their "salary expectations are too high."[7] But that's seldom the case once an offer has been made. The "disqualification" they're referring to occurs much earlier in the interview process, usually done by a lower-level external screener or someone in HR, not by the ultimate hiring authority.

Our apologies to Don McLean, who penned the '70s hit "American Pie," for borrowing a verse from another of his songs, "The More You Pay," but when it comes to how superiors think about employees, *the more THEY pay, the more YOU'RE worth*. If you're hired at a bargain-basement price, your value in their eyes is diminished. If they hire you at top dollar, you're worth more to them.

Early on we wanted you to have three possible salaries in mind: lowest acceptable, median, and pie in the sky. Now is the time to ask for as close to the high-water mark as possible. What's the worst they can do, say no? One of our favorite ploys is that when they make the salary offer, suck air through your teeth (do it now for practice) then say, "You know, I was really looking for $X. How much wiggle room is there in your number?" You will be amazed how often they will come up with more money because most companies have a *salary band range*. And if they say no, you can ask for an early review based on some of the benchmarks you set forth in your final interview POA presentation (Plan of Action).

Remember, too, that all your subsequent merit increases will be based on your starting salary. A lower starting salary means lower pay increases throughout your tenure. Think about it. If you're offered $120,000 and you ask for $132,000 (10% more) and split the difference, you've earned an additional $500 a month. And if they agree to $132K you've added a cool 12 Grand to your yearly bank account!

We gladly accept gratuities.

Other than a higher starting salary and/or early performance review, things you can ask for after you've been given an offer include additional weeks of vacation, time off if you already had a vacation scheduled, a better company car, virtual office time, and relocation and related expenses, which could include an additional house-hunting trip for your significant other.

The few of us who still read a newspaper are lucky here in the Atlanta area to have career coach Amy Lindgren's "Working Strategies" column on Sundays. In one of those columns, she wrote about the subject of what to do after you get a job offer. She says you should be skeptical when an interviewer makes an offer and tells you, "This is the top of our range." She agrees with what we stated above. "That doesn't mean that they've topped out their budget," she writes. "There's almost always more money available, but only if one asks for it."[8]

Now is the time to ask for it. Remember that of all the candidates they spoke to, you were the one they chose. Besides, they don't want to go through this process all over again. It's a pain in the keister!

Thank You, Thank You, Thank You!

Did we mention thank-you's? Fewer than 5% of candidates thank the interviewer for their time and consideration. At every step in the process, be sure to express your appreciation. We strongly suggest that you handwrite a thank-you note immediately after every interview. If you're at an office, write the note while you're in the waiting area (this often allows you to see your competition) then hand it to the receptionist to distribute. If you're at a hotel, leave the note at the front desk or with the concierge (a tip wouldn't hurt).

When we insisted on writing thank-you's during one of our small group coaching classes, a former client told about her experience of being on the receiving end of a thank-you note. She had been a member of a panel interview. One candidate wrote a short note to each of the people on the panel. The receptionist handed them out and the interviewers were so impressed that they compared thank-you's. That candidate was hired. *Can you hear us now?*

Okay, but that's anecdotal evidence. Do you have any hard facts?

In a CareerBuilder 2013 survey, 58% of employer respondents stated that a thank-you note was important while 24% said it was VERY important.[8] A thank-you note is the sort of attention to detail that employers seek. It's an indicator of what you will be like after you're hired. It can make the difference between you and another candidate.

In a Monster.com piece by business writer Margot Carmichael Lester, she quotes Carol Galle, president and CEO of Special D Events: "I recently filled an open position for which I had two highly qualified candidates, but it was a thank-you note that made the difference. [One candidate] took the time to create a custom two-dimensional note card with our company's logo and a sincere, handwritten message of thanks. I want to hire people who genuinely want to work for my company, and it was clear from her effort that was the case."[9]

Have we made our point clearly enough? *"Can you hear us now?"*

So what about emailing a thank-you? Great! Send one via email too—it's a double whammy! We suggest that you send an email thank-you the day of your interview that will get to the interviewer's inbox AFTER 5 p.m. After five means your note will reach them after working hours or first thing in the morning. If they read it that same evening, you've just made an additional impression on them: You work even after-hours.

"Can you hear us now?"

Dressing for the Occasion

When I (Al) was initially asked to have an image consultant speak about interview attire where I direct a career ministry, I almost laughed out loud. *"What a silly notion,"* I thought to myself. When that class was packed with professional-looking people taking notes and asking questions, I was astounded. I'll never again discount the need for candidates to know the currently acceptable attire for interviews. For that reason, we asked Joanne Blake, an internationally recognized expert on interview attire, if we could share some of her thoughts by including her article, "Job Interview Tips," which follows:

You've got the interview, now how do you dress to clinch the job? Employers are looking for candidates that will be ambassadors for their organizations, and the image they portray plays a significant role in how they fare in the interview. You want to make it as easy as possible for them to visualize you representing their company in that role.

For the candidate, it's a good idea to do some research in advance to determine how people typically dress in the organization. Visiting the company website will give you a flavor of the company culture and provide clues in terms of how formal or informal employees dress. If the opportunity permits, visit the company during the lunch hour to determine how the majority show up. Then take your cue from the top 25% of the employee group. It's always best to be more formal than too casual.

The guiding principle in any business setting is to be clean, presentable, and reflective of the clients you will be serving. Your choice of interview attire should be guided by what is appropriate for your future clients, office environment, and work associates.

Interview Tips for Men and Women
- Ensure that your clothing fits properly and invest in alterations
- Make sure your clothing is clean and pressed the night before
- Carry a portfolio or briefcase with your resume and related documents
- Neatly manicured clean nails
- Polish your shoes
- Grooming (things your best friend won't tell you): audit yourself daily top to bottom. Proper oral and body hygiene is imperative. Synthetic fabrics often retain body odor and cigarette smoke
- Gum-chewing diminishes your professionalism

Interview Attire Tips for Women
- Options include: suits, tailored dress, or skirt, or dress pants worn with a jacket
- If a skirt is chosen then hosiery should be worn, especially in conservative industries and ensure you can sit comfortably
- Jewelry can be used to express your personal style; however, it should not be distracting (too large or noisy)
- Classic pumps, save the stilettos for personal time
- Neat, professional hairstyle
- Natural looking make-up and omit the perfume
- Avoid sheer clothing along with bare skin, cropped tops, and low necklines

Interview Attire Tips for Men
- Suit (navy or dark grey or subtle pattern)
- Long-sleeve shirt (white or light blue coordinated w/suit)
- Belt, tie, dark socks
- Leather shoes (not distressed)

- Minimal jewelry
- Neat, professional hairstyle (1 week prior is best)
- Minimal aftershave

Let's close this chapter on interviewing with a review. You don't want to blow your interviews, so we're including the perspective of a top talent acquisition manager, Children's Healthcare IT Recruiter Caron Atteberry, who offers 10 interview tips:

1. Always wear a suit to an interview unless asked to wear business casual. Women, wear closed-toe shoes. Men, wear ties.
2. Do not wear cologne/perfume/scented lotion to an interview. Cover up any tattoos. Men should take out all earrings; women should take out any additional earrings besides one pair.
3. Always bring a portfolio to the interview with you, take notes when the interviewer is telling you about the role and have a list of questions ready.
4. Practice a firm handshake. A weak handshake or a "girly" handshake (even for women) can start the interview off on the wrong foot.
5. Be nice to everyone you meet at the company when you go to interview. You are being interviewed by the receptionist too. They are the first to give their opinion of you if you are rude to them. They can easily email the person coming to meet you up front and let them know their experience.
6. If you are going to be late to an interview, call immediately. You should always leave enough time to arrive exactly 10 minutes early to an interview.
7. If you are sick, reschedule the interview. The person interviewing you does not want to catch what you have. It's always better to just cancel and reschedule for when you're feeling better.
8. Be prepared with plenty of examples of situations that showcase your relevant experience to the role.
9. Ask checking questions in the interview and don't be long-winded. If you're not sure if you answered the question properly, don't keep rambling. Ask, "Is that what you were looking for, or would you like me to expand?"
10. Follow up every interview with a thank you note/email.

Now go knock 'em dead!

Chapter 14: Alternatives to Traditional Jobs

"Entrepreneurship is one of the most liberating experiences you are ever likely to enjoy in life...Don't let anyone tell you that it's easy or that they can eliminate the risk for you. That's a lie!"

-Milo Pinckney

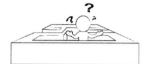

Your Next Job: Your Own?

Getting another "Job" is the immediate goal for most of us, but a full-time job like you previously had may no longer be in the cards. Luckily, it's not the only alternative.

Note: As we stated earlier, time is not on your side during job transition. If you have any inclination toward being a business owner, explore this possibility as soon as possible. A long transition period may make this option more difficult.

Many people would love to own their own small business. Unfortunately, few know how to go about it or even what sort of business to start. Small businesses can be classified three ways:
1. Franchises
2. Existing Enterprises
3. Start-Ups

Our idea of career coaching was, is, and will always be to teach clients about every option we can think of for them to get a job. Maybe considering an alternative to a traditional job is something that would make sense for you.

Franchise Ownership

Before we met Bill Williams of Axxiom Franchise Advisors, our idea of a franchise was fast food and only fast food—not that there's anything wrong with owning a food franchise. Bill is a franchise advisor and, boy, did he straighten our thinking out. Bill showed us that there is virtually no business type that's not franchise-able. Who knew?

We were conducting seminars at a local college and because it was important to introduce the attendees to many potentially different ways to make a living, we asked Bill to speak during part of those seminars. What he presented was enlightening and needs to be shared with you. A franchise might be a viable option for you. Bill offers some of his wisdom in his article, "Should Your Next Job Be Your Own?":

Fact: 72% of Americans dream of owning their own business.

Fact: Only 3% actually pursue the path of business ownership.

Fact: Job tenure in the United States is less than 2.8 years and growing shorter.

Fact: The staffing industry predicts boom times as employers turn to short-term contract staff. Employers will hire to meet business demands and cut contract staff as soon as the need decreases.

Fact: If you're over 50 and in that dreaded "Career Transition Zone," your chances of landing a new position at the same level of responsibility, at the same level of compensation, without changing location or industry, are nil.

What holds most people back from exploring having their own business are the three old ghosts:

1. **Fear**
   - Fear of failure
   - Fear of change
   - Fear of criticism
   - Fear of commitment
2. **Uncertainty**
   - Uncertainty over how to proceed
   - Uncertainty about whom to believe
   - Uncertainty about how to avoid being sold
3. **Doubt**
   - Doubt if you have what it takes to make it all work

The first step toward working for yourself is to be clear about WHY?

What do most people want from a business?
- More control of their lives and careers
- More flexibility in their day
- More balance between work & lifestyle
- Greater personal and professional challenges
- Retired, but still looking to continue a productive life or need supplemental retirement income
- Giving back to their community or making a difference in the lives of others
- To be their own boss

People really want <u>financial freedom</u>, which will provide all of the above.

So how do you reduce your risk? Invest in a franchise!

Buying a franchise includes the operating systems and a proven way of doing business. This allows the franchisee to concentrate on running the business. The franchisee receives support from the franchisor and a large network of franchisees that have been where he or she is going. You know what you're getting because of the information in the Franchise Disclosure Document and by speaking with the existing and former franchisees whose contact information must be provided. The infrastructure is defined, a product line is in place, and the marketing strategy has already been developed. The pooled resources of many franchisees allow strong promotional opportunities and group buying power.

What is a franchise?

A franchise is a group of systems that can be systematically applied by any franchisee in a step-by-step method that incorporates the systems into the operation of their franchise unit. The systems create a predictable way to produce results if the franchisee is willing to give the time and attention it requires to flourish. There are over 3,000 different franchise brands in 80 different categories!

Advantages of Owning a Franchise:
- Established product or service
- Proven Systems of Operations

- Initial Training/Ongoing support
- Experience of Franchisor
- Other franchisees in the system
- Understand your Customer
- Group purchasing power (Products and Advertising)
- Easier to get Quality Locations
- Start-up Assistance
- Assistance in Financing—(easier to obtain)
- Name recognition
- Vehicle for organized growth
- Typically, experience with the product or service is not required

How will a franchise advisor Help?

Franchise advisors provide help and guidance to people who want to own their own businesses so they can make an informed buying decision. Your franchise advisor should have a national team of advisors who help prospective buyers develop a plan for finding the right franchise opportunity. Your franchise advisor will conduct an interview to develop a personal profile that outlines your personal needs, business requirements, and financial goals. Then the franchise advisor will research and identify franchise opportunities that match your unique personal profile and present them to you for your consideration. He or she will introduce you directly to the appropriate franchise personnel. Your franchise advisor will also advise and coach you throughout your due diligence and decision-making process, but the final decision is always yours to make.

All at no cost to you!

Existing Business Purchase

Al: Unbeknownst to me, Art Lennig and I share a somewhat similar background. We were both manufacturer's reps at one point in our professional history, and he's from Michigan where I lived for a time. After meeting with him, I decided that his character and expertise were necessary additions to this book since there are many existing businesses for sale right under our noses every day. Finding something you love doing that already has a base of business as you walk in may be an option for you. (By God, Art, you'd better send me some Michigan pie cherries!) In his article, "Purchasing an Existing Business," Art offers a wealth of information:

Owning your own business gives you the opportunity to take control of your own destiny. We all know that. The questions are: How can I do that? Where do I start? Let's first consider the pros and cons of owning your own business.

Pros:

> ➢ You have an existing customer base generating revenue.
> ➢ You know the money the seller has been making historically before you buy.
> ➢ You have the seller's business model to follow.
> ➢ You receive training and support from the seller during a transition period.
> ➢ You can change things if you wish.

Cons:

> ➢ You will be paying a premium for goodwill based on the business' ability to generate profits.
> ➢ When you decide that you want to acquire an existing business, you should seek professional advice. Put together your advisory team. This should consist of the following:
>   - Your spouse/significant other (communication is very important)
>   - Attorney (Business Transaction Attorney—not the attorney who handles divorces)
>   - CPA (same as with attorney—one whose expertise is in business)
>   - Business Broker

It is your responsibility to educate your advisory team as to what your specific goal is: to buy a business. Keep in mind that these advisors work for you, the buyer. Don't allow them to derail your deal by dragging their feet or failing to meet your deadlines. Ask for advice, but never be afraid to do something different if you feel it is in your best interest—even if it means going against their advice. Many advisors have kept people from buying a business because it is safer to do nothing than to take the risk.

A business broker will help you do searches to find a business that meets your criteria, as well as help you understand the financial statements. He or she will also help you with the negotiations for the price and terms of a deal. After you have agreed on the basic terms of a deal, they will help you with the due diligence process and obtaining the financing. Business brokers have been through the process many times and will be able to offer you advice so you can avoid making very costly mistakes.

Navigating through the acquisition process can be equated with traveling through a maze. An experienced business broker has been through that maze before and can anticipate what obstacles will come up before they become problems. He or she will guide you around those obstacles and keep your deal on track and moving forward.

Buying a business can be a long process. You want to be comfortable with the broker you use. When choosing a business broker, here's what you need to know:
- ➤ How long have they been doing this?
- ➤ Have they represented Buyers before or do they only represent Sellers?
- ➤ Does he or she have a network of other brokers with whom they share listings/information?
- ➤ What is his or her background/experience?
- ➤ Does the broker understand your personal goals and objectives?
- ➤ What does your gut say?

Once you make the decision to buy a business, be focused. Don't waste your time or your broker's time. Be responsive to his or her requests. When you find a business you like, move forward. The more you like the business, the more focused you need to become. Good businesses will not last on the market. Many buyers have lost out on purchasing a good business because they could not make the decision to make an offer. They got stuck in the analysis phase. Follow your broker's advice and you should reach your goal.

Starting From Scratch

Many people have pet business ideas that they've been stewing over. For some of us, the pot has been simmering for years. As with franchises and existing businesses, a start-up needs careful consideration, much research, a sound business plan, and enough money to sustain you until it attains profitability.

As is the case in every business (as well as in a traditional job search) you'll need a recognizable brand, something that differentiates you from your competition. Your idea may seem original or unique to you, but is that originality understandable to your potential customers, and are they willing to buy into the difference?

Your ongoing tasks will include establishing a marketing campaign, finding adequate financing, developing a relationship with suppliers, and hiring the right employees. All the fundamentals of business must be in place and maintained, not to mention keeping tabs on everything.

ChancesE.com offers both positives and negatives on getting a new venture going. "[S]tarting a business from scratch," they say, "gives the person the flexibility to create the business model without having to answer to anyone."[1] On the other side of the coin, they warn, "Most new businesses fail, meaning that the risk in starting a new business is high. There is also a lot of added pressure involved with starting a new business due to having to deal with so many unforeseen factors. New businesses can also cost more than existing businesses because of the need to spend money on advertising and other ways to notify people of your new business[1]." That's pretty straightforward.

Regarding finance and failure, many bankers are highly skeptical of new businesses because of their high failure rate. Getting financing from lending institutions, including the bank you may have done business with for years, is usually more difficult than buying a franchise or an existing business.

However, not all new enterprises require a large investment. An online business is one such option. Still, you must seriously consider how you'll move customers who are unaware of your existance to your Website and then get them to actually part with their money. Your potential client base may be worldwide, but your competition could be out of this world, too.

Dee Doanes has started businesses from scratch and made them successful. She is adept at both traditional and social media marketing for business and personal promotion. We think you'll find the wisdom she offers in her article, "Two Things I Know About Being an Entrepreneur," to be worthwhile:

1. Chose a Philosophy about Life That Translates Well for Business

I've been an entrepreneur most of my life. It's something that comes naturally to me, and I love being a businesswoman. There have been ups and downs, and at times running a business can be extremely difficult, but I have persevered.

My philosophy is to be strong and flexible, which has allowed my businesses to grow. This is based on the teachings of Bruce Lee, one of my favorite philosophers. Yes, that's right, martial artist and actor Bruce Lee was a great philosopher. This is his quote that I use to run my life and business: *You must be shapeless, formless, like water. When you pour water in a cup, it becomes the cup. When you pour water in a bottle, it becomes the bottle. When you pour water in a teapot, it becomes the teapot. Water can drip and it can crash. Become like water, my friend.* This is useful advice for all entrepreneurs. Entrepreneurs are water. We have to be flexible and take the shape of many different things to survive the changing business trends and be able to compete in an unstable economy. So as I continue my path as an entrepreneur, I will always be like water.

2. Know When To Fire Clients

When first starting out, many small business owners take on as many clients as possible and charge cheap rates. This may be necessary to get testimonials and build a client list. But there comes a time when firing clients is necessary to thrive in a very competitive marketplace. As a business owner, you have to make enough of a profit to take care of operational expenses and to expand.

I started in public relations. After building my reputation, I began charging rates that were in line with my industry peers. At first I was scared that I would go out of business. But I quickly found new clients, didn't have to take on as many clients, and the bonus was making more money! I highly recommend that all new business owners do this.

Like water, enjoy taking on the many shapes and forms that your own business allows you to become.

Another alternative to traditional employment is multi-level marketing. It's not for everyone, but it might be perfect for you. We know a number of individuals who have been successful with these businesses as a second career.

Realtor, author, and speaker Peter Gibson, in his article, "Take Your Career to Another Level—with Multi-Level," offers his thoughts on multi-level marketing:

Multi-level marketing or network marketing. Is it a viable income option? It is. But are you strong-willed enough to maintain the posture necessary to succeed in it?

What do I mean by posture? Well, this industry really does create millionaires. It gave my wife and me a very secure financial foundation. With over eighteen years of experience with one company and as one of the top distributors for that company, I can confirm that an executive-level lifestyle is attainable.

Let's get back to posture. How you position and market yourself, the network marketing industry, and the products or services you represent are critical. You can rarely master any job, or business, unless you first master yourself and your mind. The mental position, posture, or attitude you hold toward this industry dictates how well you will do. Hold tight to the fact that multi-level, or network marketing, is a respectable business model, a model that is rapidly embraced by start-up companies with a widget to distribute, but a model not as easily grasped by the majority of people recruited to distribute that widget.

The discouraging fact is that few people make the six- (and seven-) figure incomes industry leaders tout, a tactic we disagree with. Good leaders present the facts. Coaching and training is their thing, not parading around displaying bling. If you enroll in this business, find a leader to coach you. For him or her to do that, you have to stand out as a team player who warrants his time; show him or her that you want to build and lead a team, too.

It's easy to enroll in this business and just as easy to quit. If you avoid the fundamentals or let them overwhelm you, you will likely wind up quitting. This business has a very high fall-out rate.

What are the fundamentals? The same ones you have to apply in any job or business. Position your multi-level (network) marketing career in your mind the same way an entrepreneur would: as a business that may take 3 to 5 years to build to the income level you want. Then, continually study the industry, your products, and the people to whom you intend to market them. Get clear—really clear—about what you will say to prospects to recruit them as marketing partners or customers in your network. I insisted that my team had a clear, naturally flowing conversational style "script" that created high interest in the business option first and in becoming a customer second. Sure, you can book appointments, rooms, or home parties to present the products, but only a bold posture that invites recruits will earn you the six-figure income.

The bottom line? You have to have system, a process that leads people through the ubiquitous "pipeline." Know what to say, how to find enough people to say it to, and how to track and discipline the willpower needed to call, meet, network, share, present, recruit, and retail until you reach your goals. Sounds simple, but it's not as simple to do. You've got to be hungry! However, reach your goals, and your income will then come less from your efforts and more from the efforts of those on your team. Do not chill out when you get to this point! Help your team do what you did.

So, you can see that the multi-level network marketing industry demands the same work ethic as any other career. It's a different mindset because you are your own boss. You determine your level of income and your direction. Surely, this outweighs the risks of going back to a job track that dictates your direction. Change tracks. Change your posture. Consider this industry as a viable income option. Let multi-level take you to another level!

Stringers

Atlanta's newspaper, the *Atlanta Journal-Constitution,* has a section called The Vent. Unlike its Letters to the Editor page, where a person's name and city are printed, individuals writing a Vent are totally anonymous. Any Joe or Jane Blow can submit something he or she wants to vent about, and it might be published. As you might expect, there are some doozies!

For example, recently there has been talk of raising the minimum wage. The outrage over the possibility of a pay increase for the lowest of the low earners has been amazing.

Al: My favorite example of how out of touch much of the population is about the reality of the working poor trying to make ends meet was expressed in the following Vent, in which this Mensa candidate wrote, *"If you're not making enough at your minimum wage job, just get another one."*

We won't get into a huge discussion about the socioeconomic ramifications, but let's do some simple math to demonstrate how hard it would be to survive, much less get ahead, by having to string jobs together. Minimum wage in most of the USA is $7.25 per hour. If working a full forty hours, the employee would make a whopping $290 per week (before taxes). A second job might bring in an additional $145 per week for a grand total of $435, or a lavish annual salary of $22,620. That's working 60 hours per week. By the way, the federal poverty line is an annual income of $23,550 for a family of four.[2]

Of course, we're making a number of assumptions here. Changing any of them could alter the equation quite a bit. For the sake of argument, here's what the Vent writer assumes a minimum wage worker could easily do:

- Get a second, part-time minimum wage job in the first place
- Travel from one job to the other seamlessly
- Get both employers to work with the employee's work schedules
- Not get sick or be forced to miss time for other reasons
- Manage to get a full 60 hours per week
- Work 60 hours per week every week of the year

Unfortunately, once a person enters the "stringer" way of life, it is virtually impossible to get out of it since survival is their driving force. There's no time for school, no time for certifications, no time for training, no time to properly raise children who are likely destined to be stuck in the same employment track.

Maybe the Vent's author should spend a year walking in the worn-out shoes of a stringer before assuming that minimum wage workers have it so easy.

The Trades

We've heard for years how the only way to get into the middle class was to get a degree. And the only way to advance is to get an *advanced* degree. No degree, no hope! As ESPN's GameDay co-host Lee Corso might say, "Not so fast, my friend!"

CNN Money printed an article by higher education editor Jon Marcus of *The Hechinger Report*, an independent education news organization, which said that people who graduated with an associate degree were making 15% **more** than those who recently graduated with a bachelor's degree from a four-year college.

Most of us *can't do stuff.*

Mr. Marcus cited a Georgetown University report in which nearly 30% of Americans with an associate degree were said to make more money than those with a bachelor's degree.[3] Still, those with four-year degrees seem to eventually surpass those with technical degrees. Some have dubbed this the "C-Factor" and the "L-Factor," meaning that people with certificates and licenses can parlay practical knowledge and ability into a comfortable living. These certificates and licenses are not limited to the trades. They also include technology.

Chances are good that we will always need electricians, plumbers, masons, and other tradespeople. Many of us would rather *write a check* than attempt to do such work ourselves. Indeed, many of us MUST hire a tradesperson since we're incapable of properly running wiring, sweating a plumbing joint, floating drywall, laying brick, etc. Seldom does the need for tradespeople completely go into recession. At the same time, we must ask ourselves if our bodies will continue to allow us to practice these trades in later life.

In the final analysis, entering the trades can be a rewarding career, but this isn't for everyone. A person can no doubt make a fine living doing this sort of work, but we would still recommend that persons in one of these trades protect themselves from the inevitable ravages of time by continuing to further their education and parlay their combination of experience and education from subcontracting or laboring into becoming a contractor who supervises a variety of tradespeople.

Regarding certifications and licenses in general, we believe it's incumbent upon those in this category to highlight those attributes prominently on all their traditional and social sites, which MUST be updated on a regular basis and reflect the ever-changing terminology of the day.

Government

Everyone has strengths and weaknesses. Knowing how to get government jobs may be our most glaring weakness. Virtually none of the methodology we espouse will work for getting a government position. The extent of our knowledge might end with suggesting you go to USAJobs.org;[4] which is an excellent source for finding available positions with government agencies.

Whereas we tend to favor the use of bullet points, people with in-depth knowledge on how to get a government job say that long paragraphs are what they require. Our goal is to shorten your time in transition, while getting an answer for a government position can take months longer than in the private sector.

We have previously quoted Nancy Collamer, a career coach, speaker, and author who writes a weekly column about careers and volunteering for PBS and Forbes.com. Here we present an abreviated version of her thoughts on obtaining work in the public sector from her *Forbes* article entitled, "5 Tips for Getting a Government Job,"[5] in which she suggests the following:

1. Acquaint yourself with the landscape by uncovering what's out there, such as these sources sponsored by the Partnership for Public Service:
   a. The Best Places to Work in the Federal Government
   b. Makingthedifference.org
2. Look for openings on the right sites
   a. USAJobs.org
3. Engage your network (Yeah! Some of our advice applies here too!)
   a. Who do you know that works for the government and can give you insight?
   b. Use some of the LinkedIn government groups
4. Reformat your resume (We told you the government was different!)
   a. Makingthedifference.org
5. Be patient
   a. 80-105 days is typical (that's only the average)

Note: We advise reading her entire article on this subject.

Catching the Next Wave

Almost every generation seems to have an exciting new wave of employment that is about to crest. The greatest challenge might be to recognize the ones that will allow you to ride high as opposed to having the break line of its bowl come crashing down on your head. You need to be aware of industries that are creating a swell or at least offering the greatest potential for growth.

What you don't want to do is to get into (or remain in) industries that are dying or on their last legs. It wasn't that long ago that selling buggy whips or typewriters, becoming a switchboard or an elevator operator were viable positions. And while farriers can still make a decent living, blacksmithing is rather self-limiting. Besides, making a living with your head below your posterior leaves a lot to be desired for most of us.

And it's not only individuals who make career choices that eventually lead to their own demise. Kodak is a prime example of a company that was once king of an industry but refused to see the future. As late as 1976, Kodak commanded 90% of film sales and 85% of camera sales in the United States that year.[6] And though they pioneered the digital-imaging industry, today they struggle for market share largely because they believed more in their marketing prowess and name than in technology and the desires of their customers.

If you're old enough to have seen the movie, *The Graduate,* you probably remember the advice a neighbor gave to young Benjamin Braddock: "I want to say one word to you, just one word. Are you listening? *Plastics.*"[7] Back in the '60s, plastics was the wave of the future. Twenty years later, personal computing was the wave that many sharp entrepreneurs rode all the way to the software and dot.com phenomenon of the 1990s. And as recently as 2008, the housing and real estate market was the place to be.[8]

There is potential for the so-called "green industries" to become our next wave depending on whether the political left and right can get their heads out of their respective derrieres. While this is neither an endorsement nor condemnation of either view, we wonder if the two sides will ever see the potential for a capitalistic tsunami.

Let's say for the moment that the left is correct and global warming is real. Wouldn't it be wiser for the right to create businesses that cater to those fears? And even if the left is dead wrong, the right could be selling things that placate the Greenies. And if the right's position is wrong and global warming is real, they would have positioned themselves as industry leaders as opposed to fighting against that possibility in the same way that Kodak refused to build a franchise outside of film? In either case, Green may be that next wave.

To that end, we offer the perspective of "Green Expert" Holly Henderson in her article, "Green Dimension":

> When making any decision from the purchase of athletic shoes to a career choice, one should consider the "triple bottom line" impacts— economic, social, and environmental. Ideally, these three dimensions would be weighed equally in decision-making. All too often, companies and individuals place more emphasis on the economics.
>
> As one of my mentors, Ray Anderson, said, *"There is no more strategic issue for a company, or any organization, than its ultimate purpose. For those who think business exists to make a profit, I suggest they think again. Business makes a profit to exist. Surely it must exist for some higher, nobler purpose than that."* (Ray is the founder of Interface

Carpet, which is known for industrial ecology and sustainability for business.)

I'd extend Ray's quote beyond organizations to each individual's goal being something that has a purpose. The good news is that being green can be integrated into any profession and make you green (money) in the process. Not only do environmental considerations matter, they can give you the edge both in current and future careers.

ECO-EMERGING
As Patti Prairie, CEO of Brighter Planet, writes, "Against a backdrop of rather tepid near-term macroeconomic projections, market forecasters predict ongoing growth rates well into the double digits for corporate sustainability services, a market already valued in the billions of dollars. Sustainability is now big business in the U.S., and the way it evolves and matures over coming years will shape the way we all do business of any kind."

Across all sectors, environmental aspects are applied in all fields from accounting to technology and everything in between. In fact, for entities such as Ford and Starbucks, sustainability has become so critical that a relatively new position has emerged in these pioneering corporations called the CSO or Corporate Sustainability Officer. This leader is responsible for the corporation's environmental footprint and typically reports directly to the CEO or Board of Directors.

For the outlook on a myriad of green jobs, check out the U.S. Department of Labor's Bureau of Labor Statistics, where you'll find helpful articles on various green job opportunities, credentials, and associated wages: http://www.bls.gov/green/greencareers.htm#articles.

KEY EMERALD TRENDS
Three trends in sustainability include life cycle, metrics, and transparency. Life cycle considers key impacts of a product and associated processes from cradle to grave, including but not limited to raw material extraction and transportation. Metrics get back to the old adage "You can't manage what you don't measure," so measuring energy and water are important factors. Transparency asks manufacturers and businesses to reveal their ingredients and supply-chain practices.

When companies integrate some of these key trends, positive results follow. In the *State of Green Business 2013 Report*, which includes data on 1,600 companies worldwide, as well as on the U.S.-based S&P 500, Joel Makeover and the editors of GreenBiz.com cited these statistics: "The number of S&P 500 companies reporting on profits from environmental activities rocketed by 61% over five years. Their environmental R&D more than doubled, despite economic gloom."

TIPS FOR GREENING YOUR CAREER
- **Do your research** with industry and professional green associations
  Examples:
  Apparel: http://www.apparelcoalition.org/
  Law: http://www.lfsnetwork.org/
  Spa: http://greenspanetwork.org/
- **Speak the lingo**—study green terms and integrate them into your language
- **Narrow your search** with green-specific Web sites such as:
  Green Jobs Network: http://www.greenjobs.net/
  Green Careers Guide: http://www.greencareersguide.com/
  Grist: http://www.grist.org/
  Indeed: http://www.indeed.com/Green-jobs
  (Also, Real Simple Syndication (RSS) feeds and aggregators can narrow job searches and provide more efficient, productive results.)
- **Engage the experts**—Did you know there are green coaches and recruiters?
  Green Coach: http://www.greencareercentral.com
  Green Recruiter: http://www.footprinttalent.com
- **Be authentic**—consider green details such as recycled paper and soy-based inks for your paper resume or opt for electronic communications.

Maybe a college or university in a southern city could adopt Green Wave as its nickname. How about Tulane University? What, it's already taken? Darn! Looks like we may need a new surfboard. Or maybe just Mrs. Robinson. Or better yet, Elaine Robinson!

Chapter 15: Future Mountains to Climb

By failing to prepare,
you are preparing to fail"
-Benjamin Franklin

Where have we been?

Possibly the best way to determine where we will go is to examine where we were and the trails we chose to get to where we are at this moment. So let's work our way backwards. You have a new job; you are no longer in job transition. Besides the insights in this book, what got you here?

- Knowledge of You (assessment)
- An Expansive List of Contacts
- A Network of Executives
- A Meaningful Resume
- Social Media Positioning
- A Marketable Brand
- Awareness of Where Jobs are Hidden
- Ability to Maximize Your Search Efforts
- Skill to Attract and Keep People's Attention
- Know-how to Set up Google Alerts
- Extensive Interview Training

You've accomplished a lot!

How much of the above list did you have before you got started? What's more, how many people do you know who still believe that the best way to get a job is by using only the traditional methods (like you once did)? Knowing what you know now, if you were to lose your job again, aren't you more confident that you'd have a shorter period of transition than all the people who haven't yet learned the lessons you have? Will your next period of transition likely be shorter than your current one?

What can we expect?

As Thomas Friedman says in his book, *The World is Flat*, "Since lifetime employment is a form of fat that a flat world simply cannot sustain any longer, *compassionate flatism* seeks to focus its energy on how local government and business can enhance every worker's lifetime employability."[1]

Here's what we know about the new, flatter world of employment:

- Shorter-term Employment (2.4 years average)
- Reduced or Eliminated Benefits
- A "1099 Future"
- Multiple Job Transitions

What can you do now to <u>NOT</u> go through this again?

"It's Looking More And More Likely That Peyton Manning Is Finished"[2]

How about you? Before you read this book is that what you were made to feel? Like the experts said Peyton Manning was in 2011, were you thinking the following about yourself:

- Washed up!
- A has-been!
- Can't cut the mustard!
- The game is over!
- Finished!

Or, like Manning's record-breaking 2013 season has shown, do you still...

"Deserve Your Own Page in the Record Book?"[3]

Maybe, just maybe:

"The reports of your death have been greatly exaggerated too."

—Mark Twain (with apologies from Al & Jeff)

Do you want THAT to happen again? Okay, what are you going to do about it?

You've learned valuable lessons and made priceless new contacts, but how many acquaintances have you had during your life whose camaraderie has not been maintained? Will your new network of contacts and decision-makers go the way of those relationships, or do you now see the value of keeping those new associates close?

You've already invested much energy in your marketing campaign, so let's take advantage of that hard work. People change jobs all the time, new positions open up, and others disappear regularly. Let's prepare now for those next opportunities. And the only way to be ready is to maintain and strengthen the relationships you've made.

Hopefully you've become more organized during this process. Your contact-management skills have been honed and you've learned how to stay in contact with people without becoming a pest. Let's put a plan into effect NOW that continues the pattern you've already set into motion.

You've worked with an online calendar to set appointments and keep in touch with contacts, including executives. Wouldn't it make sense to continue doing that? The problem is that if you don't have strict discipline, this effort will fail. And when you find yourself in transition again (and the odds say it's almost a sure thing that you WILL have to look for another job) you'll have to go through this entire process from step 1 all over again—and THAT is work. And it's costly work at that!

You aren't the only one whose employment status is likely to change either. According to a 2009 Execunet survey reported by John Zappe, executive tenure in a position declined steadily between 2005 and 2008 to 2.3 years,[4] a 15% decline! (Some of those changes may have been voluntary.) Being able to help others—which includes your executive contacts—certainly puts you in position to receive further help in the future should you need it.

We believe that once a week (every week) you should schedule an hour or so to forward your Google Alerts to the appropriate contacts. Do it by blind copy so you don't have to send out a gazillion individual emails. If you are receiving job or industry alerts, send them on to people who are in that line of work. If the information is valuable, you will never be seen as a spammer. In fact, you'll be viewed as a reliable source of information—and you'll stay in the mind of each of these contacts.

Schedule to send an email (again by blind copy) to all your other contacts with a short note of hello and an offer to help them should they ever need it. This only has to be done quarterly for you to stay on the mind of those contacts. And if you have alerts set up for specific individuals, how much time would it take to send a quick note saying, "I saw that your daughter got married", "I noticed that you took a new job", "Hey, I see that you spoke at a convention"? Think about the potential returns you might get from such a miniscule investment?

Mighty Morphin' Power?
Speaking of investments, have you ever heard someone say that they've "reinvented" themselves, or that you should? What they're suggesting is that you morph from one profession to another. That's a risky investment if we've ever heard one. But it can be done.

Bob Zartarian is a prime example of someone who has reinvented himself many times throughout his professional career. From internal sales in industrial instrumentation to manufacturing in the food service industry to telecommunications to mortgage lending, Bob has successfully morphed again and again. You may feel the need to do so, as well. In his article, "MORPH or DIE," Bob suggests that morphing is not only desirable in some cases but a necessity:

Morph or die sounds grim doesn't it? Yet that's what the unemployed and underemployed have been facing for a decade, or even longer.

With the advent of increasing use of technology in the workplace, those who didn't use a computer extensively in high school are being left behind. And that applies equally to blue collar, white collar and executives, as well. Of course the deep recession didn't help matters any. And the 1099 consultant and part-time economies that have emerged have made it even more difficult for the unemployed and underemployed to hold their families together.

Not a pretty picture, is it? But does it have to be that way? You guessed it, I don't think so.

Just over seven years ago I received an offer for my telecommunications business. I was past retirement age, had turned around that business (which was destroyed on 9/11), and was fighting a patent lawsuit that had been hanging over my head for four years. It was a tough decision. If I lost the patent suit I'd have nothing, but if I won, my business would be worth substantially more. After thinking about depositions and thousands of dollars more in legal expenses, I retired. (We won the patent suit—alas, I didn't profit by that.)

Ahhh, retirement.

The thrill of retirement lasted three weeks. Boredom set in. I started looking for things to do. My peers played golf—that wasn't for me. Volunteering, while noble, didn't give me the satisfaction I had gotten from paid work. Something was missing, and that was it. I needed to work. I needed work for the sake of my family, my health, and my self-esteem.

Elated with my discovery, I set out to find an opportunity to use the skills I had learned over the years, skills that would benefit my family and others and let me become a productive member of society again.

Whoa, not so fast. Hiring Managers were thirty years younger than I was. My resume was entered online—no response, ever. Jobs I could get were not appropriate for a guy nearing 67. Then it hit me: MORPH!

That dire saying (Morph or Die) had been above my desk for nearly 15 years. I heeded it when I had my business, and it worked. Now it came in handy again. In late 2006 the financial services industry was hot, but the barriers to entry were high. The real estate industry was booming, but you needed an established network. Then it hit me: Mortgages. No barrier to entry, high school diploma only. All you had to be able to do was prove you were still breathing. Ads everywhere for loan officers.

While I had built companies from the ground up for my family, myself, and my employers, I'd never sold anything, ever. This is where the MORPH comes in. I felt I had to change or be miserable and bring my family along with me. After four interviews I was hired just before Christmas to start in early January. Doubt set in. Could I do this? What do I have to do? I'd be trained in the business and in telephone sales. My employer provided leads. I can do this. I will do this.

I did it. Then the financial crisis hit and we went from 35 loan officers to 3. I survived. Business dried up, the phone didn't ring, and my colleagues took other jobs (they were half my age). Time to MORPH again.

I moved to another company, built a referral business, got my national and state licenses when that became a requirement and I'm now thriving again. I brought four others to my company last year. All had experience in mortgage lending but from years of being beaten down had lost their spirit.

They're back and you can be too.

You may find yourself in a situation where you need to call an audible (deviate from your original plan). Just ask Peyton Manning.

OMAHA! OMAHA!

Future Climbs

We suggest that you always keep one eye open for a new and better position. Unfortunately, industries tend to see no farther than their next earnings report, which precludes loyalty to any employee. They write the rules we must play by. So if you're going to play the game, you must take the game to them:

- ✓ Keep looking
- ✓ Continuously refine your skills
- ✓ Maintain existing contacts and expand your base of contacts
- ✓ Prepare for your next job now!

> *"I skate where the puck is going to be,*
> *not where it has been."*
> -Wayne Gretzky

We want to skate where the puck is going to be because the world has become a flatter place.

Where will you choose to skate? Let us know.

Warmest regards,

Al & Jeff

Referenced Experts:

Chapter 1:   One Size Fits All?!?
[1]Foxsports.com, February 2, 2014, Andy Nesbitt, *How Much Money Did Peyton Manning Raise by Yelling Omaha! In the Super Bowl?*, http://msn.foxsports.com/buzzer/story/peyton-manning-omaha-charity-super-bowl-xlviii-020214 (p.2)

Chapter 2:   State of the Job Market
[1]Plato (c. 427-347 BC) (p.7)

[2]National Journal, August 21, 2013, Brian Resnick, *Unemployed Less Likely to Receive Kidney Transplants,* http://news.yahoo.com/unemployed-less-likely-receive-kidney-transplants-125213185.html (p.8)

[3]Michael Thurmond, Keynote address Roswell United Methodist Church Career Ministry, 2011 (p. 9)

[4]United States department of Labor, Bureau of Labor Statistics, October 2013, http://data.bls.gov/timeseries/LNS14000000 (p. 9)

[5]United States department of Labor, Bureau of Labor Statistics, November 8, 2013 http://www.bls.gov/news.release/empsit.nr0.htm (p. 9)

[6]http://www.bls.gov/news.release/pdf/empsit.pdf (p.10)

[7] Yahoo News, December 7, 2011, Richard Johnson, *Actual Unemployment Rate Soars Above 25 Percent,* http://news.yahoo.com/actual-unemployment-rate-soars-above-25-percent-200400654.html (p.10)

[8] Trading Economics, Joana Taborda http://www.tradingeconomics.com/euro-area/unemployment-rateNew   York Daily News, April 30, 2013,

[9]Reuters, *Recent U.S. College graduates disillusioned, more than 40% unemployed: poll*
http://www.nydailynews.com/news/national/college-grads-disillusioned-unemployed-poll-article-1.1331346 (p.10)

[10]CNN Money, August 8, 2011, Annalyn Chensky, *America's Job Crisis,*
http://money.cnn.com/2011/08/08/news/economy/jobs_unemployment_rate/ (p. 11)

[11]Yahoo Shine, October 23, 2012, From Reader's Digest Magazine, quoting Cynthia Shapiro
http://shine.yahoo.com/work-money/13-things-hr-wont-tell-150000992.html (p.11)

[12]Recruiter.com, November 26, 2012, Joshua Bjerke, *Job Seekers: Criminal records easier Hires Than Extended Unemployed,*
http://www.recruiter.com/i/job-seekers-criminal-records-easier-hires-than-extended-unemployment/ (p.11)

[13]Time Business & Money, August 20, 2013, Christopher Mathews, *Long Term Unemployment: A Weak Link in a Fragile Recovery*
http://business.time.com/2013/08/20/long-term-unemployment-a-weak-link-in-a-fragile-recovery/ (p.11)

[14]Atlanta Journal-Constitution, April 22, 2012, Michael E. Kanell, *Stuck in a cycle of joblessness* (p.11)

[15]Wall Street Journal, January 18, 2012, Sara Murrya and Cameron McWhirter, *Long Term Unemployment Ripples Through One Town,*
http://online.wsj.com/news/articles/SB10001424052970204319004577084843074586190 (p.11-12)

[16]New York Times, October 17, 2013, Paul Krugman, *The Damage Done,*
http://www.nytimes.com/2013/10/18/opinion/krugman-the-damage-done.html (p. 12)

[17]Gallop Economy, September 5, 2013, Jenny Marlar, *U.S. Payroll to Population Rate Drops to 43.7% in August,*

http://www.gallup.com/poll/164273/payroll-population-rate-drops-august.aspx (p.12)

[18]Abby Kohut, *Absolutely Abby's 101 Job Search Secrets,* http://www.absolutelyabby.com/ (p. 14)

[19]CNN Money, June 10, 2009, Jessica Dickler, *The Hidden Job Market,* http://money.cnn.com/2009/06/09/news/economy/hidden_jobs/ (p. 15)

Chapter 3:   Get ready, Get Set...
Associations: [1] http://www.weddles.com/associations/ (p. 22)

Attributes: [2]http://www.missouristate.edu/assets/bms/AttributeComp.pdf (p.22)

[3]LinkedIn Contact Management: [3]http://contacts.linkedin.com (p.26)

[5]Atlanta Journal-Constitution, April 21, 2010, Jay Bookman, *Do jobless checks subsidize laziness? Research Shows,* http://blogs.ajc.com/jay-bookman-blog/2010/04/21/do-jobless-checks-subsidize-laziness-research-shows/ (p. 33)

Chapter 4:   Mental, Physical & Fiscal Fitness
[1]"The Paradox of Thrift"   Attributed to John Maynard Keynes; The General Theory of Employment, Interest and Money, 1936. Term adapted by Al Smith to demonstrate why some people in job transition should invest in themselves or a job coach. (p. 35)

Chapter 5:   Keywords and Boolean Searches
[1]From Shakespeare's *Romeo and Juliet,* circa 1600 (p. 51)

[2]CNN Money, June 10, 2009, Jessica Dickler, *The Hidden Job Market,* http://money.cnn.com/2009/06/09/news/economy/hidden_jobs/ (p. 52)

[3]Search Engine Watch, June 20, 2013, Jessica Lee, *No. 1 Position in Google Gets 33% of Search Traffic*

http://searchenginewatch.com/article/2276184/No.-1-Position-in-Google-Gets-33-of-Search-Traffic-Study (p. 57)

Chapter 6:   Personal Branding
[1]From: *Ol' Man River, 1927,* Jerome Kern & Oscar Hammerstein II (p. 64)

[2]The American Marketing Association (AMA), Brand Management Fundamentals, http://www.ana.net/training/course/id/bmf (p. 65)

[3]Fast Company Magazine, August 31, 1997, *The Brand Called You,* http://www.fastcompany.com/28905/brand-called-you (p. 69)

[4]Absolute Abby's *Top 12 Interview Questions Exposed,* Abby Kohut, http://staffingsymphony.3dcartstores.com/book-bundle.html (p. 72)

[5]My Point...and I do have one... Ellen DeGeneres, http://www.goodreads.com/book/show/71979.My_Point_And_I_Do_Have_One (p. 72)

[6]Lehigh University Career Services http://careerservices.sites.lehigh.edu/view_keyword.php?keyword_id=195 (p. 73)

[7]New York Times, March 23, 2002, Judith Rehak, *Tylenol Made a Hero of Johnson & Johnson: The Recall that Started it All* http://www.nytimes.com/2002/03/23/your-money/23iht-mjj_ed3_.html (p. 74)

[8]Forbes, February 4, 2013, Nancy Collamer, *The Perfect Elevator Pitch to Land a Job* http://www.forbes.com/sites/nextavenue/2013/02/04/the-perfect-elevator-pitch-to-land-a-job/ (p. 78)

Chapter 7:   Targeting
[1]LinkedIn Job Seeker Tips, Lisa Rangel, from CareerXRoads 2012 study http://learn.linkedin.com/jobseeker/page-how-to-build-target-company-list.html (p. 82)

[2]CareerXroads, February 16, 2012, Gerry Crispen and Mark Mehler, *2012 Sources of Hire* http://www.slideshare.net/gerrycrispin/2012-careerxroads-source-of-hire-channels-of-influence (p. 83)

[3]SHRM, Eliza Jacobson, *Examining the Relationship Between Turnover, Average Tenure, HR Investments* http://www.shrm.org/Research/benchmarks/Documents/Turnover%20by%20Type_FINAL.pdf (p. 84)

[4]Execunet, John Zappe, May 28, 2009, *Survey Says Executive Tenure Shortening* http://www.ere.net/2009/05/28/survey-says-executive-tenure-shortening/ (p. 84)

[5]New York Times, January 27, 2013, Nelson D. Schwartz, *In Hiring, A Friend in Need is a Prospect, Indeed* http://www.nytimes.com/2013/01/28/business/employers-increasingly-rely-on-internal-referrals-in-hiring.html?src=me&ref=general&_r=2& (p. 85)

Chapter 8:   Assembling the Puzzle

[1]Recruiter.com, Joshua Bjerke, November 6, 2012 http://www.recruiter.com/i/job-seekers-criminal-records-easier-hires-than-extended-unemployment/ (p. 89)

[2]Bloomberg News, May 3, 2013 http://www.bloomberg.com/news/2013-05-03/long-term-unemployment-is-turning-jobless-into-pariahs.html (p. 89)

[3]Cynthia Shapiro, Corporate Confidential http://www.cynthiashapiro.com/CCBookCareer.php4 (p. 89)

[4]Ruthie Powell, Founder and creator of *The Ruthie's List*, as stated at the Career Ministry of the Holy Spirit Catholic Church, Thursday, August 1, 2013 http://ruthieslist.org/ (p. 90)

[5]The Daily Muse, November 22, 2013, Adrian Granzella Larssen, *The 5 Biggest Resume Debates Among Recruiters-Finally Answered,* http://www.thedailymuse.com/job-search/the-5-biggest-resume-debates-among-recruiters-finally-answered/ (p. 97)

[6]Mashable, October 15, 2011, Erica Swallow, *4 Simple Tools for Creating an Infographic Resume*[5], http://mashable.com/2011/10/15/infographic-resume-apps/ (p. 99)

[7]Time Business & Money, June 29, 2012, Victor Lucherson, *Catch an Employer's Attention with a Video Resume* http://business.time.com/2012/06/29/catch-an-employers-attention-with-a-video-resume/ (p. 100)

[8]Career Builder, July 2013, *New CareerBuilder Study Reveals Nine Lessons for Job Seekers and Recruiters That May Surprise You* http://www.careerbuilder.com/share/aboutus/pressreleasesdetail.aspx?sd=10%2f17%2f2013&siteid=cbpr&sc_cmp1=cb_pr785_&id=pr785&ed=12%2f31%2f2013 (p. 102)

Chapter 11: Maximizing Your Effectiveness

[1]Donna Svie, Avid Careerist, June 17, 2013 http://www.avidcareerist.com/2013/06/17/linkedin-endorsements-search-results-serp/?goback=%2Egde_146161_member_274943728#%21 (p. 149)

[2]Daily Koz, John "gravlax" Webb, May 6, 2013 http://www.dailykos.com/story/2013/05/06/1207180/-Purple-Squirrels-and-Unemployment# (p. 157)

[3]Susan Adams, Forbes, June 7, 2011, *Networking Is Still The Best Way To Find A Job, Survey Says* http://www.forbes.com/sites/susanadams/2011/06/07/networking-is-still-the-best-way-to-find-a-job-survey-says/ (p. 161)

[4]Allison Green, *Ask the Manager*, March 14, 2011 http://www.askamanager.org/2011/03/have-you-ever-gotten-a-job-from-a-job-fair.html (p.168)

[5]Eve Tahmincioglu, NBCNews.com, April 27, 2009 http://www.nbcnews.com/id/30350209/#.UmFyC_n2-So (p.169)

[6]Manta.com http://www.manta.com/mb_51_ALL_3DZ/atlanta_ga (p.170)

7*Recruiter.com*, March 11, 2013, Miles Jennings, *5 Signs of a Great Recruiter*
http://www.recruiter.com/i/5-signs-of-a-great-recruiter/ (p.171)

8The Institute for Professional Excellence in Coaching, (iPEC), *How Effective is Coaching?* http://www.ipeccoaching.com/index.html (p.173)

9LinkedIn Post, VolunteerMatch, November 6, 2013, Greg Baldwin, *The One Thing That Makes You 27% More Likely to Get a Job,* quoting from the Corporation for National & Community Service, June 2013, *Volunteering As a Pathway to Employment:*
http://www.nationalservice.gov/sites/default/files/upload/employment_research_report.pdf (p.1175)

Chapter 12: Advanced Social Media

1Data on File, Transition Sherpa, 2013, *How Did You Find Your Current Job*(p.180)

2Wall Street Journal article, December 11, 2013, *Are You a Social Media Star? Accenture Is Looking for You,* http://blogs.wsj.com/atwork/2013/12/11/are-you-a-social-media-star-accenture-is-looking-for-you/#! (p.180)

3Social Science Research Network paper, November 21, 2013, **An** *Experiment in Hiring Discrimination* Via Online Social Networks, Alessandro Acquisti, Carnegie Mellon University,
http://papers.ssrn.com/sol3/papers.cfm?abstract_id=2031979 (p.181)

4JobVite.com 2013 *Social Recruiting Survey Results*, June 2013
http://web.jobvite.com/rs/jobvite/images/Jobvite_SocialRecruiting2013.pdf (p.184)

5Neal Schaffer, *Maximizing LinkedIn for Sales and Social Marketing*
http://maximizeyoursocial.com/books/linkedin-business-book-maximizing-linkedin-sales-social-media-marketing/ (p.184)

6Dan Schawbel, *Me 2.0*
http://danschawbel.com/books/ (p.196)

7Miriam Salpeter, *Social Networking for Career Success*
http://www.socialnetworkingforcareersuccess.com/ (p.199)

8Gina Barr and Terry Brocke, *Klout Matters*

http://kloutmatters.com/ (p.210)

Chapter 13: Interviewing

[1]Abby Cohut, *Absolutely Abby's 101 Job Search Secrets*
http://staffingsymphony.3dcartstores.com/book-bundle.html (p.217)

[2]Forbes.com, August 8, 2013, Lisa Quast
http://www.forbes.com/sites/lisaquast/2013/08/12/job-seekers-dont-forget-to-interview-the-company-and-hiring-manager/?goback=%2Egde_146161_member_270985469#%21 (p.218)

[3]Bruce Dreyfus, *Personal Marketing Strategies Program*
http://www.getthatnextjob.com/content/pmsp-book-or-pdf (p.221)

[4]WOW! Interview, http://www.wowinterview.com/ (p.221)

[5]Dynamic Business, October 1, 2013, Gina Baldassarre quoting Heidi Holmes
http://www.dynamicbusiness.com.au/news/rate-of-flexible-work-not-improving-01102013.html#sthash.mozANHUh.dpuf (p.234)

[6]Virgin Entrepreneur, October 17, 2013, Sophie Hall, *Richard Branson: 3 Tips on how to Hire the Right People,*
http://www.virgin.com/entrepreneur/richard-branson-3-tips-on-how-to-hire-the-right-people (p.239)

[7]Daily Mail, June 29, 2011, Daily Mail Reporter
http://www.dailymail.co.uk/news/article-2009404/How-cocktail-umbrellas-USA-The-bizarre-questions-job-applicants-global-companies.html (p.240)

[8]Inavero on Behalf of Career Builder, July 2013, *New Career Builder Study Reveals Nine Lessons for Job Seekers and Recruiters That May Surprise You*
http://www.careerbuilder.com/share/aboutus/pressreleasesdetail.aspx?sd=10%2f17%2f2013&siteid=cbpr&sc_cmp1=cb_pr785_&id=pr785&ed=12%2f31%2f2013 (p.241)

[9]*Atlanta Journal-Constituion*, October 27, 2013, Working Strategies, Amy Lindgren (p.242)

[10]Monster, Margot Carmichael Lester, *Should You Send a Thank You Letter After an Interview?* http://career-advice.monster.com/job-interview/following-up/interview-thank-you-letter-send-or-not/article.aspx (p.243)

Chapter 14: Alternatives to Traditional Jobs

[1]ChancesE.com, 2007-2013, *Advantages and Disadvantages of Starting a Business from Scratch,* http://chancese.com/index.php?option=com_content&view=article&id=691:Advantages-&-Disadvantages-of-Starting-a-Business-From-Scratch&catid=11&Itemid=16 (p.253)

[2]U.S. Dept. of Health and Human Services (p.257)

[3]CNN Money, February 26, 2013, John Marcus at the Hettinger Institute, *Community College Grads Out-earn Bachelor's Degree Holders,* http://money.cnn.com/2013/02/26/pf/college/community-college-earnings/index.html (p.258)

[4]USAJobs.org (p.259)

[5]Forbes, November 14, 2012, Nancy Collander, *5 Tips for Getting a Government Job[5],* http://www.forbes.com/sites/nextavenue/2012/11/14/5-tips-for-getting-a-government-job/ (p.259)

[6]The Telegraph, January 19, 2012, Jasper Rees, *The End of our Kodak Moment,* http://www.telegraph.co.uk/women/mother-tongue/9025257/The-end-of-our-Kodak-moment.html (p.260)

[7]The Graduate, 1967, Calder Willingham and Buck Henry (p.261)

Chapter 15: Future Mountains to Climb

[1]Thomas L. Friedman, *The World Is Flat,* 2005, Farrar, Straus & Giroux (p.265)

[2]Stampede Blue, November 4, 2011, Brad Wells, *It's Lookin More and More Likely that Peyton Manning is Finished*

http://www.stampedeblue.com/2011/11/4/2537483/its-looking-more-and-more-likely-that-peyton-manning-is-finished (p.265)

[3]Deadspin, September 6, 2013, Barry Petchesky, *Peyton Manning's Night Deserves its Own Page in the record Book*
http://deadspin.com/peyton-mannings-night-deserves-its-own-page-in-the-rec-1262983989 (p.266)

[4]Execunet, John Zappe, May 28, 2009
http://www.ere.net/2009/05/28/survey-says-executive-tenure-shortening/ (p.267)

Resources the Authors Recommend:

Valar Afshar
Valar is Chief Marketing Officer of Extreme Networks, a thought leader, and contributor to the Huffington Post and Information Week.

Caron Atteberry
Caron is an IT Recruiter for Children's Healthcare System of Atlanta. Her LinkedIn address is: www.linkedin.com/in/caronatteberry

Joanne Blake
Provided by Joanne Blake, AICI, CIP, Owner of Style for Success Inc. Business Image and Etiquette Speakers and Trainers located in western Canada. Creator of *Style for Success* business dining video rated #1 by the *Wall Street Journal* and co-author of Executive Image Power www.styleforsuccess.com Twitter: @styleforsuccess

Dee Doanes
Dee is founder and editor-in-chief of **Health Plus Style,** an alternative health lifestyle blog **(www.healthplusstyle.com)**. She also is a published writer with an extensive background in public relations and marketing. Dee is active in many charities, including being a board member of **The Action Not Words Project.** She has conducted youth poetry workshops for the Atlanta Writers Club Youth Writing Camp, and is the former co-chair of the Writing in the Schools Program for Georgia Writers.

Melissa Galt
Identified by *Forbes* as one of the Top 20 Women of Influence for Entrepreneurs to follow on Twitter, Melissa is a recognized business growth strategist and catalyst. Over the last decade, she has worked with thousands of business owners online and offline, showing you how to go from a best kept secret to well-known and profitable. From building your success foundation, to capturing your ideal clients, Melissa works with you to create a solid blueprint for your business success and path to a purposeful life. Systems make success simple and Melissa provides the inside track on how to make more money, have more fun, and get more done.
Find Melissa at www.xeeme.com/MelissaGalt

Peter Gibson

Peter is a Realtor®, author, speaker, and Cross Coach. Peter can be contacted through his LinkedIn profile: www.linkedin.com/in/petergibsonnikkeniwc

Chris Gilliam

Chris is owner of The Gilliam Group, an Atlanta-based Career Coaching company. She is also an adjunct Career Consultant with Right Management, the world's leading career transition and talent management organization and a Career Coach with Ricklin-Echikson Associates (REA), the global leader providing career and transition services to corporate spouses. Prior to her current roles, Chris was a HR Consultant for many years, and served The Coca-Cola Company in a variety of HR leadership positions. Chris Can be reached at (770) 354-3462 or Gilliam.Group@gmail.com.

Gene Griessman, PhD

Gene is celebrated around the world for his books, training films, and memorable presentations. As an actor and playwright, he has performed at Ford's Theater, the Georgia Dome before 25,000, the Lincoln Memorial, and aboard the famed carrier the USS Abraham Lincoln.

He has conducted exclusive interviews on TV and in print with American presidents, actors, sports stars, and business leaders. He has won numerous awards including the Benjamin Franklin Award.
He often appears on television and radio, and his award-winning productions have aired nationally.. He is the creator of whatyousay.com.

Dr. Griessman has taught at major universities in the U.S. and abroad, including William and Mary, North Carolina State, Auburn, Tuskegee University, and Georgia Tech. He served as a Fulbright professor at the University of Islamabad, the national graduate University of Pakistan; and as a visiting researcher at the National Agrarian University of Peru and the University of New South Wales in Australia.

Tyrone Griffin, MBA

Tyrone is owner of Evil Bunny Consulting, LLC, an Atlanta area employee transition management company. He conducts workshops for those soon-to-be

in job transition, helping them prepare for an effective and successful job search. In addition, for the past three years he has hosted the weekly podcast *The Bunny Slippers Are Evil Jobseeker's Call In Show*, where he interviews career coaches, motivational speakers, authors, and entertainers, while providing simple, effective job-search tips and helping people deal with the mental and spiritual challenges of job transition. He also volunteers and gives speeches at various job-transition events in the Atlanta area.
Contact Tyrone at Tweet @EvilBunnyMan www.BunnySlippersAreEvil.com

Holly Henderson

Holly is a recognized sustainability and LEED expert, author, consultant, and speaker who has been honored as an LEED Fellow, the green building industry's most prestigious professional designation. As a speaker and consultant, she inspires, informs, motivates, and shares her unique knowledge about all things LEED and green. Holley lectures and presentations have inspired audiences at keynotes, company and association meetings, training workshops, webinars, and conferences. She is also the author *Becoming a Green Building Professional*.
Contact Holley at: www.holleyhenderson.com or www.h2ecodesign.com

Raegan Hill

Raegan's 20-year career history spans marketing, volunteer management, community relations, technology, and recruiting. She is currently the Director of Client Services for the Houston branch of Onward Search, a national digital marketing recruitment agency.In 2004, she served as the Director of the Volunteer Program for Super Bowl XXXVIII in Houston, which was marked by the NFL as one of the most successful volunteer programs in the history of the Super Bowl. She has served as Program Chair on the Board of Directors for the Houston Interactive Marketing Association (HIMA), the Board of Directors for the Houston User Experience Professional Association (HUXPA), and the Houston spokesperson for The CMO Club, a global organization with over 700 corporate CMO members. Raegan's diverse experience offers a unique perspective on how to leverage social media to uncover hidden job opportunities.

Michelle Hutchinson, DMD, MPH, CPH

Michelle is the founder of Wordhelper: Editing, Writing, Resumes & More (www.wordhelper.com). She has a great deal of experience preparing resumes and cover letters that open doors to interviews. You can find her on Twitter as @Wordhelper, on Facebook at http://www.facebook.com/wordhelper, and on LinkedIn at http://www.linkedin.com/in/wordhelper.

Abby Kohut

Abby, known on the web as "Absolutely Abby," is the President of Staffing Symphony, LLC and the author of *Absolutely Abby's 101 Job Search Secrets*. For 18 years, Abby held positions such as Senior Director of Recruiting for Kaplan, Interim Director of Recruiting for Continuum Health Partners, and Manager of Global Recruiting for Alpharma. Her website, AbsolutelyAbby.com, which was selected as one of the "Top 100 Websites for Your Career" by Forbes in 2013, teaches candidates the Absolute truth about the job search process that other recruiters won't tell you. Abby has provided job-search tips on Fox 5 Atlanta, NBC, CBS, ABC, LinkedIn, Monster, Real Simple, The Ladders, Bloomberg Radio, and *Forbes*. Abby was selected as one of "The Monster 11 for 2011: Career Experts Who Can Help Your Job Search" and is one of the "Top 100 Influential People Online," according to *Fast Company* magazine.

Bruce Kromer

Bruce is a photographer and Marketing Coordinator at Haigwood Studios in Roswell, Georgia. He specializes in headshots, both corporate and personal. Bruce took the back cover shots for this book and many of the pictures on the HIREDthebook.com website. His email address is bruce@haigwoodstudios.com

Art Lennig

Art has been a Business Broker since 2000. He is a Regional Developer with Murphy Business & Financial Corporation and an active member of the Georgia Association of Business Brokers (GABB) and the International Business Brokers Association (IBBA). Art was a member of the GABB Board for more than 10 years, serving in every position from Director to President. He was awarded Certified Business Intermediary (CBI), Board Certified Intermediary (BCI), and Board Certified Broker (BCB) credentials. Call him at 770-303-0044 **or Tweet him at** A.Lennig@MurphyBusiness.com.

Asha Lightbearer

Asha Lightbearer is a Posi Music Artist, Motivational Speaker and Success Skills Trainer. (For those unfamiliar with posi music, it's a fusion of spiritual, vocal, and instrumental creativity.) On stage, Asha is an energetic, passionate leader who inspires her audiences through humor, candor, enthusiasm and vulnerability. She delivers a high-energy, no-nonsense approach that is truly refreshing, delivering powerful inspiration, healing and vision to her audiences.

Tim Morrison

Tim is president of Write-Choice Services, Inc., has an extensive writing career in addition to careers in education, ministry and alternative medicine. His publishing credits include articles for three national magazines, three regional publications and chapters in three youth ministry books. Tim has authored 4 books. For over 15 years, Tim has been helping individuals discover their writing voice and take great strides towards achieving their writing dreams. Tim holds a doctorate in ministry from Andover Newton Theological School and a doctorate in naturopathy from Trinity College of Natural Health. Tim has lived in seven states and in Ghana, West Africa.

Betsy Rhame-Minor

Betsy, with over a decade of writing and communication experience, is a holder an M.S. in English from North Carolina State University. She is currently a business communication consultant, writing coach, book editor, and resume writer for Write Choice Services in Atlanta. Follow her on Twitter @betsyrhame or connect with her on Linkedin.

Jon Newman

Jon is a Certified Business Coach at FocalPoint Business Coaching, whose fundamentals are founded on the principles powered by the proven success of Brian Tracy's world-class business strategies and passion toward coaching excellence. Contact Jon through LinkedIn at www.linkedin.com/pub/jon-newman/3/793/811.

Emile Paradis

Emile retired from the Marine Corps Reserve in 1995, as a Colonel. Upon retirement, he became a Financial Advisor where he learned the importance of marketing. In 1998, Emile started the first chapter of Business Network International in Louisiana.

Emile is currently the Managing Partner of RPM Advisors and is a franchise owner of the Referral Institute. He has been a Referral Institute Master Trainer and has developed a number of referral training programs that are taught nationally. Emile is also the Executive Director for Fast Forward Restart, a nonprofit organization that helps small businesses and nonprofits recover from major disasters. Current project areas include New Orleans and Rumford, Maine.

Lee Pence, CFP, AAMS

A free copy of the booklet *How to Survive financially after a Job Loss* is available from the Financial Planning Association FPA) at www.fpanet.org.

Marilyn Pierce, RN BSN

Marilyn Pierce is a nurse in the Emory Healthcare System. She is working on a book on diet and exercise. Contact Marilyn at marilyn@marilynPierceLLC.com.

Joellyn "Joey" Sargent

Joey provides strategic counsel to leaders in businesses ranging from start-ups to Fortune 100 companies. Joey helps clients connect the dots between corporate strategy, brand vision, and customer experience. She works in diverse industries that include financial services, aviation, transportation, technology, medical, retail, and telecommunications.

Joey is one of fewer than 40 individuals in the world certified by Million Dollar Consultant® Dr. Alan Weiss and approved to provide all three of his mentor programs: Private Roster, Guided Option, and Total Immersion.

As an author and speaker, Joey has presented at industry conferences around the world, including Digital Summit and Intel's annual customer conference. Her articles and remarks have been published by CMO.com, Inc.com, Fox Business, Social Media Today, CareerBuilder, Investors.com, Call Center Magazine, TMC.net, and CNET News.

Kathryn Siefert, PhD

Dr. Seifert, CEO of Eastern Shore Psychological Services, has worked for over 30 years in the areas of mental health, criminal justice, and addictions. Dr. Seifert has specialized in the assessment and treatment of individuals who are at risk for violence and who are emotionally disturbed. She has lectured nationally and provides training on the topics of "Assessing the Risk for Violence," "Attachment Disorders," and "Bullying." Her books include her award-winning *How Children Become Violent*; the college textbook *Youth Violence*; the guided journal, *5 Secrets to Help You Solve Problems and Relax*; and the newest top-selling ebook, *BIG B and little b bullies: 5 Proven Tips To Stop All Types of Bullying Right Now*. Dr. Seifert developed the CARE *CARE2: Child and Adolescent Risk and Needs Evaluation*, and Relaxation Journals and MP3's. She testifies as an expert witness, lectures internationally, and has appeared on CNN, Discovery ID, Fox News, and a variety of local TV and radio networks.

Rick Sullivan

Rick Sullivan is the owner of HR STAR Consulting and the Director of St. Brendan's Career Transition Ministry. For more job-search tips and tools, contact Rick via www.hrstarconsulting.com, 678-576-3550, ricksullivan319@comcast.net, or http://www.linkedin.com/pub/rick-sullivan/0/160/b35

Jim Stroud

Jim is the Director of Sourcing and Social Strategy at the Bernard Hodes Group, a world leader in integrated talent solutions. Over the past decade, Jim has become an expert in lead-generation strategies, social media recruiting, video production, podcasting, online research, competitive intelligence, community management, and training. He has consulted for such major companies as Microsoft, Google, MCI, Siemens, and a host of startups. You can Tweet Jim @jimstroud or contact him via www.linkedin.com/in/jimstroud.

Nadine Walley

Nadine is a marketing expert who has worked for the Georgia Department of Labor in Corporate & Community Relations. She brings to marketing management a passion for developing effective teams and managing people, processes, and promotions. She is a proactive voice in leadership deliberations, strategy, and creative vision. Contact Nadine via LinkedIn at: www.linkedin.com/in/nadinewalley

Bill Williams

Bill is a Franchise Advisor with Axxiom Franchise Advisors who knows what it's like to want to control your destiny through owning a business. For more than 25 years, he was a senior executive with technology companies, responsible for training, support, operations, and IT. Later he became a career consultant with Right Management Associates.

Since 2005, Bill has been a franchise consultant, building a solid track record of helping his clients choose the best possible match in a franchised business. He speaks and writes on career issues and has begun writing a book, *Golf as a Metaphor for Life*. Bill is active in the Atlanta Vietnam Veterans Business Association and is developing programs to help veterans become franchise owners. Bill can assist entrepreneurs anywhere in the U.S. from his Atlanta offices. Call 770-973-0878 or 678-524-6992, or contact Bill via http://www.linkedin.com/in/wjwilliams, Twitter: @franchiseanswer, or www.AxxiomFranchiseAdvisors.com/bwilliams.

Karen Vining

Karen is a registered financial advisor. She can be reached through her company, Vining Financial Services, Inc. Securities offered through Triad Advisors, Inc. Member FINRA/SIPC.

Bob Zartarian

Bob is Vice President of Mortgage Lending at Guaranteed Rate, offering residential buyers, investors, the self-employed, seniors, and resident aliens who need assistance in financing/refinancing both traditional and "outside the box" solutions. Clients benefit from his extensive experience with real estate agents, CPAs, financial planners, and attorneys, as well as with specific aspects of real estate acquisition, financing, investment, and property management for industrial, commercial, residential, investment, and vacation properties. Bob can be contacted through LinkedIn at: www.linkedin.com/in/bobzartarian

Acknowledgements

Many people helped make this book possible and deserve to be acknowledged. All have our deepest, most sincere thanks since without them, what you have just read would likely not exist. Our effort, with their help, will hopefully guide you to your next, and subsequent, positions much faster than you might have otherwise arrived there. Many are former clients who are living examples of the methods we teach. As unique individuals, they chose among the methods we shared, as you did.

In no particular order, we would like to thank many at the Life Lessons' Career Group. Thanks to the candor and input from Scott Bennett, Nancy Morris, Mohan Vaswani, Christy Turner, Art Jones, and Jana Caldwell. Gigi Burke, Susan Sunay and Susan Connors offered in-depth assessments and suggestions. None of it would have happened had it not been for Kathy Walsh heading this win-win opportunity.

Caroline McCoy-Hansen's support over the years and the valuable lessons learned from hearing speakers at the Career Ministry proved to be invaluable in compiling ideas we have used throughout *Hired*! Monica Vincent, Michael Hydzik, and others at the Holy Spirit Career Ministry provided welcome insight.

The insights we gleaned from speaking and volunteering at so many of the other career ministries over the past four years has proven to be invaluable in enabling us to truly understand what makes the most sense in the job-search process. Special thanks to John Marotto, Chris Ensley, and others at the Catholic Church of St. Ann for their support.

Many at Unity North Atlanta provided great insight and assistance. Through Richard Burdick and Jay Schofield's leadership, members of Men of Unity gave great help. Thanks to David Pritchard, Bradley Chatfield, Peter Breese, Rusty Morgan, and Mac Schmidt for their assistance.

Paul Abbott always made himself available as a sounding board; we could always count on his unfiltered assessment. Todd Darby gave his help in many ways. Chris Donovan, Patrick Thompson, Brent McCarthy, Chris Riker, and Jon Harris were also quick to lend a hand and support.

Max Sutherland added his C-level and international perspective while offering unfettered advice. He also caught errors of omission and commission. Thanks, Max.

Others who helped include Debbie Hoppe, Leslie Farrell, Nila Surgi, Julie Grace, Mandy Marchitello, Al Cole, Joe Dye, and Doris Smith. Thanks also to Bruce Kromer's photography for the www.HIREDthebook.com website, the back cover's portraits, and elsewhere. And let us not forget the help of the Canadian contingent, Sharon Maclean and Kate Leighton.

Although we will certainly have overlooked many who have helped us hone our message and skills over the years, we cannot fail to thank Katherine Simons, Pat Holt and Jay Litton and all the volunteers of Roswell UMC (America's largest church-based career ministry). Rich vonBiberstein at Intown Community Church, Mark Eister of Perimeter College, everyone associated with Atlanta Job Seekers, and Bill Schwartz of Community Beth Shalom have all often welcomed us warmly.

Thanks also to Georgia State University; St. Pius X; C3G; St. Thomas Aquinas Catholic Church; Dunwoody UMC; Blessed Trinity Catholic High School; First UMC of Lawrenceville, St. Brendan's Catholic Church; St. Bridget Catholic Church; First Presbyterian Church in Marietta; North Point Community Church; Suwanee Parish UMC; McKendree UMC; Eastminster Presbyterian Church; Episcopal Church of St. Peter and St. Paul; Johnson Ferry Baptist Church; Edmonton, Alberta, Employment and Career Fair; and the Technology Association of Georgia, among many others.

Above all, this work could not have been initiated, much less completed, without the unending support of Al's family: Terry and Shannon. Jeff's Family was equally supportive: Liz, Jonathan and Kerri.

If you are, or plan, to become a Hiring Manager, you'll want to check out Al's next book: "**HIRE, *HIGHER!*"** It will help you and other Hiring Managers through the interview process, thus filling prescriptions for a brighter future.

Jeff's next book is in the planning stage.